TROUBLESOME ENGLISH
A Teaching Grammar
for ESOL Instructors

Richard Firsten

Lindsey Hopkins Technical Education Center
Dade County Public Schools

Pat Killian

Salisbury State University

PRENTICE HALL REGENTS, Englewood Cliffs, New Jersey 07632

Library of Congress Cataloging-in-Publication Data

Firsten, Richard.
   Troublesome English / Richard Firsten, Pat Killian.
     p.   cm.
   Includes index.
   Contents: v. 1. Teaching grammar for ESOL instructors.
   ISBN 0-13-328840-4
    1. English language—Study and teaching—Foreign speakers.
   2. English language—Grammar—Study and teaching. I. Killian, Pat.
   II. Title.
   PE1128.A2F54 1994
   428′.007—dc20
                                       93-11940
                                        CIP

Acquisitions editor: Nancy Baxer
Editorial production/design manager: Dominick Mosco
Editorial/production supervision: Cheryl Smith Robbins
Cover design: JM Design & Illustration
Production coordinator: Ray Keating
Copy editor: Eugene Hall

© 1994 by PRENTICE HALL REGENTS
Prentice-Hall, Inc.
A Paramount Communications Company
Englewood Cliffs, New Jersey 07632

Printed in the United States of America

10 9 8 7 6 5 4 3 2 1

Printed on Recycled Paper

ISBN 0-13-328840-4

Prentice-Hall International (UK) Limited, *London*
Prentice-Hall of Australia Pty. Limited, *Sydney*
Prentice-Hall Canada Inc., *Toronto*
Prentice-Hall Hispanoamericana, S.A., *Mexico*
Prentice-Hall of India Private Limited, *New Delhi*
Prentice-Hall of Japan, Inc., *Tokyo*
Simon & Schuster Asia Pte. Ltd., *Singapore*
Editora Prentice-Hall do Brasil, Ltda., *Rio de Janeiro*

Contents

Acknowledgments

To my parents, Hy and Tess, who instilled a love of learning in me and gave me the gift of a multilingual/multicultural environment to grow up in.

To my parents, Jeanne and Jack, who always knew I would be a teacher.

To Dr. John Staczek, who gave us the professional elbow room and encouragement to spread our wings and fly at a time when we most needed both.

To all of the students we've had in TESOL courses over the years who kept asking us the question, "So when are you going to write the book?"

To Edie MacDougald, who generously gave her help when it was sorely needed.

And a special thanks to Bruce Carl Fontaine, whose constant support and faith contributed to this text becoming a reality.

Preface

Troublesome English is a grammar book for teachers of English for speakers of other languages, and it's a grammar book with many differences. Right from the start, you'll notice the relaxed, informal style of the book; books like this don't have to be written in stuffy "academese." You'll also take note of a whimsical approach throughout; if humor serves an important function in the classroom to make teaching and learning more enjoyable, why shouldn't it do the same in a grammar book?

The purpose of *Troublesome English* is to make difficult, but basic, areas of English grammar more comprehensible to a wide range of people: undergraduate and graduate TESOL students, ESOL and VESOL teachers, junior high and high school teachers, advanced ESOL students, and anyone who just wants to brush up on his/her skills in English. If you're a teacher and have a much stronger understanding of how English works, you'll be better prepared to communicate the grammar and give clearer, more effective examples to your students. If you're an advanced ESOL student or if you simply want to brush up on your grammar, this book will go a long way to help you feel more comfortable about how English works.

We haven't attempted to cover every aspect of the language; only those areas that traditionally seem most troublesome are dealt with on these pages. Nor have we attempted to give every single analytical detail of each grammar point covered; if you master the material we've provided, you'll be more than well prepared to teach grammar effectively, directly or indirectly, or to use the language more effectively.

Troublesome English contains the following unique features:

The Socratic Approach: You'll be encouraged to observe, think about, and make conclusions about each grammar point covered. This technique, also referred to as the "inductive method," will allow you to explore the grammar in a way that will make the material much more meaningful to you in the long run. Instead of being "spoonfed" the information, you'll work through it yourself to discover exactly what's going on.

And here's a tip to help you get the most out of this approach: whenever you're asked to think of a reason or interpretation, take the time to do just that and write down your own thoughts on the line(s) provided. This will be a lot more meaningful than taking the easy way out by jumping ahead to find the answers.

Troubleshooters: These "asides," which pop up in many chapters, focus on those points which you can anticipate will bring problems to the teaching and learning of English due to language interference or other causes.

Teaching Tips: To help you create a fun atmosphere in your classroom, whether you're a new or experienced teacher, these suggestions offer an array of time-honored classroom activities, exercises, and games which enhance the teaching of specific grammar points.

Mind Bogglers!: Found at the end of each chapter, these questions are meant to stimulate your powers of inductive reasoning even further to promote greater independence of thought concerning grammar.

To give you more opportunity to explore the grammar covered in *Troublesome English,* an accompanying workbook has been created to reinforce your new understanding of the material. We hope that you find the workbook stimulating and enjoyable.

Finally, to give you more suggestions to enhance your teaching skills, you'll find a set of appendixes at the end of this book which deal in great detail with teaching strategies and step-by-step procedures for creating an assortment of exercises and games that go beyond what's offered in the *Teaching Tips*.

We hope that you find *Troublesome English* an unintimidating text, reference and source book, and that you'll always find it a friend to help you out at those tough moments when your mind goes blank and you're trying to remember why we say this or why we say that.

Richard Firsten
Pat Killian

The Phonetic Alphabet

Here's a simplified version of the International Phonetic Alphabet (the IPA). We've simplified it for the purposes of this book and have replaced some complex symbols with ones easier for English speakers to recognize.

a	(father)	ɔɪ	(boil)	r			
æ	(hat)	b		s			
e	(say)	d		š	(fish)		
ɛ	(bed)	f		ž	(pleasure)		
i	(see)	g		t			
ɪ	(sit)	h		θ	(with)		
o	(no)	č	(chip)	ð	(the)		
ɔ	(saw)	j	(judge)	v			
u	(too)	k		w			
ʊ	(book)	l		y	(you)		
ə	(about)	m		z			
ər	(first)	n		ẓ	(suds)		
aɪ	(eye)	ŋ	(sing)				
aʊ	(now)	p					

Chapter 1

Word Order

Throw Mama from the train a kiss!

THE BASICS

In the cartoon on page 1, it's obvious that the person on the right is quite uncomfortable with what the other person's saying—and he's probably not alone. We're sure you, too, felt uncomfortable trying to understand what the person on the left had to say. That's because he's using a word order, or syntax, that might be fine in some other language, but certainly doesn't work in English. The question is, why doesn't it work? What rules are there that you can tell students when correcting their word order that will stick so that they don't continue to make the same mistakes over and over again?

From the outset, we want to make it perfectly clear that the aim of this chapter is <u>not</u> to cover every aspect of English word order. Most details aren't very troublesome and are covered at length in other grammar books. What we intend to show you are fresh approaches to looking at and teaching certain aspects of word order that *are* troublesome. We'll demonstrate ways of perceiving word order that may make things easier for you and for your students.

For starters, let's discover the underlying basic rules for English word order by doing the exercise that follows.

*Rearrange the following sentences to put them in the word order that you consider **basic** to English.*

1. the paper / this morning / at home / he / read.

   <u>He read the paper at home this morning.</u>

3

2. in the oven / she's roasting / tonight / a chicken.

<u>She's roasting a chicken in the oven tonight</u>

3. send / to New Delhi / right now / this telegram.

<u>Send this telegram to New Delhi right now.</u>

4. Marco / earlier / outside / took / the garbage.

<u>Marco took the garbage outside earlier</u>

5. a movie / last night / we / saw / on campus.

<u>We saw a movie on campus last night.</u>

6. north / drove / today / Yoko / to Kyoto / the van.

Yoko drove the van north to Kyoto today

The sentences should have this <u>basic</u> order:

1. He read the paper at home this morning.
2. She's roasting a chicken in the oven tonight.
3. Send this telegram to New Delhi right now.
4. Marco took the garbage outside earlier.
5. We saw a movie on campus last night.
6. Yoko drove the van north to Kyoto today.

Now let's take a good look at how these sentences are set up. There's definitely a pattern we can discern. To begin with, they all start with a **subject** except for Sentence 3 (which we'll discuss further on). We've got:

he / she / Marco / we / Yoko.

These subjects are all followed by **verbs**:

read / 's roasting / send / took / saw / drove.

We next have **direct objects**:

the paper / a chicken / this telegram / the garbage / a movie / the van.

To continue, we find **directions** or **places**:

at home / in the oven / to New Delhi / outside / on campus / north to Kyoto.

Finally, there are **time phrases**:

this morning / tonight / right now / earlier / last night / today.

For now, let's state the general rule of basic word order that English tends to follow based upon what we've just looked at:

subject - verb - object - direction/place - time

This "translates" very nicely into a certain little group of wh- words that many English speakers learn in a set order when they're children: **who - what - where - when.** These four wh- words correspond very neatly to the order of the basic English sentence. Take a good look and see for yourself.

Teaching Tips: General Information

Before we begin the *Teaching Tips*, a regular feature of each chapter, we would like to make several suggestions about them. First, you'll find that the *Teaching Tips* suggest dividing the class into pairs or small groups. The main purpose for this is that students are much more likely to get a chance to speak when they're in small groups. It would be ideal if you all had small classes, but we realize that this is a dream. Small group work is a way to increase each student's chance to speak and be heard.

Second, we'd like to suggest how to divide the class into these groups. Separate students from the same language background if you can. We realize that some of you have homogeneous classes as far as language background goes, but if you can mix the members in each group so that they all don't speak the same language, it decreases the likelihood of one student breaking into his/her native language with a classmate.

Third, as your students are doing the task you've set up, wander around the room and help out when you're called on or needed. Try to do so with a minimum of interference and only interrupt for a good reason. Your students need to talk—you don't! Be an observer and a helper, not a participant.

Fourth, you'll notice that we often suggest putting the assignment on a handout. If that's not possible for you to do, there's always the chalkboard.

Finally, we've deliberately omitted references to proficiency levels in all the *Tips*. True, articles are usually taught fairly early on and the past perfect much later, but by not mentioning any particular proficiency level, we hope that each activity can be adapted for any class you may have. It may be too advanced for your particular needs today, but it may be fine later on. This helps you to recycle teaching points: what was taught in September can be reviewed in December; what was taught in Level One can be reviewed in Level Three. And now, on to the *Teaching Tips.*

Teaching Tips

Before class, collect or write interesting phrases (choose phrases that cover different positions in a sentence—various noun phrases, verbs, prepositional phrases, adverbials, etc.). They need not be on a specific topic; in fact, it makes a more interesting activity if they're not. Distribute a set of these phrases (five to seven) to pairs or small groups of students. Have them write a coherent story using several of the phrases they've received. When the stories have been written, let the students read them aloud to the class.

In the basic pattern we've shown you, five separate segments are listed, but there are only four wh- words, so you might think that something got left out. Not so! In fact, it's amazing how this works. Follow along, and everything should become clear:

> **Who** represents the subject—whoever it is;
> **What** stands for <u>two</u> segments: the verb and object(s);
> **Where,** of course, is direction and/or place;
> **When** is the time.

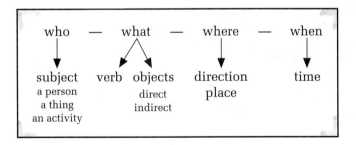

You can see that the five basic segments have been accounted for. The beauty of **what** representing both the verb and the objects is that this reinforces one of the cardinal rules of English word order which so many students have trouble with, that **you normally don't separate a verb and its object(s) and place a word or words in between.** In this case, since one wh- word stands for both segments, there's no way to separate it. As soon as your students are able to form the most elementary English sentences, start drilling them on the phrase *who - what - where - when* until they've memorized the words and their order. Make sure they consciously use this pattern whenever they speak English or write in it. As the students progress, they can start using variations on this basic pattern, but first get them to internalize it.

Even though we've given you a nice, tidy "formula" for this most basic example of English word order, we have to mention that there are variations which do occur. For example, we can have **what** as the subject (<u>The fire</u> burned out of control), and **who** as the object (The smoke almost asphyxiated <u>the O'Learys</u>). We can also have any combination of these two: **who/who** (<u>The firefighters</u> rescued <u>the whole family</u>) and **what/what** (<u>The fire</u> destroyed <u>everything</u>).

Here's a point about the objects. There are direct objects and indirect objects. For example, in the sentence *He made a promise to her,* **a promise** is the direct object and **her** is the indirect object. Even when we change the order of the words (as we can sometimes do in English by dropping the preposition) and say *He made her a promise,* the segments that have been called direct and indirect object are still just that. What's interesting to note is that **whether the direct object is before the indirect object, or vice versa, the two objects are still kept side by side,** and that's another aspect of word order that never varies. In fact, we can take this a step further and see that these three elements (the verb, direct object, and indirect object) all stay together in this basic English word order pattern.

$$\boxed{\text{what}} = \begin{array}{l} \text{I } \boxed{\text{gave the report to her}}\,. \\[1em] \text{I } \boxed{\text{gave her the report}}\,. \end{array}$$

Notice that **what** will be the appropriate question word for the following questions based upon the sentences above:

> **A:** **What** did you do?
> **B:** I gave her something.
> **A:** **What** did you give her?
> **B:** The report.

Teaching Tips

Create a scenario in which a telegram might be sent (e.g., You're on vacation and are supposed to be back on Monday. Unfortunately, the air traffic controllers are on strike and the airport is closed down. Notify your boss about the problem. / You're on a business trip and accidentally left an important document in your office. Wire your secretary to send it to you. Make sure you describe the document carefully and where it's located.) Pair the students up or have them form small groups. The students' task is to write the telegrams. (1) They must organize the information carefully and eliminate unnecessary function words (it costs less to send a telegram when there are fewer words!). (2) When they have written their telegrams, they should exchange them with the other groups and decide if any further information should be included. (3) Have the students exchange the telegrams again, and tell them to rewrite the complete text of the telegrams.

Let's get back to Sentence 3 for a moment. When we utter an imperative form, a command, we're really including the subject **you** before the verb even though we don't normally say it. Therefore, there really is a subject in Sentence 3 as well. This point can be easily demonstrated by listening to any English-speaking parent who's momentarily upset with his/her child and says something like "You stop that whining this instant!" There it is! The subject **you** has surfaced.   So Sentence 3 is just fine. It has a subject—albeit hidden—a verb (send), a direct object (this telegram), direction (to New Delhi), and time (right now).

In the segment we call **where,** we noted that it might be a direction or a place. In example Sentence 6 we can see this in action: "Yoko drove the van **north to Kyoto** today." Here we have an example containing both the direction (north) and place (Kyoto). Remember that when both elements are used in one phrase, **the direction word comes first.** Other direction words are the rest of the compass points and words like "home" and "away":

Drive **east on 42nd Street** and make a right at Broadway.

Kenji is going **home to Kobe** for the summer.

Silvia went **away to the mountains** for the weekend.

Now let's discuss the placement of time phrases. Notice where they appear in those first six example sentences? This is one segment (and there are others!) that can be pushed to the front of a sentence if deemed appropriate to do so. It's more or less up to the individual to determine if it's appropriate to place it there. The rule of thumb tends to be that **the time phrase can precede all other segments of the sentence if the speaker wishes to emphasize or linger on it:**

For the past six years, our company has made steady profits.

Teaching Tips

Before class, think up some well-known acronyms or invent some of your own (TESOL, PDQ, ASAP, AFL-CIO). Explain what an acronym is to your students and show them how one works. Then give them the list of acronyms you've prepared and have them write phrases or sentences of their own invention by using each letter of an acronym to start each word [e.g. The Elephant Sat On Louie; Please Don't Quit; A Sweet Afghan Puppy; Antony Finds Love, and Cleo Is Obliging). Make sure students use correct English word order in their phrases/sentences.

Variation

North American license plates are frequently combinations of letters and numbers. Have your students create license plates for famous people. Here are some examples: LWB 123 (Lawrence Welk's Beat, a-1, a-2, a-3); WTC 1066 (William the Conqueror, 1066); B5S [Beethoven's 5th Symphony].

ADVERBS OF MANNER (HOW?)

Note where you find the adverb in the following dialog. Then see if you can come up with a general rule for placing it.

The adverb of manner can be placed

1. _____

2. _____

3. _____

These words, which describe how something is done or how something happens, seem to have their own set of rules. Whereas adjectives, nouns, pronouns, and verbs tend to have fairly rigid, systematic placement in basic sentences, adverbs can usually be placed at three different positions in a sentence. One common position is between a subject and its verb if it isn't a complex verb: **I gladly accept** ... When we use one or more auxiliaries before a verb, we've created a complex verb. Examples of this are using "be" before the -ing form of the verb (I'm talking), modal auxiliaries such as "will" before the verb (He'll help), or putting the auxiliary "have" before a past participle (They've gone).

The other common position where adverbs of manner appear is at the end of a clause: **I accept this award gladly.**

Why, then, did Person A begin his first utterance with the adverb as his first word? The reason is that he's following the same kind of thinking as with the placement of the time phrase we discussed earlier: **by pushing the adverb of manner to the front of the sentence, he's emphasizing or lingering on this segment for whatever reason he has.** One thing to keep in mind is that placing the adverb of manner at the beginning is a very formal style observed more in written than in spoken language. Furthermore, placing it initially doesn't always work—or is it initially placing it?—because you may change the meaning. So beware!

Naturally, all of us do best what comes **naturally.**

Just for the fun of it, let's take a minor detour and look at how adverbs of manner can do some really strange things to sentences depending on where they're placed, especially in negative sentences.

Put an **X** in the boxes in front of the following sentences only if the sentences seem ungrammatical or illogical to you.

1a.	☐	He quickly did it.	1b.	☐	He did it quickly.
2a.	☐	He quickly didn't do it.	2b.	☐	He didn't do it quickly.
3a.	☐	She carefully hid it.	3b.	☐	She hid it carefully.
4a.	☐	She carefully didn't hide it.	4b.	☐	She didn't hide it carefully.

5a. ☐   I happily refused.   5b. ☐   I refused happily.
6a. ☐   I happily didn't refuse.   6b. ☐   I didn't refuse happily.

It turns out that the only boxes which should have an **X** in them are **2a** and **4a**. And something very interesting is also apparent in 6a and 6b: there's a difference in meaning with the same adverb in these two sentences. Any thoughts on the subject? If so, write them down below:

_____

_____

_____

There's really no big mystery as to why 2a and 4a don't work. How can you describe the way something is done if, in fact, it isn't done? This is totally illogical. As for the difference in meaning with the same adverb in 6a and 6b, the word "happily" in the first sentence really means that I was happy or glad that I didn't refuse; in the other sentence, "happily" in this negative context means the reverse, that I was not happy about refusing. Quite a difference! Let's just say that you must be careful about how adverbs of manner are placed and careful about how they're used in negative sentences.

To sum up, we can say that **adverbs of manner can appear at the beginning of a sentence for emphasis and formal usage, between a subject and its verb (if it isn't a complex verb), or at the end of a clause.**

But what if the verb _is_ complex? Where's the adverb of manner placed then? Look at the next dialog and notice where the adverbs appear.

A: It's awful how the human race is **continually** threatening Earth's ecosystems!

B: I know. Like the way we've been **systematically** reducing the rain forests.

A: Right! In fact, I've **seriously** spoken on that very topic at several Sierra Club meetings.

B: Have you? Well, this year I'll be **completely** focusing my attention on the problems of the ozone layer.

A: Great! It's just a shame that governmental corruption has been **dangerously** interfering with our goals.

B: Well, we'll be working **hard** to stop all that!

Whenever we want to add an adverb of manner to a complex verb form, it's really quite simple: **you can put an adverb of manner in between the last auxiliary and the verb.** So Person A can say "… we're continually threatening…" and Person B can say "… we've been systematically reducing…" (We're sure you've taken notice of the word "hard," and we'll get back to that in a moment.)

First, another question needs to be asked: If we choose to, where else can we put these adverbs of manner in the previous sentences? Take a moment to ponder this, and then draw a caret (∧) where the adverbs of manner can be alternately placed in their respective sentences.

1. It's awful how we're threatening Earth's ecosystems! [continually]
2. Like the way we've been reducing the rain forests. [systematically]
3. I've spoken on that very topic at several Sierra Club meetings. [seriously]
4. I'll be focusing my attention on the problems of the ozone layer. [completely]
5. It's such a shame that government corruption has been interfering with our goals. [dangerously]

These adverbs of manner can be placed like so:

1. It's awful how we're threatening Earth's ecosystems **continually!**
2. Like the way we've been reducing the rain forests **systematically.**
3. I've spoken **seriously** on that very topic at several Sierra Club meetings.
4. I'll be focusing my attention **completely** on the problems of the ozone layer.
5. It's such a shame that government corruption has been interfering **dangerously** with our goals.

So what conclusions can we draw from all of this? Keeping the presence or absence of direct objects in mind, come up with your own conclusions about the alternate placement of these adverbs.

_____

_____

_____

_____

Now let's see if your conclusions match ours. If a clause has a direct object, as demonstrated in Sentences 1, 2, and 4, **the adverb of manner can follow the direct object.**

As for Sentences 3 and 5, however, we need to do more thinking. Both of these sentences lack direct objects, so **we can place the adverb of manner right after the verb when there is no direct object.**

We're not totally finished yet, though. The last thing Person B says in the preceding dialog is, "Well, we'll be working **hard** to stop all that!" The final question remains, can we place "hard" anywhere else in the sentence? And the answer is, NO. In fact, the adverbs of manner **hard** and **fast** are placed after the verb if there's no direct object, or after the direct object if there is one. Here are a couple of examples:

He ate <u>**fast**</u> so he wouldn't miss his bus.

He ate breakfast <u>**fast**</u> so he wouldn't miss his bus.

Teaching Tips

Before class, select various adverbs of manner that can be acted out (strangely, noisily, carefully, quickly, etc.). Write each one on a small slip of paper. Then select various action verb phrases (drive a bus; correct homework; repair a TV; cook spaghetti, etc.) and write each one of them on a small slip of paper. Put all the slips with adverbs in one paper bag, and all the slips with action verb phrases in another. Let each student pull out one adverb and one verb. The student then mimes the combination of the two slips that he/she pulled out, and the other students must guess what's being mimed.

 Troubleshooter

Students invariably think that the adverbial form of "hard" is "hardly."

Similarly, students think that "lovely" is somehow related to the idea of "love."

Students also think that "friendly," "timely," "homely," etc. are adverbs.

ADVERBS OF FREQUENCY (HOW OFTEN?)

These adverbs are words such as **always / usually / often / sometimes / seldom / rarely / never**. Figure out the rules that govern their placement by looking over this dialog:

A: Misha's a terrific employee!

B: I know. He's **rarely** late for work and he's **never** sick.

A: Besides that, he's **always** had his work done on time.

B: And he **seldom** makes any big errors.

A: He has **never** fought with the boss.

B: And he's **always** trying to help his co-workers.

A: We could **never** have sold so much this year without him.

If the verb "be" is used, the adverbs of frequency _____

_____

If simple verbs are used, the frequency words _____

_____

If complex verbs are used, these adverbs are placed _____

_____

Let's check out your ideas. **These adverbs are always placed:**

1. <u>after</u> **the verb "be"**
   (He's <u>**always**</u> on time.)

2. <u>before</u> **other verbs in their simple forms**
   (He <u>**never**</u> gets to work late.)

3.   **in between the auxiliary and the verb if there's only one auxiliary in the complex verb**
(He'll **<u>rarely</u>** get angry.)

4.   **after the first auxiliary if the complex verb has two or more auxiliaries**
(He's **<u>never</u>** been fired from a job.)

Adverbs of Frequency in Initial Position

All languages have their peculiarities, and English is certainly no exception. One case in point is the strange phenomenon that occurs if we place the following adverbs of frequency at the start of a sentence for emphasis:

Seldom does it snow in Vancouver.

Rarely will he complain about anything.

Never have I seen such a beautiful sunset!

What do you see happening with the word order in the sentences above? Write a statement or two to explain this phenomenon.

If these adverbs of frequency are placed in initial position, _____

_____

_____

_____

In case you haven't hit upon this particular way of looking at what's happening, think about the phenomenon this way: **If those adverbs of frequency are placed as the first word of a sentence, a yes/no question pattern follows** (… does it snow … /… will he complain … /… have I seen …). There's another interesting observation we can make about those frequency adverbs: **Keep in mind that the action or state of being has a "negative" connotation; that is, it occurs less than 50% of the time. Only these "negative" adverbs of frequency can be fronted as in our examples and then trigger the yes/no question patterns that follow.**

Teaching Tips

Before class, prepare several questions that use adverbs of frequency (How often do you read a newspaper? / Do you usually do your homework in the library? / Haven't you ever been uncooperative?, etc.) and present them to the students. Now have them brainstorm similar questions and then use the questions to interview one another (they can even interview you) and give reports to the class on what they've just found out.

Other Peculiarities of Word Inversion

Another example we should note of this phenomenon in English happens when we use conditional sentences (covered in Volume 2, Chapter 8). Examine the following dialog and describe on the lines below what you see happening to the parts of certain sentences in bold:

A: Have the data on those stock market reports been faxed to us yet?

B: No, not yet.

A: Well, **should they come in** before the close of business today, please bring them in to me.

B: Right. But I don't expect them today. **Had Kirby collected** all of them as planned, he would have faxed them to us already.

A: **Were he to do** his job efficiently, we wouldn't be sitting around waiting for those data. In fact, **were he** here right now, I'd tell him so to his face!

In Person A's second utterance, _____

_____

_____

In Person B's second utterance, _____

_____

_____

In Person A's third utterance, _____

_____

_____

In Person A's fourth utterance, _____

_____

_____

In the more common pattern that conditional sentences have, the phrases in bold would be "if they come in," "If Kirby had collected them," "If he did his job," and "if he were here." Have you noticed that we're using yes/no question patterns again in the dialog?

There's still one more pattern to look at. In this one, the word "should" can be added before the verb in the If-clause ("If they <u>should</u> come in ...."). This is just an optional form of the future conditional with "should" being equal to the expression "happen to" ("If they <u>happen to</u> come in ...."). In the inverted form, however, "should" is a necessary element because the word "if" has been eliminated ("<u>Should</u> they come in ...."). A similar situation exists in the past conditional sentence; when we make the inversion, the word "if" is again eliminated ("Had Kirby collected all of them ....").

Make a note once again that the inversions in these two phrases have taken on yes/no question patterns just as we saw happen when those three adverbs of frequency were placed in the initial position. Also note that these optional forms are very formal sounding and not as commonly used. As for the phrase "were he here" (if he were here), it, too, is an optional form which eliminates the need for "if" when we make the inversion.

As for the phrase "were he to do his job ...." (if he did his job), it's also an optional form of the subjunctive/conditional and is much more formal sounding. Let's take a moment and look more deeply into how we've come up with the strange-looking form "were he to do his job." We need to backtrack to how the phrase appears in the indicative form (a sentence stating reality) and we come up with the sentence "He **is** to do his job." The sentence means *he is supposed to do his job,* and we'll be covering this idiomatic form in detail when we get to Chapter 6. Now we'll take this indicative form and change it into the subjunctive (a sentence stating an imaginary idea) and put it into a conditional phrase: "If he **were** to do his job ...." From this point it's just one more step to make the inverted word order and eliminate the unnecessary word "if": "**Were** he to do his job ...." Looking at it in a nutshell, this is what we see happening:

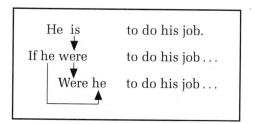

Before we leave these observations on the phenomenon of word inversion, there are five more we can mention. Consider these sentences:

The cake was so delicious that she didn't leave a crumb.

He was such a good boy that everyone loved him.

An optional form for these sentences, although again taking on a much more formal air, is

> *So delicious <u>was the cake</u> that she didn't leave a crumb.*
>
> *Such a good boy <u>was he</u> that everyone loved him.*

Note again how the inverted forms contain the word order for a question ("...was the cake..." / "...was he..."). This yes/no question pattern is the common thread found in all of these unusual forms.

Next we have a sentence like:

> **He not only wrote the music, but he also wrote the lyrics.**

With this sentence construction, you can opt for:

> *Not only <u>did he write</u> the music, but he also wrote the lyrics.*

Moving right along, there's a sentence like the following:

> **They have considered our proposal only recently.**

In this case, you can front the adverbial part (beginning with the word "only") and end up with:

> *Only recently <u>have they considered</u> our proposal.*

Other examples of this occurrence are:

> *Only now <u>does he admit</u> his errors.*
>
> *Only by sheer luck <u>was his life spared</u>.*

Finally, there's the matter of certain exclamations. Once again, we'll use the word order common in yes/no questions to create these statements:

> **Boy, <u>was it</u> hot this afternoon!**
>
> <u>**Can I make**</u> **a wonderful spaghetti sauce!**
>
> **Wow! <u>Did they mess up!</u>**

Teaching Tips

Before class, completely scramble a paragraph, but be sure to leave the punctuation intact (scramble the words within each sentence and re-arrange the sentences within the paragraph). Dictate the scrambled sentences to your students sentence by sentence. Have the students un-scramble the dictation at the sentence level first and then arrange the sentences into the correct order for the paragraph to make sense. This exercise can be done individually or by pairs or small groups.

Mind Bogglers!

We all like our minds to be challenged. Here are the first of many curious questions which you will find at the end of each chapter in this book. They're here for you to have fun with, to use your intuitive or linguistic powers in order to find the answers. Try to solve these little mysteries here before you look up the answers in Appendix 4 at the back of this book. Good luck with the first ones!

Do the first three words have the same meaning? And what about the following two? If they differ somehow, how can you explain the differences to your students? Have fun!

stomach / belly / tummy

neck / throat

Chapter 2

The Presents

Timeless Form

Simple Present

Present Perfect

Present Progressive

Present Perfect Progressive

"These are the times that try men's souls."

THE PRESENT PROGRESSIVE

---

auxiliary **BE** + VERB + **ING**

I **am** work**ing**   we **are** work**ing**
you **are** work**ing**   they **are** work**ing**
he, she, it **is** work**ing**

Let's get started by asking you a question. After looking at the "brain teasers" given below, can you determine the time or meaning of the present progressive in these sentences? There's a blank line after each example on which you can write your descriptions. We've done the first one for you to get you started.

1. He's starring in *Macbeth* on Broadway.   _____ real present _____

2. Tommy's being good for a change.   _____

3. What are you doing?   _____

4. They're touring Southern France.   _____

5. I'm working in a drugstore for the summer.   _____

There are two basic uses of the present progressive in these examples, and sometimes they overlap a little. Sentences 1, 3, and 4 show the real present, that is, that the action is <u>at this time</u>, and there is no other major focus. If you wrote something like "the real present" on the blank lines after these examples, you're doing fine. Sentences 2 and 5, however, have a slightly different focus. True, they communicate that these situations are in the present, but the speaker is focusing on the fact that the situations are <u>temporary</u>, and that's what he wants you to understand. If you wrote something like "temporary present" on the blank lines after those examples, you've got the idea.

Present Progressive as the Real Present

Some of you may know the present progressive as the "present continuous." Whatever its name, among the important points to remember about it is that **its primary function is to communicate the <u>real</u> present.** We find that the name "progressive" is more appropriate than "continuous" because it implies that the action is "in progress," and that's a fairly accurate description.

Teaching Tips

The most effective way to demonstrate the primary use of the present progressive is to plan various simple activities that you can do in front of your class. For example, before class, have items like these on your desk: some paper, a pair of scissors, a ball, a comb, etc. Also before class, draw the time line which appears at the end of this section (**The Present Progressive in a Nutshell**) on the board, and write any pertinent vocabulary on the board that the students may not know yet. (1) At the start of class, take an item or two and say what you're doing: "I'm cutting the paper." "I'm throwing the ball in the air." "I'm combing my hair." (2) After you've gone through all the activities, ask the class, "What am I doing?" as you repeat one of the activities. Call on a student to reply, and continue with more activities and the key question. (3) Now plan on doing other simple activities. Appoint one of the students to ask the question, "What's the teacher doing?" or "What's he/she doing?" Continue this part of the exercise as before. (4) You can now use selected pictures from your picture file (see Appendix 1) to continue the same sort of exercise. (5) Move on, when it's comfortable, to teaching the question forms (which shouldn't be a big problem since the class should already know how to make questions with "be"). Hold up pictures and call on various students to make appropriate questions. At the same time you reinforce question making, teach and reinforce the short answers such as, "Yes, he is." or "No, they aren't."

Note

One cardinal rule about current teaching techniques that we'd like to reiterate is **plan for your lessons to go from being teacher-centered to student-centered as quickly as possible so that the "burden" of work lies with your students, and not with you!**

More Teaching Tips

Show the class a picture with lots of action going on and let them look at it for a minute or two. Put it away and have them write down as many things as they can remember about it (using the present progressive, of course). The one who has the most examples is the "winner" (make sure that those actions are really there and that the forms used are grammatically correct). This can also be done as a group activity; the group with the greatest number of examples is the "winner."

One of the most difficult things for teachers to get across to their students is that, except for a relatively small number of verbs, English normally uses the present progressive to communicate that the action is in the true present. (We'll deal with that small number of verbs at length under the heading "Stative Verbs.") Here are a couple of sample dialogs to demonstrate this focus:

A: Where are Shuwei and Min?
B: They're out in the backyard.
A: What **are** they **doing**?
B: They**'re planting** rose bushes.

A: Is Ari at work this week?
B: No, he isn't.
A: Why not?
B: He**'s moving** into his new house.

Notice how both dialogs deal with the concept of "now," but "now" doesn't represent the same idea in both. In the first dialog, "now" literally means "at this very moment"; in the second, "now" refers to "this week." Make it a point to explain to your students that the concept of "now" can mean this moment, this week, this month, this year, etc.

Teaching Tips

Write up brief situations that use the present progressive on slips of paper (e.g., you're a dentist checking the teeth of one of your patients; you're frying an egg; you're waiting for a bus to come; you're trying to cross a busy road, etc.). You need at least one slip for each student in your class. The students mime their activities individually while their classmates guess what's happening.

Variation

Provide activities that are much more complicated (tying your shoes while answering the phone; feeding a baby while trying to type a term paper; putting on make-up while eating breakfast, etc.). Again, students mime the actions while their classmates figure out what's happening. Make sure your students are aware that they must prepare their pantomimes precisely in order for their classmates to be able to understand them.

More Teaching Tips

For more advanced students and those who know the vocabulary of clothing, colors, and patterns, this is an ideal activity for practicing the present progressive. Present a fashion show, complete with walking across a mock stage, pirouetting, indicating the important features of the garments, etc., just as a real model might do. Before the show begins, divide the class into small groups. Each group will prepare commentaries that will be used to describe the clothing of the various models in their group. The commentaries need to focus on the actual items the students are wearing and the colors and patterns of the various garments. The show begins! Students model their clothes and their group members give a running commentary on the clothing that the models are wearing.

Present Progressive as a Temporary Situation

When we use a verb that can either focus on a temporary situation or a long-term (or permanent) situation, **we use the present progressive to communicate that the situation is temporary.** Look at this sample dialog:

A: Scientists say that the earth **is getting** warmer.
B: I didn't know that. How come?
A: People **are putting** too much CO_2 into the atmosphere.
B: That sounds serious!

In the dialog above, speaker A could choose to communicate that this situation is long term or permanent by using a different form for the verbs (i.e., the simple present, which we'll get to shortly). The speaker has deliberately chosen the present progressive to show not only that this situation is in the present but also may not be long-term.

Teaching Tips

Delay drilling this particular use of the present progressive until you've taught the simple present. Comparing the temporary aspect of the present progressive to the more permanent or routine simple present is a very comfortable, natural way of reinforcing this verb form.

There's one more use of the present progressive that we should consider. It's a use which is not typically covered in ESOL classes, but it's one that we can certainly hear on any day in any conversation. Take a look at the following dialog and identify how the present progressive is being used. Also notice the use of the simple present, which we'll get to next:

A: Happy birth-
day!

B: Oh, you knew!
Well, thanks
very much.

A: So, any big
plans for after
work?

B: You know, it's
funny. When I
got home last
night, I couldn't
find the kids
anywhere. My
husband **isn't puttering** in the garden as usual, and the kids **aren't watching** TV. Noises **are coming** from the basement, so I go down the stairs, and there they are. They**'re making** decorations for a surprise birthday party for me. They don't see me, so I go back upstairs quietly and say nothing the rest of the night.

A: So they're throwing you a surprise birthday party, eh?

B: It looks that way.

Doesn't it seem odd that speaker B is talking about something that happened in the past but uses two forms of the present to do so? For the moment, let's concentrate on the present progressive in this dialog. Can you think of a way to categorize it for this use? If you can, write down your idea on the following line:

_____

The use of the present progressive in this dialog is very common in conversational English, especially in what we call *colloquial speech*. We call it the **narrative style** because it's used to help narrate a story. Many people opt to use this form when they want to bring the listener into more of a sense of temporal involvement with the action of the story. Using the present progressive in this way (and the simple present, too, for that matter) tends to make the story *come closer* to the listener in time.

Troubleshooter

 Students have a tendency to drop or simply forget the auxiliary BE when making the present progressive. Be prepared for this eventuality! Stress the use of the auxiliary and drill it in context as much as possible so that your students won't tend to ignore it.

The Present Progressive in a Nutshell

 the <u>real</u> present (for most verbs):
She's cooking.

 temporary actions:
We're spending this summer at the beach.

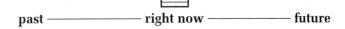

past ——————— right now ——————— future

 the narrative form:
"She's waiting for the bus, so I ask her if I can drop her off anywhere in my car, and she says . . ."

THE SIMPLE PRESENT

> I, you, we, they **work**
>
> he, she, it **works**

Here we have the one verb form in English that has the most inappropriate name. Why? Because the form is neither "simple" nor "present" in its broader usage. Here are some more brain teasers for you to consider. When you think you know how the simple present is being used, describe its time or meaning on each accompanying blank line.

1. Birds fly and fish swim.   _____generalization_____
2. She gets up at 6:30 on weekdays.   _____
3. I work in my uncle's drugstore.   _____
4. I don't like soup.   _____
5. What do you do?   _____
6. "He takes aim. He shoots. He misses!" _____

Most of the uses of the simple present in the examples above share a common thread, but there are fine points that change the focus of the meaning. Sentence 1 doesn't really deal with time at all; it's a **timeless** use which communicates a fact about birds and fish. It can be considered a **generalization or fact.** Sentence 2 shows **habitual or routine** activity. Sentence 3 communicates that this is a **long-term or permanent** job. (Compare it with Sentence 5 in the section on the present progressive.) Sentence 4 is just like 1, a simple fact. Sentence 5 is really idiomatic as it means "What's your job or career?" and has nothing to do with a present activity. Sentence 6 is called the **narrative style**, the form commonly used by someone witnessing an event such as a sportscaster talking to the audience.

Let's take a look at another way we hear the narrative style used in everyday conversation by examining the following dialog. As we've seen with the present progressive, it can also be used in this way:

A: I saw in the paper that Sludgeco's been fined again for polluting Silver Bay.

B: That's right, and I witnessed the pollution first hand. I **go** down to the bay to take some photos at sunset and I **smell** something awful. I **realize** that I'm right near Sludgeco's drain pipes. So I **walk** over to the pipes, and tons of foul-smelling waste are pouring out of these pipes into the bay. I **take** some pictures—lucky I **have** my camera with me!—and **send** them to the nearest Environmental Protection Agency office.

A: You mean, *you* proved Sludgeco was polluting again?

B: Just me and my little old camera!

One curious point that we should clear up about using the simple present and present progressive in this narrative style is to determine when the speaker opts for the simple form and when he/she opts for the progressive form. Can you think of any reason to choose one and then the other? Write your thoughts on the following lines:

_____

_____

_____

There's a very interesting rule that's being put into use in the dialog: **when the verb could be used in the past progressive, the speaker opts for the present progressive; when the verb could be used in the simple past, the speaker opts for the simple present.** In other words, there's a mirror image, so to speak, of one form with the other in the narrative style.

Teaching Tips

An excellent way to practice the simple present is by having students narrate skits. An added benefit of the activity is that you can recycle other grammar points. This skit recycles imperatives (commands) and possessive forms. (1) Before class, write up two or three skits using commands that, when acted out and narrated, tell a story. For this example, you have a narrator and two actors. One actor leaves the room with these commands: (a) Open the door. (b) Look around the room. (c) Spot a friend. (d) Smile at him/her. (e) Enter the room. (f) Take your seat. (2) Give the second actor these directions: (a) Return your friend's smile. (b) Wave at him/her. (3) Give the narrator all the commands in proper order and some concluding remarks: "It's 10:00 A.M. What happens then?" (4) The skit begins! While the actors are acting out their commands, the narrator describes what's going on using the simple present. "Kenji opens the classroom door and looks around. He spots his friend and smiles at her. She returns his smile and waves at him. He enters the room and takes his seat. It's 10:00 A.M. The bell rings and class begins." (5) Have the students produce their own skits in small groups.

Variation #1

Tape bits of TV programs with the sound turned down; select programs that have action suitable for narration. (Be careful! Too much action and students can't narrate the story fast enough; too little and there's nothing much to tell.) Have them prepare the narration to be presented along with the taped TV bits.

Variation #2

Tape a series of sound effects that have potential story lines (knocking on doors, machines running, footsteps, screams, etc.). Have students write up narratives to go along with the sound effects.

Variation #3

If you have a video camera, this is the perfect opportunity to use it. Let your students prepare skits with accompanying narration and then record them for presentation to the entire class. Quiz the class orally about the skits after viewing them.

As you can see, the so-called "simple present" is not at all simple or the true present. The examples presented show the most common uses of this verb form. Take a look at the following dialog which shows some of the uses of the simple present just mentioned:

A: Look at that big shark in the tank over there!
B: Wow! Is it big!
A: Did you know it **loses** a row of teeth every time it **eats**?
B: How **do** you **know** that?
A: I **read** lots of nature magazines.

Two great mistakes are committed in most grammar books that lay the foundation for student confusion which is very hard to straighten out later on. The first great mistake is teaching the simple present before teaching the present progressive. There are probably two reasons for this. First, old-style grammarians felt that the simple present was easier for students to deal with since it's just the base form of the verb with only the addition of an -s on the end for 3rd person singular. "No conjugations to speak of plus no auxiliaries to deal with in the statement form equal an easy verb form to teach." Nothing could be more erroneous since there's the immediate challenge of introducing the auxiliary DO/DOES in the negative and question forms.

Second, those same grammarians realized that a number of high frequency verbs are among those which almost exclusively use the simple present and not the present progressive. Since they're such high frequency items, the grammarians figured they should be taught early on, and therefore the need to teach the simple present right off. This was an arbitrary decision, but one that's proven to be more of a hindrance than a help. Since it's the first verb form students are typically exposed to, and since it's called the simple *present*, students naturally assume that it's indeed the present—the real present—in English. This is where the confusion begins. Another reason to reverse the order in which these forms are taught is that it's much easier to get across the idea of the real present to students than it is to communicate the abstract, vague concept of habitual, general, or timeless situations. To sum up, **we recommend that you teach the present progressive** (affirmative and negative statements, question forms, and short answers) **before teaching the simple present.**

Teaching Tips

Use selected pictures from your picture file. (1) Hold up a picture and describe something about the picture in the simple present. For example, you hold up a picture of a bus driver sitting behind the wheel and say, "This bus driver starts work at 6 o'clock every morning. He usually drives the same bus. He goes along the same route day in and day out. He quits work at 2:00 P.M." (2) Now ask the students, "What does this man do first?" Slightly emphasize the auxiliaries DO or DOES when you ask the question, and keep emphasizing them in every question you model for the class. When you get a correct response to your first question, continue making questions to cover all the descriptive sentences you've modeled for your students. Be sure to mix yes/no questions (Does this man drive a truck?) with wh- questions (When does he start work?) (3) Show the students another picture. This time, see if they can make yes/no questions about what they see in the picture. Let them make the questions and have other students give the answers. That's what we mean by saying you should get the activities student-centered as soon as possible.

Note #1

Whenever you use pictures from your file, make it a habit to write on the board a list of any vocabulary items (individual words or phrases) applicable to a picture you've chosen to use and which you can anticipate will be new for your students. Then, when you get to that picture, first point to the list on the board, and then have them repeat each item after you as you point to whatever it refers to in the picture. Let them know they can use these terms when forming sentences about the picture. Not only will things go more smoothly, but the students will also learn and retain the new vocabulary much faster because it's been taught in a meaningful context.

Note #2

In the *Teaching Tips* just listed, we dealt mostly with yes/no questions. When you feel that your students have these under their belts, begin introducing wh- questions (who/what/where/when/why/how) which simply stick one of these words at the beginning but maintain the DO/DOES structure. Two exceptions are the words WHO and WHAT, but for more information on these, you'll have to read Chapter 12.

More Teaching Tips

Put a grid on the board similar to the one below. Use items that your students may either like or dislike. Have students go up and check the choices that are true for them and then discuss what they've checked off. Be sure that the students use the simple present.

	ice cream	poetry	movies	flowers	tennis	ballet
Rubina	✓		✓		✓	
Jiro	✓	✓		✓		✓
Farideh	✓		✓	✓		

Variation

Students copy a blank grid on a piece of paper and go around the room filling in the information about their classmates. They then give a report about what they've found out.

More Teaching Tips

Give students pages from travel guides that use international symbols. Have the students write up a description of the information they've got using the simple present.

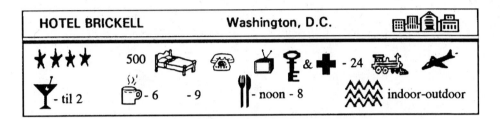

Here's a sample hotel description. We've put the symbols in parentheses to show you how they might be interpreted. Hotel Brickell is a 4-star hotel (★★★★) in downtown (🏢🏢🏢)Washington, D.C. The hotel has 500 beds (🛏) and a telephone (☎) and TV (📺) in each room. The hotel has a concierge (🔑) and medical personnel (✚) available 24 hours a day...

More Teaching Tips

Before class, write up a list of animals, professions, or things for students to describe using the simple present. If your students have research skills, give them topics that they don't know much about or that they don't know at all (planets, famous people, etc.). Example: **Horse:** it runs fast; it has a mane; it loves apples; it often lives in a barn. **Farmer:** he grows crops; he plants seeds; he milks cows.

Stative Verbs*

We've twice alluded to that relatively small group of verbs which uses the simple present almost exclusively. They're called **stative verbs**, which means that they deal with states of being rather than actions. To make these verbs more manageable for your students, you might want to teach them that these verbs can be subdivided into five basic groups: verbs of **liking, the senses, possession, mental processes,** and **states of being.** Here are the ones of higher frequency. (The verbs followed by an asterisk indicate that these are the special words that go

---

*Including Special Verbs: If you change their form, you change their meaning.

through a change of meaning peculiar to English if the present progressive is used instead of the simple present. These changes will be discussed in more detail later on.)

Stative Verbs

LIKING	SENSES	POSSESSION	MENTAL PROCESSES	STATE OF BEING
adore	hear*	belong	believe	astonish
desire	perceive	have*	doubt	be
detest	resemble	lack	feel	concern
dislike	see	own	forgive	cost
hate	seem*	possess	guess	depend
like	smell*		imagine	deserve
love	sound		intend	equal
mind	taste*		know	fit*
prefer			realize	matter
want			recall	mean
wish*			recognize	need
			regard	owe
			remember	tend
			suppose	
			think*	
			understand	

Here's an overview of the stative verbs in bold face shown in the preceding list. (SP = simple present; PP = present progressive)

feel: SP = the involuntary sense of touch anywhere on the body
           Susan **feels** something crawling up her leg!
       SP = believe
           The jury **feels** that the defendant is innocent.
       SP or PP = physical or mental states
             I **feel** ashamed that I lied to her. / I'm
               feeling ashamed.
             Jim **feels** a little ill today. / Jim's
               feeling a little ill.

hear: SP = the involuntary use of the ears;
        to be told
        We **hear** that you've quit your
        job.
        Oh, no! I **hear** the baby crying
        again.

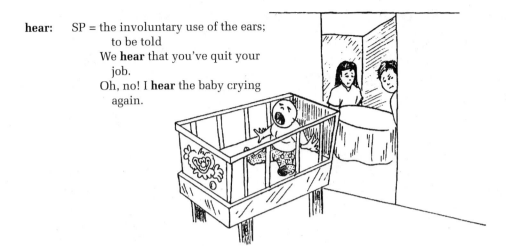

PP = witness what others are saying; imagine sounds
        She needs psychiatric help. She**'s hearing** voices.
        What we**'re hearing** from the government is talk of war.

see: SP = the involuntary use of the eyes; understand
        Jo **doesn't see** well without his glasses.
        I **see** what you mean, but I don't agree with you.

PP = witness what others are doing; have a romantic involvement; hallucinate

What we**'re seeing** is the end of communism in Europe.

I **don't see** anything in that field. You**'re seeing** things!

Did you know that Boris **is seeing** Natasha?

smell: SP = the involuntary use of the nose; how the odor of something is perceived; have a bad odor

I think I **smell** something burning in the kitchen.

These flowers **smell** so good!

Throw out those old boots. They **smell**!

PP = the voluntary use of the nose
Mom**'s smelling** the milk because she thinks it's spoiled.

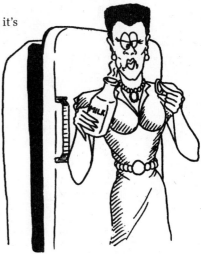

taste: SP = how food or drink is perceived
This soup **tastes** wonderful!

PP = the voluntary use of the taste buds
The chef**'s tasting** the soup for seasoning.

Remember that most sensory verbs have a difference in meaning and usage depending on whether they're voluntary or involuntary actions. **Make it a point to stress to your students that the form used depends on whether these verbs are voluntary or involuntary actions.**

fit: SP = harmonize; conform
Her current project **fits** the company's immediate goals.
Your qualifications **fit** what we're looking for.
SP = able to be put into or on a certain area without difficulty
Does that carry-on bag **fit** in the overhead compartment?

I love this new shirt. Look how well it **fits**.

PP = put something into a certain area without difficulty

I won't need two boxes. **I'm fitting** it all into this one.

have: SP = possess, own
The Kims **have** a lovely house.
SP = be sick
Carla **has** the flu.
PP = a situation that the subject is involved in

Peter**'s having** trouble with his car again.
We**'re having** a party. Would you like to come?

think: SP =believe

Let's postpone the picnic. I **think** it's going to rain.

PP   (sometimes with prepositions "of" or "about") = use the mind; imagine; consider

Be quiet for a moment. I**'m thinking**.

Are you **thinking** of what to serve at the party?

Gus **is thinking** of moving to Canada.

What**'s** he **thinking** about?

wish: SP =communicate unhappiness with a situation; tell people what you would like for them

Philip **wishes** he earned more money.

We **wish** you long life and happiness!

PP   (with preposition "for") = say a type of short prayer for something

Now that I've blown out the candles on my birthday cake, **I'm wishing** for another great year like the one I just had!

At this point, let's see if you can distinguish the differences in meaning between the following pairs of sentences:

1a.   **Did you know that Ken's grandparents are living with him?**

1b.   **Did you know that Ken's grandparents live with him?**

2a.   **Harriet's writing an article for *The New York Times*.**

2b.   **Harriet writes articles for *The New York Times*.**

3a.   **Ali's being a brat.**

3b.   **Ali's a brat.**

Here's how it goes: In **1a,** the idea is that Ken's grandparents are with him **temporarily** and that the situation is taking place now. Perhaps they had a fire in their home or their own home is being remodeled. Whatever the case may be, it's a temporary situation. In **1b**, however, Ken's house is their **permanent** residence (since no specific time is mentioned).

The next two sentences work along similar lines. In **2a**, Harriet is probably a freelance writer who's just writing this one article for the newspaper at the present time, and it's safe to assume it's a **temporary** assignment. In **2b**, Harriet seems to be a **regular** contributor to the paper.

The last two sentences follow suit. Some people might consider the use of "be" in **3a** idiomatic. That doesn't change the basic meaning, which is a **temporary** situation. The speaker is communicating that Ali isn't always a brat; he's acting this way just today or just right now. In **3b**, however, it's clear that Ali is a brat **all the time**; this is his personality. And that leads us to a little rule that we can remember about the verb "be": **We can use the verb "be" in the present progressive to describe temporary states of personality as opposed to how someone behaves all the time.** Two more examples follow:

Don't mind him. He**'s being** petty.

Why **are** you **being** so stubborn?

Teaching Tips

Once your students have learned the basic concepts of simple present, you should begin contrasting this form with the present progressive. (1) Select pictures from your file, some of which will lend themselves to describing actions in progress at this moment or seem temporary, and others that lend themselves to describing activities that are routine, habitual, or more permanent. Ideally, find pictures which can be applied both ways, let's say a picture of a family having a picnic in the park. "The Carlsons go on picnics every two weeks in the summer. They're going on a picnic today. They picnic in different parks. This time, they're having a picnic in Biscayne Park. Mr. Carlson usually prepares the barbecue. Today, his son, Rob, is preparing the barbecue." (2) After you've modeled the patterns for the class, go over the pictures again, this time asking questions and getting students' answers (short answers for yes/no questions and complete sentences for wh- questions). (3) Remember to get the activity student-centered as soon as you can. Turn over the job of asking questions, answering questions, and describing the pictures to your students, sit back, and let them experiment with the language on their own. Correct when necessary, but do so "gently" so as not to intimidate the students and inadvertently make them feel less like participating.

More Teaching Tips

If you choose to recycle this grammar with an intermediate or advanced group, bring in some examples of proverbs: A stitch in time saves nine; Familiarity breeds contempt; Absence makes the heart grow fonder, etc. Discuss the meaning of those with which the students aren't familiar and then have them provide examples from their own languages. Stress the fact that you want only those proverbs that contain the simple present.

A Special Note About the Word "ALWAYS"

In more traditional grammar books, "always" *always* appears with the simple present. That, of course, is reasonable since one of the key meanings of simple present is "all the time." Language, however, isn't always reasonable or logical.

A case in point is the very common use of joining up "always" with the present progressive: **She's always making fun of my dog Butch!** The best explanation for this phenomenon is that we use "always" with the present progressive to emphasize the habitual, unrelenting nature of an action. This usage has become so widespread that it must be considered an acceptable alternative to using the simple present.

The Simple Present in a Nutshell

- **the real present** (only for a select group of verbs):
  I hear you.
- **general, timeless facts:**
  She cooks very well.
- **habitual, routine actions:**
  We spend every summer at the beach.
- **narrative style:**
  ". . . and runner no. 3 wins the marathon!"
  "So when I call her a witch, she slaps me in the face and storms out of the room!"

THE PRESENT PERFECT

---

auxiliary **HAVE + PAST PARTICIPLE** of VERB

I, you, we, they **have** work**ed**
he, she, it **has** work**ed**

There is many an English teacher who wishes that the present perfect would just disappear overnight from the language. This is probably because it contains many subtleties and nuances. If you take each use one by one, you can manage to do a good, clear, concise job of teaching this complex form.

Teaching Tips

The present perfect provides an additional problem for students—the past participles, especially those for the irregular verbs. A fun way to practice these forms is to do "Body Spelling." Prepare a list of irregular verbs before class begins. Divide the class into groups of seven to eight. You may need to make the groups larger if the verbs that you're using have more than eight letters (e.g., forgotten, understood). And if you have verbs that have fewer letters than the groups have members, two or more students can "become" one letter. Distribute several verbs to each group. The students then have to spell the past participles using their bodies as the letters and their classmates have to figure out what they're spelling:

"Body Spelling" is a fun way to practice present participles, too.

Present Perfect as a Bridge from Past to General Present

Read these sentences and answer the questions.

1. **Rolf lived in Budapest for many years.**
   Does Rolf live in Budapest now?   Yes ☐   No ☐
2. **Rolf has lived in Budapest for many years.**
   Does Rolf live in Budapest now?   Yes ☐   No ☐

The answer to the first question is NO. We're clearly given to believe that Rolf either moved out of Budapest some time ago or he's now deceased. The answer to the second question is YES. We know for a fact (from the grammatical form) that Rolf still lives in Budapest. He moved there many years ago and he's still there. So how did you do?

There's one other point to mention here. Present perfect can be used for an action that's been uninterrupted since it began in the past: "Rolf has lived in Budapest for many years" is an example of an uninterrupted action. Compare it to this sentence: "Maria has visited Budapest many times." Maria made many visits to the city, and each one of them was completed in the past. You'll learn why we use present perfect in this case as you read further.

We know the answers to the two questions above because we understand the use of simple past versus present perfect: With the simple past, the action is completely finished in the past; with present perfect, **the action began in the past and comes to an indefinite time in the general present**. Here's a dialog that will demonstrate this use more fully:

A: I **have**n't **had** a hot meal in a long time.
B: That's because you**'ve been** too busy to cook one.
A: And nobody**'s invited** me to dinner either.
B: You poor thing! Come over to my house tonight.

Teaching Tips

By the time you get around to teaching the present perfect, your students will already have learned the simple past. They should understand that the simple past means that the action is completely finished and stays in the past. Use this as a base to start explaining the present perfect. (1) On the board, draw the time line you'll find in **The Present Perfect in a Nutshell** at the end of this section and explain to the students that the present perfect is used for an action begun in the past which comes to the present. Another visual aid that works well is to draw a bridge on the board. Label the land it's attached to on the left side "the past," and label the land on the other side "the present." Show the class how you can cross over the bridge from the past to the present. (2) Before class, think of a number of things that began in the past and continue into the present, preferably things that your students can relate to. Again on the board, list these things in the simple past. For example, "We met each other a month ago." "We bought our textbooks last week," etc. (3) At the start of class, after you've demonstrated the time line and the bridge, say the first sentence in the list out loud. Then create a sentence from this base in the present perfect: "We've known each other for a month." "We've had our textbooks for a week." Continue in this way with the other simple past sentences you thought of before class. (4) Use pictures from your picture file for similar practice. Let's say we use the picture of the Carlsons on their picnic again. "The Carlsons began to go on picnics four years ago. They've gone on picnics for four years." "Mr. Carlson prepared the barbecue on their first picnic. He's always prepared the barbecue." (5) Again, get the lesson student-centered whenever it seems comfortable to do so by having the students recreate your original sen-

tences about the pictures and then by creating some of their own. (6)
Work with questions and short answers when appropriate.

Present Perfect as a Foot in the Door to the Future

Read each of the following sentences and answer the questions.

1. **My grandfather traveled from Europe to Africa many times.**

    Is grandfather alive or dead?   Alive ☐   Dead ☐   Don't know ☐

    Do you think he'll take the trip again?   Yes ☐   No ☐   Maybe ☐

2. **My grandfather has traveled from Europe to Africa many times.**

    Is grandfather alive or dead?   Alive ☐   Dead ☐   Don't know ☐

    Do you think he'll take the trip again?   Yes ☐   No ☐   Maybe ☐

It's really amazing how the change in a verb form can create such subtle but important differences. Let's see how you did with the questions. In the first sentence, which uses "traveled," most people would guess that grandfather's dead, although others would be justified in saying that they don't honestly know. As for whether or not grandfather will take the trip again, most people would check NO. (We'll discuss the reasons for these answers in more detail when we get to the past forms of verbs.)

In the second sentence, which uses the present perfect, most people would guess that grandfather's still alive, and as for whether or not he'll take the trip again, most people would check YES or MAYBE. Quite a difference from the answers to the first two questions! So how did you do this time? Coming up is the explanation that will make it all clear.

Troubleshooter 🔫

 You may have students who speak French. If that's the case, they will probably confuse the English present perfect with a form of the simple past in French known as the "passé composé." They will invariably think that present perfect means the simple past and end up using it in sentences with words like *ago*. Anticipating this problem may save you a lot of grief!

Why should the sets of answers be so different? The reason lies in this second important meaning of the present perfect, that the action happened in the past, comes up to the present, **and may happen again at some point in the fu-**

ture. In other words, we're leaving the door open a little in case the event should happen again; we're not shutting the door forever on this possibility. The simple past communicates the idea that an action is completely finished in the past and has no real connection to the present, much less the future. This is where the simple past and the present perfect differ so greatly. Let's look at another sample dialog to see this in action.

A: **Did** you **watch** TV last night?
B: No, I **didn't.**
A: Then you **haven't seen** that new show.
B: No, I **haven't,** darn it!
A: Don't worry. It'll be on every week.

Teaching Tips

Since your students already know that the simple past means the action is finished, this concept of present perfect shouldn't be too hard to get across. (1) Before class, think of two or three things that happened in the past and won't be repeated in the future. For example, "Columbus saw various parts of America." "The Egyptians built enormous pyramids at Giza." (**Note:** Think of sentences with themes familiar to your particular students.) (2) Write these ideas on the board, but next to each one, write the same sentences in the present perfect: "Columbus has seen various parts of America." "The Egyptians have built enormous pyramids at Giza." (3) At the start of class, ask the students if they think all the sentences on the board are correct, and if they don't, why not? Clearly explain, if necessary, that the present perfect doesn't work with these sentences simply because Columbus can't see any more parts of America, and the Egyptians have no intention of building any more pyramids. (4) Use selections from your picture file to continue practicing this use of the present perfect, and also prepare a part of your lesson plan for asking your students questions about their lives with ideas that can be in the simple past (finished) or present perfect (possible again in the future).

Present Perfect as a Recent Event or an Event from the Past That Affects the Present

Once again, read these sentences and answer the questions:

1. **Brendan and Maureen got engaged.**
   When did Maureen accept Brendan's proposal?
   Some time ago ·☐   Recently ☐   Don't know ☐

2.   **Brendan and Maureen have gotten engaged.**

When did Maureen accept Brendan's proposal?

Some time ago   ☐   Recently   ☐   Don't know   ☐

The answer to the first question is SOME TIME AGO or DON'T KNOW. We know it took place in the past, but it could have been a hundred years ago or two days ago for all we know. It's vague and leaves us guessing about the time in the past unless we have additional information. The answer to the second question, however, is RECENTLY. We know that because present perfect was used. We still don't know the exact time in the past, but we certainly understand that the event happened so recently that friends and family are probably still excited about the news. This is what we mean when we say that another important use of the present perfect is **to communicate that an event happened recently and still touches on, or affects, the present.** That's why Brendan's and Maureen's relatives are probably still excited.

A: **Have** you **heard** the news?
B: What news?
A: Brendan**'s** just **proposed** to Maureen!
B: Well, **has** she **accepted**?
A: Yes! And they**'ve** even **set** the date.

Teaching Tips

Your trusty picture file will be a big help once again. (1) Choose pictures that show actions which have just taken place or are finished, but still affect the present. As an example, let's go back to that marvelously versatile picture of the Carlsons on their picnic: "Rob has lit the charcoal for the barbecue." "Mrs. Carlson has set the picnic blanket on the ground."

"The girls have brought the cooler from the car and placed it near the blanket." "Mr. Carlson has fallen asleep under a tree." (2) Have the students review the model sentences and ask one another questions about the scene. Then continue with other pictures. (3) Ask the students to think of actions that happened in the past, but still have an effect on the present. For example, "The government has raised taxes again." "I'm feeling very nervous. I guess I've drunk too much coffee today."

More Teaching Tips

Pass out various short exclamations to students. Students will read their exclamations out loud, using appropriate intonation, and add explanatory statements to clarify the reason for their exclamations. Here are some exclamations to distribute to the students:

Oh my gosh!	Ouch!	Stop it!	So?	Rats!	Do it again!
No, thanks.	Oh, no!	No way!	Why?	Ahhh!	Why not?
Good luck!	Yes!	Bye bye!	Yes?	Damn!	Congratulations!
Fantastic!	Sorry!	Please?	What?	Wow!	Please!

These are the kinds of responses that you might expect students to produce: "Oh my gosh! I've just swallowed something strange!" "Ouch! I've just stuck myself with this needle." "Congratulations! You've just passed your driving test." "Ahhh! I've never tasted anything so good!"

More Teaching Tips

Because the present perfect is a difficult verb form for most students, it may be helpful for them to be able to analyze how native English speakers use the various forms in actual speech. This activity gets them thinking about these difficulties. Record bits of TV or radio news reports before class. Or, if you prefer, collect items from newspapers or magazines. Note instances of the present perfect. Present the tape or clippings to the students and have them write down some examples of the present perfect forms that they hear or find. Have them analyze why present perfect was used.

Variation

After the students have done their initial analyses, have them write their own news stories, record them, and then play them for the entire class. Even if a tape recorder or video recorder isn't available, the students can still present their stories to the class.

The Present Perfect in a Nutshell

- uninterrupted actions from the past to an indefinite time in the general present:
  They've raised horses ever since they bought that farm.

  past —————— general present —————— future

- completed actions from the past to an indefinite time in the general present:
  She's received several promotions since she started working there.

  past —————— general present —————— future

- actions from the past to the present that may occur again in the future:
  We've seen that movie three times.

  past —————— general present —————— future

- actions from the past that still affect the present:
  They aren't setting up the school gym for tonight's dance because the dance has been cancelled.

THE PRESENT PERFECT PROGRESSIVE

> auxiliary **HAVE BEEN** + VERB + **ING**
>
> I, you, we, they **have been** working
> he, she, it **has been** working

This form of the present perfect is quite troublesome for students and should be taught slowly and cautiously.

To begin with, a very simple but effective rule can be made about the present perfect progressive: **any verb that can be used in the present progressive can be used in the present perfect progressive.** For example, if we can say "he's doing," we can say "he's been doing"; if we can say "they're living," we can say "they've been living." It's as simple as that.

Take a look at the following sets of sentences and see if you perceive a difference in meaning between them.

1a.   **She's worked here for three years.**

1b.   **She's been working here for three years.**

☐   A difference   ☐   No difference

2a.   **We've traveled in South America.**

2b.   **We've been traveling in South America.**

☐   A difference   ☐   No difference

There's really no important difference in meaning between 1a and 1b. Native speakers will use them interchangeably. There's a difference in meaning, however, between 2a and 2b. Remember that we discussed the fact that some actions in the present perfect can be completed, repeated, and may happen in the future? Do you also recall that these actions can be uninterrupted from some point in the past to now? This is why we perceive a difference between 2a and 2b, but not between 1a and 1b.

Because she's been a steady employee for the past three years, we don't perceive any difference between the simple form or progressive form of the present perfect. In 2a, we perceive that there was either one completed trip or various completed trips, but we're using present perfect to communicate that there may be a future trip as well. In 2b, we're talking about one uninterrupted trip that began at some point in the past and is still going on at this moment. Which leads us to the next important use of present perfect progressive: **it brings the action from the past to this very moment in the present** and not to the general concept of the present as the simple form of present perfect does. Here are some more examples to show you this difference:

3a.   **Claire has taught biology for over ten years.**

3b.   **Claire has been teaching plant reproduction since Monday.**

4a.   **The Taylors have played golf since they were teenagers.**

4b.   **The Taylors have been playing golf since 8:00 A.M.**

In 3a, we're bringing the action from ten years ago to the general present, but it doesn't necessarily mean that Claire has a biology class this term. In 3b, not only do we know that Claire's teaching biology this week, but we also know that she began teaching plant reproduction on Monday and is <u>still</u> teaching it now.

The next two sentences work the same way. Sentence 4a tells us that the Taylors began playing golf when they were teenagers, and it's still a sport they practice. However, they may not be playing today. The action comes to the general present. Sentence 4b tells us that they began playing a round of golf at 8 o'clock this morning, and they're <u>still</u> on the golf course.

Let's try an experiment to clarify this difference between the simple form of present perfect and the progressive form. Read these four sentences and check off the one which is ungrammatical:

☐ **The Taylors have played golf since they were teenagers.**

☐ **The Taylors have been playing golf since they were kids.**

☐ **The Taylors have played golf since 8:00 A.M.**

☐ **The Taylors have been playing golf since 8:00 A.M.**

The ungrammatical sentence is the third one ("The Taylors have played golf since 8:00 A.M."). The questions we need to ask at this point are, why is the third one wrong?, and why doesn't it *sound* right? We can arrive at the answers by going over each sentence methodically. To begin with, one technique which frequently works to find out where the action began and where it is now is to break a sentence down into two smaller chunks. First of all, we need to establish the starting point of the action, and that's easily found by looking at the prepositional phrase with "since" or "for." Next, we can see that the rest of the sentence deals with the action as it's come into the present or into the general realm of time. If we do that to the first sentence, this is what we arrive at:

The Taylors began to play golf when they were teenagers.

The Taylors still **play** golf.

This works because we're using the simple present in the second chunk as a generalization or a timeless idea. We certainly don't mean that they're playing golf at this moment.

The second sentence is an alternative form which really doesn't change meaning, and we've already discussed how the speaker can do that.

If we break down the fourth sentence, we end up with:

The Taylors began to play golf at 8:00 A.M.

The Taylors **are playing** golf right now.

This also works because we know the present progressive means the real present, what's occurring right now.

But if we break down the third sentence, this is what we get:

The Taylors began to play golf at 8:00 A.M.

The Taylors **play** golf right now.

Here's the problem! We can't use the simple present for the verb "play" if we mean that the action is going on now. Remember: **the present perfect progressive is usually a reflection of present time.** The typical changeover would be:

simple present	$\longrightarrow$	present perfect
(The Taylors play)	$\longrightarrow$	(The Taylors have played)
present progressive	$\longrightarrow$	present perfect progressive
(The Taylors are playing)	$\longrightarrow$	(The Taylors have been playing)

Teaching Tips

You don't have to go crazy teaching the fine points of distinction between present perfect and present perfect progressive because there are so many times when they seem to overlap in everyday usage. The only thing to concentrate on is the type of situation that we gave you previously when the present perfect just doesn't work because a particular action is in progress at this very moment and doesn't just come to the general present. (1) When you start teaching this form, show your students a time line like the one you'll find in **The Present Perfect Progressive in a Nutshell.** (You want to clearly show the students the difference in time lines between the present perfect and the present perfect progressive.) (2) One way to introduce the progressive form is to break the sentences down into their two basic components like the example you've just read. Put the second component in the present progressive, and when you combine the two parts, you'll have the present perfect progressive. For example: "She started working on that project two weeks ago. She's still working on that project." These two components will combine as "She's been working on that project for two weeks (now)." (3) Create various situations that your students can relate to to produce more sentences. Your picture file will certainly come in handy, too.

The Present Perfect Progressive in a Nutshell

🥜 **uninterrupted actions from the past to the general present (as an alternative to the present perfect):**
They've been raising horses ever since they bought that farm.

past ——————— **right now** ——————— **future**

◕ **uninterrupted actions from the past to this moment:**

You've been reading about present verb forms in this chapter.

past ————————— right now ————————— future

A Note About the Words "SINCE" and "FOR"

When the perfect forms of the verbs are taught, the first words that always seem to accompany them are "since" and "for." Here are some sentences containing one or the other of these words. Study these examples and see if you can determine what common elements can be found in each group of sentences and, therefore, what rules are in play to determine whether to use "since" or "for."

1. **He's been a teacher for a long time.**

   He's been a teacher for twenty-six years.

   He's been a teacher at this school for three terms.

   He's been a teacher here for just a couple of months.

   He's been a teacher here for only a little while.

2. **He's been a teacher since he graduated from college.**

   He's been a teacher since 1962.

   He's been a teacher since he got his teaching certificate.

   He's been a teacher since he moved to this city.

   He's been a teacher since the early '70s.

Have you figured it all out? Here's what's happening: phrases like "a long time," "twenty-six years," and "a little while" all deal with a **quantity of time**. The rule is, **use the word "for" after the perfect forms of the verbs if you're going to talk about quantity; for everything else, use the word "since."** (Note: "1962" is considered the name of a year, not a quantity.)

Some Other Companion Words with the Present Perfect

Traditionally, the present perfect has been the verb form to use when the following words or phrases are employed: **already, still, yet, lately, so far**, and **up to now.** Here are some examples:

We've already seen that movie. / We've seen that movie already.

We haven't seen that movie yet.

We've seen some very good movies lately.

We've seen two movies so far this month.

Videos haven't put movie theaters out of business up to now.

It just seems to be the case that when these words or phrases are employed, present perfect is the verb form to use. Notice, however, that we said "traditionally" the present perfect is used with all of these words. In modern, colloquial speech, it's very common to hear the simple past used with several of these expressions:

We already saw that movie. / We saw that movie already.

We didn't see that movie yet.

We saw two movies so far this month.

True, most educated speakers of English tend to feel that using the present perfect with <u>all</u> of these words is "better English." This, nonetheless, is a matter of style nowadays, not hard-and-fast grammar.

Mind Bogglers!

Here are some tricky words that every ESOL teacher should be able to deal with—and will certainly need to deal with!

What's the difference between:

see and **look at**

look at and **watch**

Chapter 3

The Articles

a book ~~X~~ books

~~A~~ artist
An artist

~~a~~ rain
the rain

~~A~~ Yukon
The

~~a~~ sky
the

~~the~~ life

~~a~~n union
a

AN UNCLE

the mail

~~a~~ apple
an

~~the~~ Robert's bike

The Mona Lisa
The Mona Wilson **?**

The Yucatan

~~The~~ God

~~a~~ weather
the

~~a~~ honor
an

~~an~~ house
a

~~X~~ Nile
The

~~The~~ Love

a beer X
a beer ✓ **?**

It wasn't just a party, but the party to end all parties!

THE INDEFINITE ARTICLE

It's odd how this chapter wouldn't even appear in, let's say, a Russian or Chinese or Latin grammar book, and only the second part of this chapter, which deals with the definite article, might appear in an Arabic or Hebrew grammar book. Very curious indeed! The reason is that the articles (indefinite = a/an; definite = the) are features which don't exist in many languages—and the speakers of those languages get on perfectly well without them. This little bit of information may help you anticipate certain problems when you teach students whose native languages have no articles or at least no indefinite article.

Pronunciation

Before we go on with the standard usages of the indefinite article, let's discuss its pronunciation for a moment. The usual pronunciation is like the unstressed syllable (first syllable) in the words *about* or *agree*. The symbol *schwa* /ə/ in the International Phonetic Alphabet represents this sound.

We do have an alternate pronunciation, however. It's the same sound as the name of the letter, "a" /e/ and is used more for emphasis or in slowed-down speech. Make sure your students understand that it is <u>not</u> the standard sound in normally flowing speech.

"A" Versus "An"

We showed above that the word "a" has a variant form, "an." How can we know when to use "a" and when to use "an"? Here's a hint: it has to do with sound. Look at the following examples and see if you can figure out the two phonological rules that govern "a" and "an":

a plum	an apple
a melon	an orange
a nice apple	an old banana
a ripe pear	an overripe peach

First Rule: _____

_____

Second Rule: _____

_____

As it happens, the rules are quite clear cut: if the noun or adjective begins with a consonant, use the word "a." If the noun or adjective begins with a vowel, use the word "an." Simple, right? Well, almost.

a harp	a university
a happy child	a united faculty
an hour	an uncle
an honorable man	an ugly wart

Above are some exceptions to the rules—or are they? Figure out what's going on with the indefinite article in front of these words and write your conclusions below:

_____

_____

_____

Come to think of it, we really haven't come across any exceptions to the rules after all; in fact, the examples above make our case even stronger. We use "a" before "harp" and "happy child" because the words after the article begin with a consonant, or rather, a consonant <u>sound</u>. We use "an" before "hour" and "honorable man" because, even though the words after the article begin with a consonant, they don't begin with a consonant sound but with a <u>vowel</u> sound since the initial **h** is silent in both words.

One possible exception that bears mentioning is the adjective "historical." Even though the traditional rule dictates that we say "<u>a</u> historical novel," more and more native speakers tend to say "<u>an</u> historical novel." It seems that there's a tendency to drop the **h** in this word and this triggers people into using "an" instead of "a." A possible explanation might involve the change of stress between the noun "**HIS**tory" and the adjective "his**TOR**ical." After all, no native speaker would say "an history."

Taken to its farthest limits, this phenomenon can be observed regularly in what we refer to as Cockney English, a dialect spoken in a certain section of London. It's a standard rule in Cockney phonology to drop all initial **h**'s and, by so doing, use the article "an" instead of "a": *an 'ammer* (a hammer); *an 'and* (a hand).

Getting back to our previous list, we say "a" before "university" and "united faculty" because the initial sound isn't a vowel (onion / ooze), but a *glide* like the sound of "y" in "youth." We say "an" before "uncle" and "ugly wart" because the words after the article in these two cases do begin with vowel sounds.

So, our rules should be amended a bit: **use "a" before words that begin with consonant <u>sounds</u>; use "an" before words that begin with vowel <u>sounds</u>.**

Teaching Tips

Realia is very useful for ESOL teachers to have; it can be used in many different ways (role plays, for example). In this case, bring in realia that represents occupations, sports, or actors and their roles. Examples might be a pilot's cap, stethoscope, wig, book bag, swimming goggles, mortar board, Mickey Mouse ears, etc. If you don't have any of these items, you can often get them at toy stores, second-hand shops, and yard sales. Your students may even have some they'll bring in to class. Hand out the props, or let the students choose them, and say as you point to a student: "She's a rock star." "He's a doctor." "She's a professor." If you have duplicate props, you say: "They're pilots." "He's Mickey Mouse." Have the students repeat after you individually or as a group. Continue with questions ("Who's the doctor?" "Is Jenna a chemist?") or by pointing to a student and saying: "clerk." Student responses may be the following: "Who's a dentist?" "Is Genghis a teacher?" "I'm a swimmer." "She's not an actor; she's a ballerina." When the students are comfortable with the articles, let them take over the questioning.

More Teaching Tips

Before class, select several pictures from your picture file. Be sure that the pictures you choose have plenty of items in them. (It's also possible for you to let your students select a picture themselves.) Ask the students to describe the various items in the pictures, using articles where necessary.

Meaning and "A" Versus "One"

What does the word "a" mean? It represents one way that we communicate that **something is singular and countable** (a book, a flower, a cat). **It's also the article we use in general statements** (An apple is a fruit).

But the number "one" does the same thing, doesn't it? In some cases that we'll discuss later, it does, but right now let's look at some comparisons and see if we can find a distinction between "a" and "one":

I bought **a** book.
They have **a** parakeet.
He gave her **a** flower.

I bought **one** book.
They have **one** parakeet.
He gave her **one** flower.

Do you discern a difference? If you do, write down the difference you find between "a" and "one" on the lines that follow.

_____

_____

_____

For students whose native languages have only "one" word for the indefinite article and the number "one," such as Spanish with "un[o]" (masculine) or "una" (feminine), there's usually some confusion as to when to use the article and when to use the number in English. If your observations are the same as ours, they'll include the explanation that some of your students will need. As it happens, **the indefinite article means that the noun is singular, countable and just <u>one of many</u>;** the number "one," on the other hand, tends to be used when we respond to the question "How many . . . ?" or "How much . . . ?" In other words, **we normally use "one" when counting, but we use "a" just to communicate that something or someone is singular.**

Are there times when "a" and "one" can be used the same way? Let's find out. Here are some examples for you to look at. If you can substitute "one" for "a/an," check the box after each sentence.

1.   Would you like to hear **an** interesting story?   ☐
2.   I found close to **a** hundred old coins in my basement!   ☐

3. I told my brother and he said it was probably **a** treasure somebody had hidden there. ☐

4. In fact, what I had found was only **a** third of the total treasure hidden in my basement! ☐

5. I looked closely at some of the coins. There was **a** dollar, **a** dubloon, **a** kroner, and **a** ruble. ☐

6. I put some of the coins in **a** little leather pouch. ☐

7. That tiny pouch must have weighed at least **a** kilo! ☐

Do you see any rules at work? In a moment we'll look into what rules there may be. The boxes we'd check go with Sentences **2, 4, 5,** and **7.** In all of those sentences, the word "a" can be substituted perfectly well with "one." So why is that? Why can't we do the same for the other sentences? Think about how you'd categorize the words following "a" in the sentences you checked and list the categories below:

a / one hundred	_____
a / one third	_____
a / one dollar, etc.	_____
a / one kilo	_____

The categories we hope you came up with are numbers, fractions, money and weights or measurements. With words in these categories, "a" and "one" can be used the same way.

An Idiomatic Offshoot

We'd like to mention here that there's an idiomatic use for the word "one" which is currently quite popular. It's used as another way to show emphasis or to substitute for the phrases "a really" or "a very." For example, one person might say to another, "That's **one** beautiful car!" Translation: "That's **a really** beautiful car!"

One last point we should discuss is in answer to the question, what is the plural of the indefinite article? The answer is simply NOTHING. When a noun that has "a" before it is pluralized, it drops the article:

a pin	pins
an anchor	anchors
a grape	grapes
an unpaid bill	unpaid bills

Among many linguists, this lack of an article actually has a name of its own; it's called the "zero article."

Teaching Tips

Bring in 20 to 25 items that represent a variety of count and non-count nouns (a book, some sand, a newspaper, some paper, etc.). Spread them out on your desk before class and cover them up. When the students come in, have them gather around your desk and uncover the items. Give the students a few minutes to remember as many items as they can before you cover them up again. Have the students return to their desks and ask them to list the items, making sure they use articles in their list.

More Teaching Tips

Divide your class into pairs or small groups and have them plan a party, barbecue, picnic or trip, etc. Ask them to write up a list of the equipment and items that they'll need for the event. Again, make sure that they include appropriate articles on their list. When each group has made up its list, bring the class back together and compare the lists.

THE ZERO ARTICLE

As we've just mentioned, the zero article is used when a countable noun that takes "a" in the singular is made plural. It's also used when we deal with uncountable nouns (butter / water / snow) in general terms.

There are some peculiarities in its usage, though, that we should also mention. Compare the words in bold in the following dialogs and see if you can make any conclusions about when the definite or indefinite article is used as opposed to the zero article.

A: You just bought **a car**, didn't you?
B: Well, it's really **a used car**.
A: Do you go everywhere **by car**, or do you use **the bus**?
B: Now I hardly ever go anywhere **by bus**.

A: Are you going **to church** now?
B: Yes, I am.
A: Is **the church** the one at the corner?
B: That's right.

A: I'm staying **in bed** all day today!
B: Uh-oh. That's what <u>you</u> think.
A: Oh? What do you mean?
B: Our St. Bernard just broke **the bed!**

Before you become totally perplexed, we'll make it easy for you. The simple fact is that there's often a zero article in what we can refer to as "pat phrases" (preposition + noun). These phrases usually deal with abstract uses of concrete nouns. In other words, they don't refer to one specific item but rather to an item in a general activity.

For example, "a car" is a concrete item; "by car" is an abstraction which deals more with the general activity of using this means of transportation. "Going to church" refers to an activity rather than one specific building; "the church" does that. "Staying in bed" is another example of a general activity, while "the bed" refers to a concrete item.

Other examples of pat phrases with the zero article are:

in or **to**: jail / class / school / college / town / court

at: school / work / sea / home

on: top / land / consignment / call

Another interesting example of the zero article is with some verbs of movement or motion such as:

leave: home / work / town

go / fly / drive: home / uptown / downtown

<u>You</u> should understand why the zero article is used in this way—your students don't have to. They should simply learn these kinds of pat phrases just as they are and not bother analyzing them. As you'll read later on in this chapter, part of good language learning is to be accepting of the idiosyncracies that the target language may have.

Teaching Tips

Have your students write down (1) 10 to 15 items that they'd like to have, given unlimited money, or (2) 10 to 15 things that they'd like to change about themselves, their lives, or their world. Make sure they use articles with their items. Collect the lists and redistribute them. The students need to interview one another to find out whose list they have. Students must use appropriate questions in order to discover who the lists belong to.

A Word About Change

In just about every prescriptive English grammar we've come across (the ones that tell you what you *should* say), the lesson dealing with countable and uncountable nouns is quite straightforward: here are the nouns that you can count (in which case, you can use the indefinite article or a number accompanied by a plural marker on the noun), and here are the nouns you cannot count (in which case, you can't use the indefinite article or a number and a plural marker on the noun).

In the list of uncountable nouns, we find words such as *beer, coffee, tea, water, bread,* and *lettuce.* The lesson goes on to tell us that we must use such words as a *glass, two cups, a loaf,* and *two heads* in order to count the uncountable items we've just mentioned. Then we go out into "the real world" and listen to what people really say. Go into any restaurant and you may just hear:

"Let's see, that'll be a vodka on the rocks and two beers, right?"

"Hey, Antoine, the chef's gotta make a little more salad, so go get a lettuce, an endive, and a can of anchovies, okay?"

So what should English teachers do? Are we to "go by the book," remain staunch defenders of prescriptive grammar and be blind to the changes that are taking place in the language? After all, if enough native speakers decide to contradict what the grammar books say, what should we do?

Our advice, for the time being, is to say that you should teach the prescribed grammar, but that it's perfectly acceptable to mention the current alternatives that your students will surely hear once they're exposed to enough native speakers. We can call these alternatives when dealing with countable and uncountable nouns "fast food English." It could have developed out of the need for restaurant people to abbreviate their messages whenever possible in order to keep up a certain pace on the job. After enough time passed and enough customers kept hearing these usages, they caught on with the general public and have now become fairly acceptable alternatives.

You may not choose to have your students use these alternative forms actively, but your students can at least be made aware that they do exist. Sometimes it can be dangerous to judge what's right and what's wrong in language.

Teaching Tips

Before class, collect or prepare various menus. Divide the class into small groups; one student will be the "waiter" or "waitress" and the others the "customers." Have the students role play ordering food. The waiters and waitresses should write down the orders as they're being given so that they can repeat the orders at the end to see if they're correct. Make sure that everyone uses appropriate "restaurant English."

THE DEFINITE ARTICLE

Pronunciation

We've already mentioned that the definite article is the word "the" and the first thing we should consider is its pronunciation. Just as when choosing to use "a" or "an," we have rules for the standard pronunciation of this word as well. Read the following examples out loud and see if you find yourself using two different pronunciations for "t-h-e."

the angel	the plant
the onion	the fruit
the elm	the birch
the ink	the pen

There are some people who would pronounce "t-h-e" the same way with all these nouns, but that's considered nonstandard. Note any observations you can make about how you pronounced "t-h-e" in the column on the left, and how you pronounced it in the column on the right.

In the left-hand column, _____

_____

In the right-hand column, _____

_____

If you harken back to the rules we figured out for "a" and "an," you recall that it all depended on whether the first sound in the following word was a vowel or consonant sound. That holds true for these pronunciation rules as well. **If the following word begins with a vowel sound, pronounce the vowel in "t-h-e" as the name of the letter, "e" /i/. If the following word begins with a consonant sound, pronounce the vowel in "t-h-e" the same way you pronounce the "a" in** ***about*, /ə/.** This also holds true for those deceptive words which begin with silent "h" (honor) or the glide "y" /y/ (union). Since the "h" is silent, we treat those words as if they begin with vowel sounds; since the "y" is a glide, we treat those words as if they begin with a consonant sound.

One other pronunciation to keep in mind is that we often pronounce the "e" in "t-h-e" as the name of the letter when we emphasize the noun it precedes:

A: Did you say that his name's Jason Rockefeller?

B: Yes, I did.

A: Is he one of ***theee*** Rockefellers?

B: No, I'm afraid he isn't.

Meaning and Usage

We've already said that "a" is the article to use in general statements; the same can be said about "the" (The orange is a fruit of Oriental origin). Is there a significant difference if we substitute "An" for "The" in the example in parentheses? Not really; at least, not for the purposes of this book. In fact, there are three ways that we can talk in generalities about subjects: using the indefinite article (a), using the definite article (the), or using no article (the zero article) and making the noun plural. Here's an example of the three ways we can discuss the same topic in a general statement:

1. **A rabbit** is an animal loved by all children.
2. **The rabbit** is an animal loved by all children.
3. **Rabbits** are animals loved by all children.

Keep in mind that the use of "the" in Sentence 2 is restricted and doesn't reflect the usual meaning of this article. To discover the most typical use of "the," let's examine another group of sentences. If the sentences sound right to you, write the word *okay* on the lines after them; if they don't sound right, put the word *odd* on the lines.

1. Where's **a** newspaper I was reading?   _____

2. A: Look at that peeling paint!
   B: Where?
   A: On **a** front door!   _____

3. Want to see some card tricks? Good!
   Take **the** card out of **a** deck.   _____ _____

4. Hey, Pete, we ate at **the** great restaurant!   _____

In case you were wondering about your better judgment, don't be alarmed. You should have written *odd* on <u>all</u> of the previous lines. But why are they all odd? Let's examine each one and find the reason.

The question in the first example refers to a specific newspaper that the person was reading earlier, and **"the" is the article we choose when identifying a specific thing which both speaker and listener are aware of.** The corrected sentence should be, "Where's <u>the</u> newspaper I was reading?"

In Example 2, Person A is talking about a specific door, the one and only front door that the house would have. Since the door being referred to is specific, we again need to use "the" and the corrected version should be, "On <u>the</u> front door!"

Example 3 has two misuses. The corrected sentence should read, "Take <u>a</u> card out of <u>the</u> deck." The speaker needs to say "a" card because it can be one of fifty-two and refers to a general or vague thing (this card, that card—any card); the speaker has to say "the" deck because our amateur magician is referring to the specific deck which the participant sees, not any deck of cards in general.

If left alone, Sentence 4 would probably force Pete into wondering whether he'd previously recommended some outstanding restaurant to the speaker. He'd be uncomfortable because the speaker is making no reference to a previous conversation that he can pinpoint. The sentence should be, "Hey, Pete, we ate at <u>a</u> great restaurant!"

By now, we realize that **the all-important use of "the" is to refer to something or someone specific, <u>not</u> general.**

How about the following sentences? All four of them are right, but information about the direct object in each one is different. What assumptions can we make? Write your thoughts about the direct objects (depending on which article is used with them) on the accompanying blank lines.

1a.   Please pass me **a** salt shaker.   _____

1b.   Please pass me **the** salt shaker.   _____

2a.   Did you see **a** film last night?   _____

2b.   Did you see **the** film last night?   _____

In 1a, we can assume that there are at least two salt shakers on the table. The speaker is saying he doesn't care which one of the two the other person passes to him. In 1b, however, there can only be one salt shaker on the table, and the speaker needs to use "the" because it's the one and only specific item he's asking for.

 Troubleshooter

 In many languages, e.g., Spanish and French, the definite article is more commonly used than in English. In fact, contrary to English usage, the definite article is typically used when making statements about things in general, not just specific things as in English. Some cases in point:

- In French, it's "C'est $\boxed{la}$ vie," but in English it's "That's $\boxed{X}$ life."

- In Spanish, it's "$\boxed{El}$ agua es un tesoro," which is "$\boxed{X}$ Water is a treasure" in English.

So be prepared to deal with this if your students add "the" where we would not normally use it in English!

 As we mentioned at the beginning of this chapter, there are many languages which have no articles at all—definite or indefinite. If you have students whose native tongues fit into this group (Russian and Japanese are two good examples), plan accordingly for the double challenge of getting your students to understand the concepts involved and getting them to use the articles appropriately.

In 2a on the previous page, the speaker is asking the other person if he saw just any movie last night; it doesn't matter which one. In 2b, the speaker is asking if the person saw a specific movie that they'd previously discussed, probably at some recent point in the past. In other words, both speaker and listener know exactly which movie is being referred to.

To sum up everything we've touched on so far, all we need to do is remember this basic difference between "a" and "the": "a" is for generalities about people, places, things, or ideas, and the "zero article" works this way, too. "The," on the other hand, is for specific people, places, things, or ideas.

An interesting way to look into other uses and misuses of the definite article is to put ourselves right in the classroom and deal with situations as they arise. Here are examples of typical questions that students ask their English teachers. See if you can figure out what to say to these students. Let's start out with just a couple of questions:

1.   Is it all right to call her **the Roxanne**?

2.   Why can't I say **It's the Roxanne's book**?

Things get quite interesting right away with our first question. Can we ever say "the" before a person's name? Absolutely! Just check out the following examples:

1.   **The Roxanne** you're talking about isn't my sister; she's my cousin.
2.   I've just bought a new sailboat. I'm calling it "**The Roxanne**."
3.   A: Isn't Roxanne's last name Bergerac?
      B: Yes, it is. In fact, **the Bergeracs** live next door to me.

In our first example, the rule is that we can use "the" before a person's name if we're speaking about one out of two or more people with that same name. In this situation, there are two Roxannes.

In Sentence 2, the rule is that we can use "the" before names when referring to things like ships or boats, aircraft, paintings, and any other things that we've given names to.

Example 3 is a little different. When we refer to a couple, a whole family or any group of people with a collective name, it's customary to put "the" before the name and then add the plural marker (-s or -es) onto the name.

While we're on the subject, is it ever possible to put "a" or "an" before a name? Again, the answer is YES, although it's more common to do so before a last name. When speaking of one member of a group or family, it's quite proper to use the indefinite article before the name, signifying this is just one of many (which the indefinite article represents under any other circumstances, too).

You've disgraced the whole family! **A MacDougald** never gives up!

Let's go back to the students' questions. As for our second typical question, the reasoning that students often have for coming up with a phrase like "the Roxanne's book" is really intriguing. They know it's <u>the</u> book, and they know it's <u>Roxanne's</u>, so their sense of efficiency dictates that they should combine the two phrases to produce "the Roxanne's book." Quite clever actually, but the reason it can't be done is that **we cannot put the definite article before the possessive form of a name.**

Now let's look at two more typical questions that students have been known to challenge their English teachers with.

1. I'm confused. I don't understand why you changed my words. When you asked me what I'd done over the weekend, I said, "Last Sunday I went to see <u>the</u> tennis match. The match was very exciting." You corrected me and said, "Last Sunday you went to see <u>a</u> tennis match." Why?

    _____

    _____

    _____

2. English is very crazy! You tell me I can't say that I come from <u>the</u> Iran; that I should say only "Iran." But when Boris said that he comes from <u>the</u> Caucasus, you didn't correct him. Why not?

    _____

    _____

    _____

For some people, the question posed in Example 1 is a real "head scratcher." What we have here is a simple rule that even most native speakers aren't aware of: **when you mention something countable for the first time, you normally say "a"; if you happen to mention it again, you change "a" to "the."** Here's a longer example of this rule at work:

When I got home yesterday, I saw **a** cat up **a** tree in front of my house. **The** tree was very tall and **the** cat was very scared. I asked **a** passerby if he'd help, but **the** man wasn't interested. Anyway, I finally managed to coax **the** cat down from **the** tree.

The answer to the next student's question is perhaps one of our favorites. We just grin broadly and say, "That's English!" Sometimes this is really the only answer to give. There are times when students should understand that the best way to learn another language is simply to accept how that language operates and not try to analyze everything. This is a good case in point.

For reasons that you as the teacher don't need to get into with your students, there are some names for geographical designations which use the definite article. The student mentioned the Caucasus; we can also mention the Crimea, the Yucatan, the Taiga, and the Yukon among others. Just keep it simple sometimes and tell your students to be accepting, not always analytical.

While we're on the subject of geographical designations, let's discuss one other area that can be perplexing. Fill in the blanks with the word **the** before the following names of these natural or man-made features or places if you think you should.

1. _____ Nile
2. _____ Himalayas
3. _____ Mt. Ararat
4. _____ Stockholm
5. _____ Hague
6. _____ Puget Sound
7. _____ Lake Como
8. _____ Vatican
9. _____ Vatican City
10. _____ Niagara Falls
11. _____ Panama Canal
12. _____ Steppes
13. _____ Tokyo Bay
14. _____ Bay of Biscay
15. _____ Tierra del Fuego

Confusing, isn't it? The definite article should appear in the blanks after the following numbers in this list: **1, 2, 5, 8, 11, 12,** and **14.** Of course, the question is, why don't we use the definite article before the other names listed?

Once again, we can make this relatively easy for you. Remember we mentioned that there are many pat phrases which have the zero article? The same basic explanation holds true for using the definite article before most of the previous examples. To try analyzing all of them could create quite a linguistic nightmare, so we're better off just accepting that this is how English has named these geographical features—and that's that.

Here are a couple of concepts that may help you if you feel uncomfortable with our philosophy. The first one is that when places created by people have become "institutionalized," that is, when they've been accepted as special, lasting places that are recognized as such universally, we tend to use the definite article along with their names (the Vatican / the Panama Canal / the Hague). It's part of the psychology of language more than anything else. At any rate, just tell your students to accept the names as they are, and learn them that way.

The other concept has to do with geographical designations and their names. What tends to happen is that the definite article is used when the name comes <u>before</u> the geographical term. For example, we say *the Nile (River), the Yukon (Territory),* and *the Andes (Mountains).* But if the name comes <u>after</u> the geographical term, we drop the definite article: *Lake Titicaca, Mt. Fuji.* One notable exception is when mentioning waterfalls: *Niagara Falls, Angel Falls,* and *Victoria Falls.*

Teaching Tips

Before class write up or collect various newspaper headlines. Have enough headlines so that each group of students has three to four to work with. Divide the class into pairs or small groups and have them reconstruct complete headlines by adding articles, helping verbs, etc.

Variation #1

Have the students reconstruct telegrams instead of newspaper headlines.

Variation #2

Ask the students to write newspaper headlines or telegrams using the shortened "telegraphic" style.

More Teaching Tips

This activity is commonly called "The Alphabet Game." Students build up vocabulary lists based on a predetermined category (a supermarket, drugstore, nouns, adjectives, etc.). One student begins the game by saying: "I went to the supermarket and bought an avocado." The first word must begin with an "a." The next student repeats what the first student said and adds an item of his/her own, this time a "b" item. "I went to the supermarket and bought an avocado and some butter." The third student repeats what's been said by the other two, adding a "c" item, and so on.

Variation

Have the students write an "Alphabet Poem": "A is for Austria, the country of the waltz. B is for bananas, the fruit I love the most. C is for chocolate, my passion, yum, yum. D is for . . . etc.

Mind Bogglers!

To finish up this chapter, we thought it might be interesting for you to figure out what differences there are between the following pairs of sentences. Here's the first pair in which one sentence has no article and the other has the indefinite article:

> 1a.   "Mr. van Straten is on the phone, sir."
> 1b.   "A Mr. van Straten is on the phone, sir."

And now, here's the other pair of sentences. One contains the indefinite article and the other has the definite article:

> 2a.   She's going to have a baby.
> 2b.   She's going to have the baby.

We think you'll find it amazing how those two little words—or the lack of them—can change meaning so much!

Chapter 4

The Pasts

"What's past is past."

THE SIMPLE PAST

A: I call**ed** you on the phone like a hundred times last night!

B: Really? Well, I **was**n't home.

A: I figur**ed** that out myself.

B: So, why all the calls?

A: I **made** those calls to try out my brand new cordless phone. My wife **bought** it for me.

B: You tri**ed** somebody else then, **did**n't you?

A: No. The battery **went** dead after all those calls to you!

First Use

The parts in bold in this dialog show us that the time is in the past, the simple past. It's called the "simple" past because we have a verb form that's relatively uncomplicated.

There are three uses of the simple past. The first one is shown in our dialog with examples of regular verbs (called / figured / tried) and irregular verbs (was / made / bought / did / went). What simple description for this use can you come up with? Think about the verbs in the dialog, and then write down how you'd define the simple past on the lines below:

_____

_____

_____

What we see in the dialog are examples of **actions that happened before and a state of being that existed before, and both are finished;** this is our first use of the simple past. Keep in mind that the verbs in the simple past in the dialog have no connection with the present and are like a closed door. Compare this to the discussion we had in Chapter 2 about how verbs in the present perfect can keep that door open.

 Troubleshooter

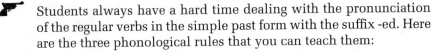 Students always have a hard time dealing with the pronunciation of the regular verbs in the simple past form with the suffix -ed. Here are the three phonological rules that you can teach them:

- If the verb ends in a voiced consonant <u>sound</u>* except for /d/ [b, g, j, l, m, n, ŋ, r, v, z, ə] or in a vowel sound, the -ed suffix is simply pronounced /d/.
- If the verb ends in a voiceless consonant <u>sound</u> except for /t/ [f, k, p, s, č, š, θ], the -ed suffix is simply pronounced /t/.
- If the verb ends in /d/ or /t/, the -ed suffix is pronounced /ɪd/ or /ɛd/.

*Note: We're talking about <u>sounds</u>, not letters. Be careful that your students don't look at the final letter of the verb; they have to think about the final sound!

Teaching Tips

Have the students bring a photo of themselves or any picture that means something to them to class. Bring one yourself. You can start the activity by showing the picture and explaining the reasons that the picture is important, why the picture was taken, and any pertinent information about it. Urge the students to ask questions about the pictures, being sure to focus questions, answers, and discussions in the past. Then students can take turns explaining their photos and their stories. For homework, the students can write up short passages of their photos in the past.

Second Use

There's another use of the simple past in the opening dialog that isn't so apparent. Maybe you can figure it out by looking at this next example. Compare the alternative responses that Person B could say at the end of the dialog and see if you perceive a difference.

A: I hear you had some excitement outside your house last night.
B: I'll say! I got into a fight with my neighbor.
A: Why? What happened?
B: He **hit** his dog. / He **was hitting** his dog. I really hate that.

Ask yourself which one of Person B's options would make it clearer why he got into that fight. When you've answered that question, you'll probably have figured out what the difference is between the two verb forms. Write your conclusions on the lines below.

_____

_____

_____

It turns out that Person B's saying "He was hitting his dog" seems to explain more clearly why the fight took place; with the response "He hit his dog," it just doesn't seem as much of a justification for a fight between neighbors. Why is this so? It's because Person B's response in the simple past (hit) leaves us with the impression that he only hit the dog <u>once</u> if no further information is supplied; the verb form "was hitting" makes us think that he did this many times— but more about that later on in this chapter.

So here we have the second use of the simple past that isn't so apparent: **the simple past can mean that the action happened only one time.**

Don't think we've forgotten about that third use of the simple past. We're going to put it on hold for a little while.

Teaching Tips

Provide a model of a family tree (it can be an imaginary one, one for a famous person, or even your own). Tell each student to write a letter to an artist asking him/her to draw a family tree for the student's photo album. The letter should include brief details about each family member in order for the artist to draw the tree properly. ("My grandfather was born in 1908. He married my grandmother in 1931. They had six children.") Have the students exchange letters and become the artists. When the "artists" finish their "commissions," tell them to return their work to their "clients" who will check the work for accuracy.

More Teaching Tips

Record a variety of sounds—cars beeping, a train going by, doors slamming, interesting noises (swoosh, creak, pop, etc.). Make sure you have enough sounds—eight to ten will work well. Divide the students into small groups and have them construct a story about the events that occurred, for example, "on their way home from class," incorporating the sounds into the story line. The students then tell their stories adding in the sound effects at the appropriate moments.

Variation

Have the students record their own sound tracks to accompany a story or skit they'll write and/or act out.

The Simple Past in a Nutshell

   actions finished in the past:
I sent the letter.

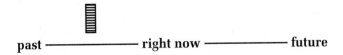

past ———————— right now ———————— future

THE PAST PROGRESSIVE

> auxiliary **BE** + VERB + **ING**
>
> I, he, she, it **was** work**ing**
> we, you, they **were** work**ing**

First Use

We're going to talk about three uses of the past progressive, but to start off our investigation into this form, let's look at the following dialog:

> **A:** What **were** you **doing**?
> **B:** Doing? When?
> **A:** Last night around eleven.
> **B:** Oh! I **was rummaging** through the trash cans outside my house.
> **A:** I know that! But why?
> **B:** I **was looking** for my watch. My little boy thought the trash can was a big jewelry box!

All the verbs in bold are in the past progressive. There's something very subtle, but very useful, that this form is imparting to the verbs, and there's a good reason that the speakers have chosen this form over any other.

All the actions in bold have really been caught at the moment they were happening. Let's see how you perceive this form as it appears in the dialog above. Read the following statements about the verbs in bold from this dialog and check the boxes in front of the statements that you agree with.

☐ The verbs in bold tell us when they began.
☐ They don't tell us when they began.
☐ They tell us when they ended.
☐ They don't tell us when they ended.
☐ These actions are finished.
☐ These actions were in progress.

Because of the way these verbs appear in the context of the dialog, the boxes to check are the 2nd, 4th, and 6th, and this leads us to our first observation about this verb form: **we use the past progressive when the actions were in progress and there's no focus on any definite beginning or end.** It's the activity in progress that counts, nothing else.

Second Use

Now let's look at a conversation between a police officer and a motorist.

A: I **wasn't doing** anything, Officer!
B: You **were speeding**.
A: It's just that I **was hurrying** to City Hall.
B: And why **were** you **rushing** there?
A: To pay some overdue speeding tickets!

The easiest way to begin examining this verb form as it appears in this conversation is to ask the question: If we change the verbs in bold to the simple past, will the conversation work?

*"I **didn't do** anything, Officer!"*

*"You **sped**."*

*"It's just that I **hurried** to City Hall."*

*"And why **did** you **rush** there?"*

"To pay some overdue speeding tickets!"

It doesn't completely work, you say? You're right, it doesn't. But why not? What difference is there between using the past progressive in the dialog and using the simple past? Take a few moments to compare each verb as it appears in both versions of the dialog. Decide whether they're grammatical in this context and then write down any thoughts you may have about why one form works and the other doesn't, if you've found that to be the case.

(wasn't doing) _____

(didn't do) _____

(were speeding) _____

(sped) _____

(was hurrying) _____

(hurried) _____

The most important reason that the past progressive seems to work better for most of these verbs is that there are implied, but unspoken, ideas in each utterance. For example, when the motorist says "I wasn't doing anything," the unspoken idea might be ". . . when you pulled me over." Can you supply other implied ideas for the following lines from the dialog?

1.   "You were speeding _____ ."
2.   "I was hurrying to City Hall _____ ."

Some possibilities for filling in the implied idea for Sentence 1 are: . . . when I stopped you /. . . when I spotted you /. . . when I pulled you over.

Some options for Sentence 2 are: . . . when you made me stop /. . . when you caught me /. . . when you pulled me over.

Let's digress just for a moment and talk about the meaning of a couple of the sentences in this dialog when the simple past is used. How about the lines "You sped" and ". . . I hurried to City Hall"? Why do you think we're uncomfortable with the simple past in these sentences in the context of this dialog? Can you figure out the reason?

_____

_____

_____

If you recall what we said earlier about the first use of the simple past, it was that <u>the action is completely finished</u>. Let's test out the two lines we've cited and add implied ideas to see if they work.

"You <u>sped</u> **when I spotted you**."

"It's just that I <u>hurried</u> to City Hall **when you saw me**."

What do these sentences really say now? Check the box that precedes the description you agree with.

Both sentences mean that:

☐   one action was in progress when the other happened.

☐   the first actions were the results of the second actions.

The second box is the one we should check. The truth is that if both verbs in each sentence are in the simple past, we get the feeling that we're dealing with cause and effect. In other words, the motorist only began to speed when the police officer spotted him, and he hurried to City Hall only when the officer saw him. These verbs in the simple past might work in a different context, but they're not the ideas we're trying to convey in this dialog.

To compound the confusion, if the motorist says that he " . . . hurried to City Hall," it gives us the impression that he'd already reached City Hall before he spoke to the police officer, so how could he be sitting there on the side of the road talking to him? There's no logic in this.

The all-important reason for using the past progressive with these verbs is to show that the actions were <u>not</u> finished, **and that they were interrupted by some other actions**. That's why these two sentences won't work in the simple past. You may have heard this verb form referred to as the "past continuous," but we prefer to call it "past progressive" to reinforce the idea that the action was still in progress.

Let's go over some basic points about the past progressive before we go on to anything else. Look at the following sentences and focus on the verb forms *in italics*. Write **G** in the space provided if the verb is grammatical, or **U** if it's ungrammatical.

1. A: What *were* you *doing* when I called you last night?   _____
    B: I *slept*.   _____
2. A: What *did* you *do* when the fire alarm went off?   _____
    B: I *was leading* my frightened students out of the building. _____
3. A: I *was hearing* that you were sick last week.   _____
    B: I *was having* a terrible cold.   _____
4. A: That boy's a brat. He *yanked* that little girl's hair.   _____
    B: It's awful that he *was yanking* her hair!   _____

Let's check your perceptions of these verb forms in the context we've put them. **1A** is **G** but **1B** is **U**; **2A** is **G** but **2B** is **U**; **3A** and **3B** are both **U**; **4A** is **G** but **4B** is **U**.

1B is ungrammatical. Remember that the past progressive is used to show that the action was in progress and was interrupted. The simple past doesn't communicate that the speaker was already in the midst of sleeping at the moment that the phone rang. The sentence should read "I **was sleeping**."

2B is ungrammatical for exactly the opposite reason: it communicates that the speaker was in the midst of leading his frightened students out, but he wouldn't have been doing so before the alarm went off. The sentence should be "I **led** my frightened students out of the building." Using the simple past here shows cause and effect which is logical in this case, and it also shows that the action was completed.

3A is ungrammatical because "hear" is one of those sensory verbs we talked about in Chapter 2 that normally don't take the progressive form. The sentence should read "I **heard** that you were sick last week."

3B is ungrammatical for a similar reason; the verb "have" is only used in the simple form when referring to illness, so the sentence should be "I **had** a terrible cold."

4B is ungrammatical in the context of this dialog. "He **yanked** that girl's hair" suggests that he did it one time. "He **was yanking** that girl's hair" suggests many times, and, if the second speaker is reiterating what the first speaker said, he'll be doing so inaccurately if he uses the past progressive.

Third Use

What's the third use of the past progressive, and what third use can we find for the simple past (remember we put off talking about this use earlier in the chapter)?

To find the answers, let's take another look at Sentence 1A on the previous page:

> What **were you doing** when I **called** you last night?

We have two actions, both in the past, but there's an important difference between them. As we've previously seen, **do** (the first verb, which is in the past progressive), deals with an activity that was already happening when the other action occurred. The action **call** (the second verb, which is in the simple past), interrupts or cuts into the first action and takes but a few seconds. So, with this comparison in mind, what can we say about the <u>length of time</u> for the simple past and the past progressive? Check the box for the statement which best describes the verbs in the previous example:

- [ ] Both verbs lasted the same amount of time.
- [ ] The first verb (do) was of longer duration than the second verb (call).
- [ ] The first verb (do) was of shorter duration than the second verb (call).

This is the basic rule to show you if you've checked off the right box: **when two actions occur at the same time in the past, but one action is longer than the other, the longer action is put in the past progressive, and the shorter action (which seems to cut into the other) is put in the simple past.** So, you should have checked off the second box.

Here are a few more examples to demonstrate this point:

1. We **were playing** soccer when it **started** to pour.
   (longer action)   (shorter action)
2. I **dozed off** while my aunt **was singing** some folk songs.
   (shorter action)   (longer action)

Here's an interesting question: Of the two actions in the past, what if one wasn't significantly longer than the other? Look at the following examples and see for yourself. (Only one of these four sentences is ungrammatical. Can you find which one it is and then explain why it doesn't work?)

1. While I **was preparing** the salad, my son **was setting** the table.
2. While I **prepared** the salad, my son **set** the table.
3. When the car **backfired**, I **jumped** out of my seat.
4. When the car **was backfiring**, I **was jumping** out of my seat.

Sentence _____ is ungrammatical because _____

_____

_____

_____

Sentences 1 and 2 are really quite interesting. They use different verb forms, and yet both seem grammatical. The reason is that **when the two actions are of more or less the same duration, they can both be placed in the same verb form**, and in the case of these two sentences, it doesn't much matter if they're both in the past progressive or simple past; they still communicate that the two people began their tasks more or less at the same time and completed those tasks also at about the same time.

Well, if those two sentences are grammatical, that only leaves us with Sentence 3 or 4 to be the ungrammatical one. The answer is that **Sentence 4 is ungrammatical.** Reason? It goes back to the concept we mentioned before about the simple past representing short actions. How long does it take for a car to backfire? How long does it take to jump out of one's seat? The answer to both questions is NO TIME AT ALL, or shall we say, only a second at most. If we try to use the past progressive for this kind of action, it seems odd because we're using a form that normally represents long duration, and our two actions have almost no duration.

Teaching Tips

Prepare a daily schedule sheet similar to the one below. Have the students go around the room and interview several of their classmates about what they did the previous day. After they've gotten enough information, have them give a report about what they've discovered. Make sure they use the various pasts and time words. (While Nur was taking a shower, Hassan was getting up. Carla ate breakfast at 7:00 yesterday, etc.).

TIME	NUR	HASSAN	CARLA	?	?
6:00					
6:30	shower	got up			
7:00			ate		
7:30					
8:00					
8:30					
etc.					

The Past Progressive in a Nutshell

> actions that are unfinished, in progress in the past, which don't focus on any beginning or end:
> Pardon me, but I wasn't talking to you.

past —————— right now —————— future

The Past Progressive Interacting with the Simple Past

> when two actions are at the same time in the past, but one action is longer than the other:
> She caught up on her correspondence while she was recuperating.

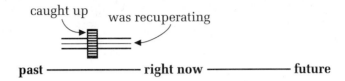

past ——————— right now ——————— future

A Special Note About the Words "WHEN" and "WHILE"

In most standard grammar books, the following sort of statement is made about how to use "when" and "while":

> Use "when" with the clause in the simple past.

> Use "while" with the clause in the past progressive.

According to this, we should always say:

"When he lived in London . . ." and "While he was driving to work . . ."

That's all well and good, but it really doesn't completely reflect the way native speakers use these words. It should be mentioned here that there seems to be a great deal of overlap between the two words, and you very easily may hear people say:

"While I lived in London . . ." or "When I was driving to work . . ."

What, then, accounts for this switch-over? Look at the following and check off the boxes for those sentences which you feel are <u>un</u>grammatical. Leave the verbs alone; they're fine just the way they are! Focus on "when" and "while," and consider whether they both work in the sentences. Then see if you can figure out why some of these sentences don't work, but the others do.

1a. ☐ While he fell, he hurt his knee.

1b. ☐ When he fell, he hurt his knee.

2a. ☐   When I was watching TV, I fell asleep.

2b. ☐   While I was watching TV, I fell asleep.

3a. ☐   While she left the house, she forgot to lock the door.

3b. ☐   When she left the house, she forgot to lock the door.

4a. ☐   While the dog was napping, the cat stole his bone.

4b. ☐   When the dog was napping, the cat stole his bone.

First, let's see which boxes are ungrammatical. You should only have checked off **1a** and **3a**. Now take a moment to think about why only those two sentences don't work (considering the use of "while" and "when"), and write your conclusions on the lines that follow.

_____

_____

_____

The reason those two sentences don't work with "while" is that the verbs following are not of long enough duration to warrant the use of this word. Remember that "**while" is normally used with verbs of relatively long duration**, and we're fairly consistent about when it is or isn't appropriate to use.

So now we have to find a reason that explains why "when" works in all of the previous sentences. It's simply that "when" is more loosely rule-governed than "while." In prescriptive grammar books, the student is led to believe that "when" should be as strictly regulated as "while," but that's misleading. The plain truth is that **native English speakers don't consider it a cardinal sin to use "when" in place of "while."**

Teaching Tips

Invent a crime with specific details (time, place, witnesses, etc.). Call on two students to play the suspects. Have them leave the room, inventing an alibi while outside. Tell the suspects that their alibis must be as detailed and specific as possible. While the suspects are planning their alibis, have the rest of the class prepare questions to ask the suspects. Bring the suspects back into the room one at a time; this way neither suspect will hear what the other one has said. After the interrogations, poll the students to decide which suspect is guilty.

More Teaching Tips

Start out a story "Once upon a time there lived a little girl named Suzanne and her brother, Kevin. They were very funny children, always telling jokes and doing silly things. One day while they were walking home from school, Suzanne . . ." Have the students add on bits to the story, letting their imaginations go where they will, but making sure they keep to the story line that's being created. Every once in a while, have a student go back and retell what's gone on up to that point. That reminds the students about what's happened and helps to keep the story line from wandering.

Variation

At the end of each student's contribution, the student suggests a verb that he/she wants incorporated into the next student's bit of story.

THE PAST PERFECT

> I, you, he, she, it, we, they **had** work**ed**

Here are some sentences for you to examine. If they're grammatical, write **G** on the line following each one; if they're ungrammatical, write **U** on the line after each one.

1. When I met Carlos, he lived next door for only a short time. _____
2. The company went bankrupt because they didn't show a profit for over two years. _____
3. Mintsu admitted that she didn't like cooking very much. _____
4. As I reached the corner, the light turned red. _____
5. He couldn't write because he broke his thumb. _____

The sentences are as follows: **1** is **U**; **2** is **U**; **3** is **G**; **4** is **G**; **5** is **U**. If we correct the three ungrammatical sentences, this is how they look:

1. When I met Carlos, he **had lived** next door for only a short time.
2. The company went bankrupt because they **hadn't shown** a profit for over two years.
5. He couldn't write because he **had broken** his thumb.

Why should we use the past perfect in these three sentences and not the other two? What difference in time do you perceive between the two verbs used in Sentences 1, 2, and 5, and in Sentences 3 and 4? Take a moment and write down your impressions on the lines that follow.

In Sentences 1, 2, and 5 _____

_____

However, in Sentences 3 and 4 _____

_____

Notice that Sentences 3 and 4 have both verbs in the simple past (admitted and didn't like/reached and turned). That's because the two verbs in each sentence take place during the same period in the past. In Sentence 3, when Mintsu made the admission, her feelings about cooking were current. In Sentence 4, both verbs happened at approximately the same moment. It makes sense grammatically that both verbs in each sentence should be placed in the same form to show that they were basically concurrent.

On the other hand, Sentences 1, 2, and 5 have verbs that didn't take place at the same time in the past, and that's the reason we should use the past perfect. **If two or more verbs in the past didn't happen at more or less the same time, you need the past perfect for one of them.**

But now the question arises, which verb should be in the past perfect? What would you say? Look back at those sentences and write down your answer to the question.

We should use the past perfect _____

_____

In Sentence 1, Carlos moved in next door first, and the speaker met him some time later. In Sentence 2, profits didn't exist for the company for two years prior to their declaring bankruptcy. In Sentence 5, he first did the damage to his thumb and, as a result of the mishap, he couldn't write. We can clearly see that the two verbs in each of these sentences can't be put into the same time frame. Now we can answer the question about which verb should be in the past perfect: **when two or more verbs are in the past, but they didn't happen at the same time, the verb that happened <u>first</u> is put in the past perfect.**

But is this always the case? Do we have a hard-and-fast rule to go by? Not necessarily. There are many cases in which the past perfect is avoidable, especially in informal or conversational speech. One example of this is when we use **time words** that clearly set up the chronology for us so that there's no confusion over the sequence of events. Look at the following sentences which demonstrate this:

1. **Before** he got home, he stopped at a grocery to buy some bread.
2. I lay down on the couch to take a nap **after** I had lunch.
3. **As soon as** they reached the beach, they dove into the water.

As you can see, there's no confusion about the chronological order of the actions in these three sentences. Conservative speakers would say that the past perfect should still be used in these sentences, but in informal or conversational English, it really isn't necessary. Impress upon your students, however, that in formal usage (especially like that found on tests such as the TOEFL and the Cambridge University Test of English), they should always use the past perfect when appropriate.

Teaching Tips

Ask the students to write down several things that they had never done before this year, entered high school, or began learning English, etc. The students should begin their sentences with "Before I ____, I had ____ ." Collect the answers and have the class arrange their seats in a circle, or in any fashion so that they can all see one another's faces. Tell the students that you're going to read some of their responses and that they should guess who wrote them. Have them write down their guesses and be sure to tell them to keep straight faces when the responses are being read; otherwise, they may give themselves away. When you've read all the statements that you've chosen and the students have made their guesses, reread them and ask each person to identify him-/herself. To find out who the best "detective" in the class is, see who guessed right the most times.

The Past Perfect in a Nutshell

 when two or more actions happened at different times in the past, use this form for the verb that happened first (further back in the past):
I hadn't known her age until she told me.

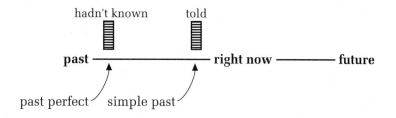

THE PAST PERFECT PROGRESSIVE

> I, you, he, she, it, we, they **had been** work**ing**

You'll recall that one of the distinctions we made in Chapter 2 between the present perfect and the present perfect progressive was that the present perfect starts in the past and continues to the <u>general</u> present rather than to one specific moment (or right now). The progressive form is more *pinpointed* since it comes up to the primary sense of "now."

This same basic principle holds true with the past perfect progressive. Let's see how this works by having you look at some pairs of sentences. Decide whether using the past perfect or past perfect progressive makes any noticeable difference.

1a.   He'd worked here for twenty-five years when he retired.
1b.   He'd been working here for twenty-five years when he retired.
    ☐ A difference   ☐ No difference
2a.   She told me she'd written some letters.
2b.   She told me she'd been writing some letters.
    ☐ A difference   ☐ No difference

There's really no perceived difference between Sentences 1a and 1b, but there certainly is a difference between 2a and 2b. Sentence 2a communicates that her letter writing activities were completed by the time she talked to me. In 2b, we understand that she began the letter writing some time before she talked to me, but that she wasn't finished. Another way of looking at this is that our conversation interrupted her letter writing.

What rule, then, can we come up with to explain the use of the past perfect progressive? Simply put, **with certain types of activities, the past perfect progressive does what its name implies: it shows that the activity was still in progress from some earlier time in the past when another past action happened.**

The Past Perfect Progressive in a Nutshell

    this verb form shows that one action began earlier in the past than other actions, but instead of being completely finished before the other actions happened, it overlapped onto them:
He said he had been waiting for over an hour.

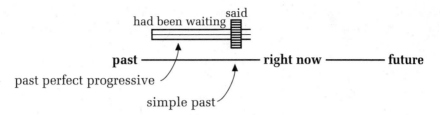

THE EXPRESSIONS "USED TO" AND "WOULD"

"USED TO"

Read this sentence and interpret what it means to you without any further context offered. Check off the descriptions of this sentence that you agree with.

I got up at 6:00 A.M.

☐	1.	The action is in the past and finished.
☐	2.	The action is in the past, but not finished.
☐	3.	This happened repeatedly.
☐	4.	This happened one time only.
☐	5.	I'm not sure how many times it happened.

What information is given to us in this sentence, and how should we go about interpreting it? We know that the simple past has been used, meaning that the action is completely finished, so we should check the box for **Sentence 1.**

What we're uncomfortable with, lacking more context, is whether or not this happened one time or repeatedly. We might assume that it happened only once, but we just don't have enough information to be certain, so we should check off **Sentence 5.**

Suppose we want to embellish our idea. How can we get more information into our sentence? The answer is that we have a very efficient way of doing so simply by adding **used to** (often considered a semi-modal) after the subject:

I <u>used to</u> get up at 6:00 A.M.

This little phrase adds important extra information to our basic idea. What further information can you interpret from this addition? List whatever comes to mind on the lines below.

1. _____

2. _____

There are two additional pieces of information that have been added to our basic idea. The first is that the action we're discussing **occurred repeatedly over a rather long span of time**. The second extra detail is that **we assume this isn't so today**. We've now included an implied meaning just as we did with the second use of the past progressive. Here's how the sentence might look if we include the implied idea:

> I used to get up at 6:00 A.M., **but I don't anymore**.

The negative form of "used to" is quite interesting. We can form the standard negative and say **didn't use to**, but many native speakers tend to use the adverb of frequency "never" and create the negative by saying **never used to**. Remember that we can often assume that the contrary is true for the present, just as it is in the affirmative:

> She never used to like spinach, **but now she does**.

We should mention that the British have another negative form, **used not to (usedn't to)**, but it's not very commonly heard these days:

> She **used not to** like spinach, but now she does.

Teaching Tips

Have the students write down examples of how their lives have changed in the past ten or twenty years (brief descriptions are okay). Then have them give reports on those changes, using "used to" where appropriate.

 Troubleshooter

 Students almost invariably confuse "used to" with the expression "be used to." Be aware that this problem will surely arise. Whenever it's appropriate to do so, point out that the grammar involved with these two expressions is quite different:

- "be used to" needs the verb BE, and any verb that follows the expression has -ing attached to it.
  (They're used to hav<u>ing</u> dinner by 7 P.M.)
- "used to" never has BE, and the verb after this expression is always in the base form.
  (They used to have dinner by 7 P.M.)

"USED TO" in a Nutshell

 state of being existed or action happened repeatedly over a relatively long span of time in the past with the implied idea that the situation isn't so any longer:
The Sahara Desert used to be a fertile, lush area.

 something didn't exist or happen before, but now it does:
There never used to be a hole in the ozone layer.

"WOULD"

There seems to be a fine point of distinction between "used to" and "would" when discussing events of the past. Remember that one of the meanings of "used to" is that the activity or state of being took place over a relatively long period of time. Now let's see if you discern any difference between the following sentences. Check the boxes for the statements you agree with.

1. I <u>used to</u> play chess with my roommate.
2. I <u>would</u> play chess with my roommate.

☐ Both sentences can stand alone.

☐ Sentence 1 offers more information than Sentence 2.

☐ Sentence 2 offers more information than Sentence 1.

Most native speakers would only check off the second box. The reason is that only Sentence 1 can stand alone; it doesn't need anything added to be a complete idea because we have enough information in the expression "used to" to feel comfortable with it.

Sentence 2 doesn't supply us with enough information and creates some sort of gap in our understanding of the idea. What if we add some more information? Let's try it:

When I was in college, I would play chess with my roommate.

Suddenly it works! That extra information about when this happened has now made the sentence a more complete idea. What if we were to substitute "would" with "used to"? The sentence would now read:

When I was in college, I used to play chess with my roommate.

Is there any major difference between the two sentences now? No, not really. The commonality between "used to" and "would" is that we understand they both took place over a rather long period of time in the past, but the sentence that contains "would" seems to suggest that this was **traditional, something done routinely,** and there's a tie-in with another activity, namely, being in college. We should keep in mind that the addition of the word "would" is really superfluous—even redundant—because most everyone can arrive at the same interpretation with just the use of the simple past; the clause "When I was in college . . ." prepares us for this. So it is in general with the word "would." There's really no need for it; we use it simply as a reinforcement. The big difference between "used to" and "would" that we should keep in mind is that "used to" doesn't necessarily need extra information about the time period in order to stand alone; "would" must have this extra information.

One other way we use "would" is to communicate that certain activities were in a sequence as well as parts of a routine. Look at the following passage which demonstrates this:

During my high school years, I would get up at 6:00 A.M. I'd take a shower and wake up my little brother. After that, I'd get dressed and go to the kitchen to make my own breakfast. I wouldn't eat much, just some toast and cheese, and I'd have some coffee, too.

Clearly, the word "would" serves to reinforce the routine nature of these activities and gives us to understand that they were more or less a set pattern in this person's daily life. Would the passage convey the same feeling if the word "would" were eliminated and replaced with just the simple past? Let's take a look and see.

During my high school years, I got up at 6:00 A.M. I took a shower and woke up my little brother. After that, I got dressed and went to the kitchen to make my own breakfast. I didn't eat much, just some toast and cheese, and I had some coffee, too.

What difference, if any, is there now that the simple past has replaced the word "would"? Most people agree that there's no real difference, but we tend to lose something by eliminating the word "would" which helps us remember that we're listening to or reading about someone's past <u>routine</u> activities. This isn't to say that we should use "would" before every single verb. On the contrary, the best plan is to use a combination of "would" and the simple past to enrich the communication.

What about "used to"? Can we apply this expression in place of "would"? Yes, we can, even though there's that slight change in focus since "used to" includes the idea that this might not be true nowadays.

Teaching Tips

Write the following topic and phrases on the board: "Five Years Ago"; "My Family"; "My Friends"; "School"; "Holidays"; "My Appearance"; "My Hobbies", and so on. Pair up the students and have them interview each other, writing down the information that they learn about their partners. Brief statements are acceptable. (**Family**: lived in Canberra; bought their first home; got a new dog. **Hobbies**: sang with a choir; went swimming al-

most every weekend, etc.) After the pairs have collected their information, have each one give an oral report (or write up a report) based on
his/her classmate's life, using the appropriate pasts and "used to" / "would."

More Teaching Tips

Have the students brainstorm things that they or others use, have, or do
in their daily lives (electrical appliances, transportation, entertainment,
clothes). Then tell the students that they're going to consider how their
ancestors lived their lives in the year 10,000 B.C. and A.D. 1500. Have the
students compare their lives today with those of their ancestors. ("I use a
hairdryer to dry my hair, but in 10,000 B.C., my ancestors didn't even
wash their hair!" "I wash my clothes in an automatic washing machine,
but my ancestors in 1500 used to wash all of theirs by hand." "In the year
1500, my relatives wouldn't travel more than a few miles away from home
because traveling was too dangerous.")

"WOULD" in a Nutshelll

- can be used the same way as "used to," but doesn't necessarily imply that
  the contrary is true now:
  Even as a child, I would have coffee in the morning.
- tends to communicate that the past activities mentioned were parts of a routine, and . . .

  must be used with a clause which supplies additional information to place
  it accurately in a time frame:
  During those long winters when I lived up north, I'd start a fire in the fire
  place after waking up, and then I'd boil some water for tea.

Mind Bogglers!

See if you can explain the differences between the following pairs of
sentences.

1. We have few good friends.
    We have a few good friends.

2. They have little money.
    They have a little money.

3. I remembered to do it.
    I remembered doing it.

Chapter 5

Adjectives

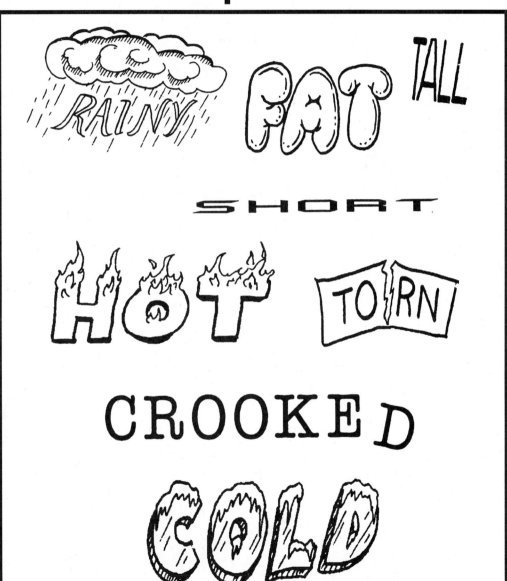

"It was an itsy-bitsy, teeny-weeny yellow polka dot bikini."

Some readers may wonder why we've included a chapter devoted to adjectives; after all, are they really a troublesome part of English? The answer is YES, but we hope they won't be by the time you've finished this chapter! What we have to say about adjectives won't deal so much with problems as it will with helpful insights and ways of understanding and teaching some interesting phenomena that occur with these descriptive words.

VERBAL ADJECTIVES

We call these two kinds of adjectives "verbal" because they spring from verbs. Look at the following dialog to see both kinds in action:

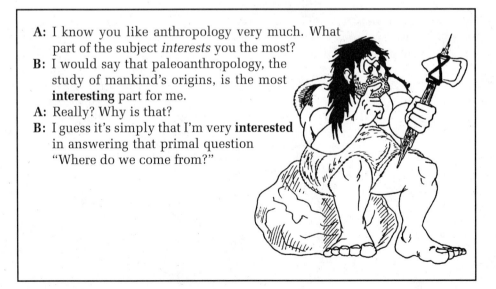

A: I know you like anthropology very much. What part of the subject *interests* you the most?

B: I would say that paleoanthropology, the study of mankind's origins, is the most **interesting** part for me.

A: Really? Why is that?

B: I guess it's simply that I'm very **interested** in answering that primal question "Where do we come from?"

As you can see in the dialog, we've taken the verb "interest" and created two kinds of adjectives out of it, "interesting" and "interested." The question which we know you can anticipate our asking is, what's the difference between these two adjective forms? What does the -ing adjective (the present participle of the verb) describe, and how is that different from what's described by the -ed adjective (which is really the past participle of the verb)? Think about these two points for a moment and write down any thoughts you have on the following lines.

Let's look at a basic idea that Person B supplied in the dialog:

Paleoanthropology interests me.

Paleoanthropology is the subject, of course, but more important, it's responsible for creating or causing the interest in Person B. This gives us the answer to one part of our question: **the -ing adjective describes the person, thing or situation that's the <u>cause</u> of the feeling or reaction in the direct object.**

Conversely, the direct object (Person B in this case) is receiving the reaction or feeling. **We use the past participle adjective to describe the person or thing that receives the feeling or reaction; it describes the state or condition of the recipient.** So, paleoanthropology is interest**ing**, and Person B is interest**ed** (in it). Remember that we said the -ed adjective is really the past participle, or third form of the verb; if the verb is irregular, there won't be an -ed on the end (freeze, froze, <u>frozen</u>)!

At this point, we'd like to offer you a list we've compiled of one hundred verbs from which verbal adjectives are made (not that there aren't others). Note that some verbs are followed by an asterisk; we'll get to the reason for that in a little while.

absorb*	astound	civilize	damage	discourage	enlighten
addict	baffle	clean	dazzle	disgust	entertain
aggravate	bewilder	comfort	deafen	dishearten	entice
alarm	blind	compromise*	deceive	disquiet	exasperate
amaze	bore	confuse	defeat	distinguish*	excite
amuse	calm	connect	demoralize	disturb	exhaust
annoy	challenge	convince	depress	embarrass	exhilarate
appall	charm	corrupt	devastate	encourage	fascinate
astonish	chill*	crush*	disappoint	engross	freeze*

frighten	inspire	minimize	pierce*	soothe	thrill
frustrate	interest	mislead	please	stabilize	tire
gratify	intoxicate*	mortify	punish*	stimulate	touch*
hearten	intrigue	move*	puzzle	strike*	trust
horrify	invigorate	mystify	refresh	stun*	upset
humiliate	invite*	nauseate	relax	surprise	vex
incriminate	jangle	overwhelm	satisfy	tempt	
infuriate	love	perplex	shock	terrify	

And now to the verbs which have asterisks. The most important reason that they've been singled out is to show that the adjectives made from these verbs have figurative meanings besides the literal ones. Below is a list of the figurative uses.

absorb: mentally occupy completely
It was an **absorbing** account of life in Antarctica.
He was fully **absorbed** in his work.

chill: frightening, scary
I read a **chilling** report on the increase in AIDS cases.
(**chilled**: literal meaning only)

compromise: expose to danger, suspicion or dishonor
By asking me to disregard the corruption I've seen, you're putting me in a **compromising** situation.
When the judge realized that he knew the defendant personally, his **compromised** position forced him to take himself off the case.

crush: devastate emotionally
The **crushing** realization that his brother had betrayed him sent him into the depths of depression.
When he realized what his brother had done, he was **crushed**.

distinguish: dignified
He looked very **distinguished** in his new navy blue suit.
(**distinguishing**: literal meaning only)

freeze: extremely cold (rather than water becoming solid)
It's **freezing** in here! Turn on the heat.
I'm **frozen** stiff. I don't think the furnace is working.

intoxicate: stimulate, excite, arouse
That's a very **intoxicating** perfume you're wearing.
The steady rhythm of the drums made the dancers feel **intoxicated**.

invite: alluring, enticing, tempting
I must admit that that's a very **inviting** offer you've made me.
(**invited**: literal meaning only)

move: affect deeply (emotionally)
We found her patriotic speech very **moving**.
The audience was so **moved** that a total hush fell over the room.

pierce: a high-pitched, sharp sound; penetrating
I can't stand the **piercing** noise of jet planes flying overhead.
Her **piercing** stare unnerved me.
(**pierced**: literal meaning only)

punish: physically painful; injurious
We made that **punishing** ride through the mountainous region of the country in a Land Rover.
(**punished**: literal meaning only)

strike: immediately or vividly impressive (**-ing** adjective)
I love that gown you have on. It's really **striking**.
This sonata is a **striking** example of his musical genius.
afflicted with emotion or disease (**-ed** adjective)
People **stricken** with Parkinson's disease suffer from uncontrollable shaking of the hands and head.

stun: astonishing; excellent (**-ing** adjective)
Her **stunning** performance in the opera brought the audience to their feet for a standing ovation.
stupified; shocked (**-ed** adjective)
We felt **stunned** when we heard about his sudden death.

touch: move emotionally; elicit a tender reaction
It was **touching** to watch the little boy help that injured bird.
I sincerely appreciate this gift. I'm very **touched**.

Because there are two primary concerns with adjectives in this chapter (formation and ordering), the *Teaching Tips* will be located in just two places. The tip that deals with the formation of verbal adjectives is located below; the tips that deal with ordering are at the end of the chapter.

Teaching Tips

An effective way to practice the -ed and -ing adjectives is to prepare situations in which you can use the phrase "What do you call _____ ?" The blanks are filled in with phrases that provide the noun to be described and an appropriate verb. Here are some examples. "What do you call a fluid that cleans? / lies that convince people? / information which misleads you? / events which puzzle the police? / people who exasperate you? etc." Note that all the answers to these questions use the -ing adjective (cleaning fluid, convincing lies, misleading information, puzzling events, and exasperating people).

The same question can be asked to elicit the -ed adjective: "What do you call a friend you trust? / an enemy who you've demoralized? / customers that you satisfied? / sleep disturbed by phone calls? / pipes the plumber disconnected?" (They are: a trusted friend, a demoralized enemy, satisfied customers, disturbed sleep, and disconnected pipes.)

You can make this activity more challenging by setting up pairs of "What do you call" questions that use both verbal adjectives. "What do you call fluids that clean and carpets cleaned by the fluid? (cleaning fluid and cleaned carpets) and service that satisfies and customers that you satisfy? (satisfying service and satisfied customers)."

 ## Troubleshooter

 There are certain adjectives that look like they've been derived from the past participles of verbs, but they haven't. Here are some typical ones:

*aged	naked
crooked	peaked
*learned	ragged
wicked	

Note that the -ed on all of these adjectives is pronounced / ɪd / which goes against the phonological rules we covered in Chapter 4.

The reason that "aged" and "learned" have an asterisk is because a very unusual thing happens to them. If their pronunciations follow the phonological rule and we say / ejd / and / lərnd /, we have the literal meanings as past participle adjectives:

aged cheese / a learned behavior.

If we pronounce them / ej-ɪd / and / lər-nɪd /, though, they have different meanings:

That aged philosopher is a very learned man.

Other Uses of -ING Adjectives

There are two other important uses of this verbal adjective form that we should take a look at. See if you can figure out one use by looking over the following dialog, and write your guess on the lines that follow:

A: Gustav, have you seen the **watering** can? I've got to water the potted flowers in front of the house.

B: Look in the tool shed out back.

A: Are the **pruning** shears there, too?

B: Probably. By the way, we need some more **potting** soil so I can transplant the mums into larger pots.

In these phrases, **the -ing adjectives serve to tell us what purposes their nouns have**. For example, the can is used for <u>watering</u> the flowers, so it's a **watering** can; those shears are used for <u>pruning</u> plants, so they're **pruning** shears; the soil that Gustav needs is used for <u>potting</u> plants, so it's **potting** soil. We'll be discussing this use of the -ing adjective more in Chapter 7, which is on compounding.

By the way, did you notice the use of "potted" in the phrase "potted flowers"? Why must we use the past participle form of the adjective to describe the flowers?

The past participle adjective is used here because, as our rule said, it describes the state or condition of the flowers which received the action of being put into pots!

Now look at these sentences which exemplify one use or more of the -ing adjective and figure out what they tell us in these cases. Write down your thoughts on the lines that follow:

She's a nursing mother.

Professor Fouad is Acting Dean this semester.

When you scuba dive, never go near feeding sharks.

_____

_____

_____

In this other use, the **-ing adjectives explain the activities that are being carried out by the nouns they describe**. For example, a **nursing** mother is a mother who's <u>nursing</u> her baby; an **acting** dean is a school administrator who's temporarily <u>acting</u> as dean until a person can be found for the permanent position; **feeding** sharks are sharks that are <u>feeding</u> on some sort of prey.

THE ORDERING OF ADJECTIVES

Incredible as it may seem, we're going to deal with eighteen categories in which adjectives can be placed. It follows then, that there's a similar number of positions in which adjectives can be put before the head noun, that is, the noun that's being described. Luckily, we've never heard anyone utter a phrase that included even close to that many adjectives, and we're sure you haven't either!

One note before we get under way. In many cases, words that are actually nouns will be referred to as adjectival forms in this chapter. These nouns are actually going to be used as adjectives since they describe the nouns we're going to focus on. We'll get into all the details about these specially used nouns in Chapter 7. For right now, though, we'll just concentrate on the order of real adjectives and the nouns that can function as adjectives.

Let's begin our investigation of adjective order by looking at three mixed-up phrases and seeing if we can rearrange the adjectival forms to make the phrases grammatical. (The bold words that are boxed in are the head nouns, the ones that get all the description.)

1. coffee electric | **pot** | _____
2. water gas | **heater** | _____
3. alarm battery-operated | **clock** | _____

Without much trouble, we can see that the things being described are an **electric coffee pot, a gas water heater, and a battery-operated alarm clock.** So what rule for ordering the descriptive words can we come up with? We see that the words "coffee," "water," and "alarm" tell us what the pot, the heater, and the clock are used for or how they're used, i.e., what purpose they serve. These three words are examples of the nouns, not adjectives, that we've mentioned you'll be coming across in this chapter.

The other three words, "electric," "gas," and "battery-operated" all have their own common feature: they're the power sources. Now we've discovered the order of these two categories of adjectives:

power   purpose |head noun|

Let's describe these items in more detail, but before we do, we'd like to explain that just for the sake of demonstration, we intend to work with phrases that are longer than what people normally utter.

We want to describe what materials our items are made of. The pot is stainless steel, the heater is aluminum, and the clock is plastic. So where should we place these descriptive words? Take a moment, think about where you'd put them, and jot the phrases down on the following lines:

_____ *coffee pot*

_____ *water heater*

_____ *alarm clock*

The answer is that they should be placed before the power source words: **stainless steel electric coffee pot; aluminum gas water heater; plastic battery-operated alarm clock.** Now we have another category, material, and we can expand our ordering rule:

material   power   purpose |head noun|

Let's get back to our coffee pot for a moment. Suppose we want to describe it even more. We could talk about whether we think it's an attractive or ugly piece, we could mention whether we thought it was reasonably priced or expensive when we bought it, and we could tell where it came from. So let's opt for the adjectives "expensive," "Brazilian," and "elegant." Now the question is, in what order should we put these words and where in our phrase should we place them? Try it out yourself and then we'll see if your solution fits in with ours:

_____ *coffee pot*

It turns out that these three words should be placed before all the others we've already used to describe the pot, and this is how your newly-expanded phrase should look: **elegant, expensive, Brazilian stainless steel electric coffee pot.** But perhaps you had "expensive, elegant" instead of "elegant, expensive." The truth of the matter is that both of these versions are correct; the question is, why?

Let's see what categories are being used this time. Words like "expensive" and "elegant" are really opinions. Maybe you think the price for that coffee pot was high, but I might think it was reasonable. The same holds true for "elegant"; I might think it's very attractive, but you might think it's nothing special. As for "Brazilian," this is obviously a word describing origin. So now we have two more categories, opinion and origin. Our new version of the rule for ordering adjectival words is:

opinion   origin   material   power   purpose   ⌐head noun⌐

Why is it, though, that we can say "expensive, elegant" or "elegant, expensive," and the ordering works both ways? It's because, in the opinion category, the position of the adjectives is interchangeable.

(One thing we'll throw in for free at this point is where you place the articles (a, an, the) or demonstratives (this, that, these, those); in short, they go before everything else. For the sake of efficiency, we'll refer to these words as "determiners.")

Now, how about going back to our heater and our clock. If you recall, we said it was an aluminum gas water heater and a plastic battery-operated alarm clock. Here are some words for you to play with:

stylish / Swiss / energy-efficient / Cosmos (brand name)

Place two of these words in the phrase describing the heater, and the other two in the phrase describing the clock, and write both complete phrases.

1.   (heater)   _____

_____

2. (clock) _____

_____

Your expanded phrases should now be:

      1.   **an energy-efficient Cosmos aluminum gas water heater**
      2.   **a stylish Swiss plastic battery-operated alarm clock**

    What about color? We'll make the coffee pot white, the water heater black, and the alarm clock pink. Where should the colors be placed? Write in each color above its appropriate pen.

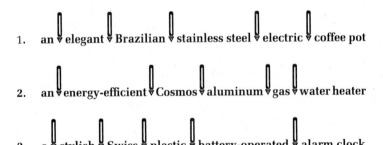

    This is how it goes: "white" should be between "elegant" and "Brazilian"; "black" should be between "energy-efficient" and "Cosmos"; "pink" should go between "stylish" and "Swiss." Do you think you've solved another piece of the puzzle? We certainly do!

determiner opinion color origin material power purpose | head noun |

    We know when you've had enough of coffee pots, water heaters, and alarm clocks! Let's move on to something else to continue our exploration into adjective order.

Let's talk about clothes for a change; in fact, let's specifically talk about a dress and a coat. First of all, we can describe these items by mentioning the **seasons** they were made for. Let's say that the dress was made for the summer, so it's a **summer dress**. The coat was made for the winter, so it's a **winter coat**.

Now choose two of the following words to add to the description of the dress, and choose the other two for the coat:

brand-new / heavy / old / light

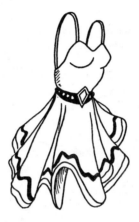

a _____ *summer dress*

a _____ *winter coat*

What you've probably come up with is either **a light, brand-new summer dress** and **a heavy, old winter coat**, or **a light, old summer dress** and **a heavy, brand-new winter coat**. The important thing to keep in mind is whether you placed the descriptive words in the same order as we did. How can we categorize words like "light" and "heavy"? One way is to consider them **conditions**. As for "old" and "brand-new," these are obviously words concerning **age**. Now that we have two more categories to add to the whole picture, these additions to our adjective order are:

determiner   condition   age   season   ⟨**head noun**⟩

Where can we stick the words "long" and "short" which, of course, fall into the category of **measurement**? Give it a try and copy the two complete phrases on the lines that follow:

a _____ *summer dress*

a _____ *winter coat*

Most native English speakers would opt for putting "short" and "long" before the words describing condition, so two of the four possible phrases could now be expanded to **a short, light, brand-new summer dress** and **a long, heavy, old winter coat**:

determiner   measurement   condition   age   season   ⟨**head noun**⟩

The dress and coat that we've been talking about probably belong to somebody, but we haven't accounted for this yet. If we want to mention who the owners of these clothes are, we've got to figure out where to place the possessive adjectives. Let's use "her" and "Vladimir's" and see what happens. Think about where you'd place these possessives into our phrases about the dress and coat and fill in the next two lines:

a _____ *summer dress*

a _____ *winter coat*

What happens is very interesting. For the first time, we have to come up with a different kind of strategy in order to use the possessive words; it's not merely a matter of sticking these words in some place. Instead of finding a spot where they can be inserted, we have to take out the determiners we've been using and replace them with the possessives. In other words, the possessive adjectives take over that spot in our ordering rules when they're needed: **her short, light, brand-new summer dress** and **Vladimir's long, heavy, old winter coat**. Why is this? Simply because a possessive adjective is a kind of determiner, too, and needs to take the same spot!

possessive   measurement   condition   age   season   ┃head noun┃

Before moving on to some other subjects, let's discuss one more way we can define a different dress and a different coat. The dress is one that many women would think is a style <u>not suitable for daytime hours</u>; it's something fancier or more elegant. The coat is one that some gentlemen wore <u>in the early part of the day</u> at the turn of the century. Can you think of the two adjectival words that would identify these articles of apparel?

her _____ *dress*

Vladimir's _____ *coat*

So, how good are you at answering such riddles? We were thinking of **an evening dress** and **a morning coat**. And, to be nice, we'll let you know right off where this category, which we simply call **time**, is placed relative to all the other categories we've been working with. **Time** normally appears in the same slot as **season**, and it would be quite rare, if ever, that you'd find a phrase containing both season and time.

How about switching to another subject now? Let's talk about cars. Imagine that there's a long line of cars just coming out of the factory. There are all kinds of cars in the line, but we're looking to pick out specific ones. Here's what we're looking for:

1. **Three** of them should be **large**.
   They should be the **first** ones we see in the line.
2. **Two** of them should be **small**.
   They should be the **last** ones we see in the line.

Using the information supplied by the descriptive words in bold, produce the two phrases we need to describe the specific cars we're looking to pick out.

the _____ *cars*

the _____ *cars*

The order in which you probably put these words is **the first three large cars** and **the last two small cars**. How did we come by this particular order? First, we need to examine what kinds of words we're using now and decide what categories they fall into.

Words like "first," "next," and "last" are called **ordinals** or "position words"; words like "one," "two," and "three" are called **cardinals** or "counting words." So what order do we see these words falling into?

determiner   ordinal   cardinal | head noun |

And notice where we put the words "large" and "small": they were placed after the ordinals and cardinals ("the first three <u>large</u> cars" and "the last two <u>small</u> cars"). We can call this category **size**.

determiner   ordinal   cardinal   size | head noun |

Now we're getting near the end of all the categories that adjectives can be sorted into. We just have two more to go. Let's talk about two objects found in the heavens, the sun and a comet. Here are adjectives we can use to describe them: "round," "oval," "hot," "cold." First, let's determine what categories we can place these adjectives in. "Round" and "oval" are **shapes**; "hot" and "cold" are **temperatures**. At this point, write a phrase to describe each one by using these adjectives.

The sun is a _____ , _____ *object.*

A comet is a _____ , _____ *object.*

You most likely came up with **The sun is a hot, round object**, and **A comet is a cold, oval object**. What further rule for ordering adjectives can we discern? It appears that temperature comes before shape:

determiner   temperature   shape | head noun |

Believe it or not, we just have one more category to go, and that happens to be **location**. Let's say we have more than one telephone in our home. There's one in the kitchen and one in the bedroom. How can we refer to them for easy identification? Well, we could use color if they have different colors, so let's say the one in the kitchen is beige and the other's blue. But how do we add the information about where the phones are located? Think a moment and see what order you come up with.

a _____ *phone*

a _____ *phone*

The answer is that we should place location closer to the head noun since it's more important for our needs of identification: **a beige kitchen phone** and **a blue bedroom phone**.

The one last question we'd like to pose is about how we would place two adjectives describing location. Let's say one of our phones is hung on a wall in the kitchen and the other one is on a little desk in the corner of the bedroom. Fill in the following lines with a full description of each phone including location and color.

One's a _____

The other's a _____

This is what we've come up with: **a beige kitchen wall phone** and **a blue bedroom desk phone**. We can see that **the general location comes before the spe-**

cific location. So we've come to the last ordering rule for adjectives that we need to deal with in this chapter:

determiner color location location **head noun**
(general) (specific)

At long last, we've covered them all! We've accounted for eighteen categories (seventeen positions) that adjectival words fall into, and we've worked on various combination phrases to show how they're positioned with one another. The last step we should consider is how all of them look in theory if we could devise a hypothetical phrase that would include every single one of them. In that way, we can always pick and choose among the categories to describe anything we want and keep the basic order that we've seen emerge from all of this work. Generally speaking, English adjectives precede head nouns in the following order:

Determiners / Possessives	Ordinals	Cardinals	Opinion	Size
18	17	16	15	14

Measurement	Condition	Age	Temperature	Shape	Color	Origin
13	12	11	10	9	8	7

Season / Time	Material	Power	Location	Purpose	**Head Noun**
6	5	4	3 / 2	1	

What we'd like to reiterate is that you can pick and choose among all these categories to place adjectives in their usual positions before the head noun. Think of any two or three head nouns, and then come up with two or three adjectives belonging to different categories for each head noun you've thought up. Place your adjectives by category before your head nouns in the order appearing above. It should work out every time!

By the way, an interesting viewpoint that some people hold about why the adjective order developed in this way is that **we tend to place the more crucial descriptions closer to the head noun**. In other words, purpose is more crucial for describing a heater than is power, but power, in turn, is more crucial for our description than is opinion or determiner—and that's how we end up with **an energy-efficient gas water heater**.

Yet another way of looking at this ordering of adjectives is to think of the adjectives as being either more specific features for identification or less specific features. **The more specific the adjective, the closer it is to its head noun**. In our minds, at least, both of these viewpoints seem to hold up quite well.

Just to have some fun before we end this chapter, we're going to talk to you about a hamper. There are all kinds of hampers, but according to our rules for ordering adjectives, telling you its purpose would be the most important item of identification we can give you—and it is.

It's a **laundry** | hamper |.
1

That eliminates any other kind of hamper. Laundry hampers can be kept in all sorts of places, but this one is kept in the bathroom.

It's a **bathroom** laundry | hamper |.
2   1

Laundry hampers don't have power sources, but they're made of some sort of material. In this case, we're thinking of wicker.

It's a **wicker** bathroom laundry | hamper |.
5   2   1

Not only have we eliminated all hampers not used for laundry from our discussion, but we've also eliminated any hampers not kept in the bathroom or made of wicker. We've already narrowed down the identification tremendously. (Have you noticed that our numbered categories seem to be fitting in just right?) Our hamper could be lost among thousands of other hampers made anywhere, but ours was made in China.

It's a **Chinese** wicker bathroom laundry | hamper |.
7   5   2   1

We've narrowed the identification a lot more now. Our hamper is that gorgeous shade of red that China is famous for, and telling you the color at this point will eliminate thousands of other Chinese wicker laundry hampers.

It's a **red** Chinese wicker bathroom laundry | hamper |.
8   7   5   2   1

What about its shape, age, condition and size? It's cylindrical. It's also large. It's old, too. Besides all that, it's brittle because it's so old, and it's mine. So, it's . . .

my large, brittle, old, cylindrical, red Chinese wicker bathroom laundry

 18   14   12   11   9   8   7   5   2   1

                                    | hamper |!!!

WHEN NOUNS ARE ADJECTIVES

Probably every language there is has the wonderfully practical means of generating new vocabulary which is known as compounding, and we have a whole chapter devoted to this phenomenon. It's appropriate, though, that we discuss one compound form in this chapter. Technically speaking, **compound forms are created by using two unrelated elements stuck together in order to create a new word**. For the purposes of this chapter, we're going to talk only about | noun + noun |. Examples of these are *ranch house* and *bank vault*. Consider the fact that the word "ranch" and the word "house" are two words that don't have any natural connection, but when stuck together, they create a third word. The same holds true for "bank" and "vault."

Why, you may ask, are they going on about nouns when this is a chapter on adjectives? The reason is that **the first element in this compound form acts exactly as an adjective does; namely, it describes the second element**. Let's go back to the word "house." Of course there are all kinds of houses used for all kinds of purposes, and a very efficient way of describing them is by placing a compound element in front of "house." So, we end up with such items as *schoolhouse, bathhouse, gatehouse, courthouse,* and *jailhouse*. Notice how the first element describes the following word—just as an adjective does.

ATTORNEYS GENERAL?

If you think about it, the title for this section is really strange. It seems to contradict a basic rule of English, that adjectives come before nouns.

So how do we explain this? To find the answer, we need to look at how other languages operate. In quite a few of them, the adjective normally comes after the noun (French and Arabic are examples of such languages). And that's where our answer lies. Over the centuries, English has borrowed many words and phrases from other languages, and in so doing, has sometimes anglicized the borrowed bits and pieces. At other times, it's retained the original placement of the elements as they appeared in the foreign languages. Here's a case in point:

We've borrowed the French job title *notaire publique* without changing much at all. True, "notaire" has evolved into "notary," and the spelling of "publique" has changed to "public," but we've kept the French word order in this noun phrase and call the job a *notary public* instead of a "public notary"—even though the adjective should normally be placed before the noun in English.

But what should we do about making this title plural? Is it okay to say *notary publics*? What would be your guess? Write down your opinion and your reason for saying so. By the way, if you don't think it's okay, what should the plural form be?

_____

_____

_____

In short, the answer is that it's <u>not</u> okay to say *notary publics* even though it probably doesn't hurt your ears to say it. So what should the correct plural form be? It should be *notaries public*. The reason goes back again to that rule about adjectives: in English, we can't put a plural marker on an adjective which accompanies a noun. That means our only choice is to put the plural marker where it belongs, on the noun, and the noun in this case is *notary*, not public. Other examples of this are:

> * ⟨attorney⟩ general   →   ⟨attorneys⟩ general
> * ⟨court⟩ martial   →   ⟨courts⟩ martial

Even though the following examples really don't belong here since they don't contain adjectives, we're going to throw them in for free. They're not words that have been borrowed from other languages, but they do fit the same pattern for making plurals, and here they are:

> ⟨man⟩-of-war   →   ⟨men⟩-of-war
> * ⟨mother⟩-in-law   →   ⟨mothers⟩-in-law
> * ⟨spoon⟩ful   →   ⟨spoons⟩ful
> ⟨passer⟩by   →   ⟨passers⟩by

The following *Teaching Tips* all deal with describing people, places, and things and using adjectives in their descriptions. Although it isn't specifically

---

*Here's a special note about a number of these terms. Because so many native speakers have consistently used the more standard pluralization pattern by sticking the plural marker at the end, we now accept *court martials, mother-in-laws, attorney generals,* and *spoonfuls* as alternative plurals in <u>informal</u> speech.

mentioned in any of the following tips, make sure you remind your students that they should use a wide variety of adjectives **and** that they need to concentrate on the order of those that they do choose to use.

Teaching Tips

#1 Before class, think up four or five nouns for each student you have, and write each noun on a slip of paper. Then think up two adjectives for each of the nouns and write them in any order on a separate slip of paper. Put all the slips in a bag to mix them up and then have each student pull out 8 to 10 slips. The students should then go around the room to their classmates and find slips that will appropriately match the slips they have. Many different combinations are possible, not just the ones you originally thought up. Have them report their combinations to the class, making sure that they've ordered the adjectives correctly.

#2 Before class prepare several grids similar to the one below. (You can draw them on the board if it's easier.) Fill in the boxes in the grids with appropriate vocabulary or have the students brainstorm their own vocabulary and then fill them in. Once the grids have been filled in, have students write down their preferences and collect their sheets of paper. Redistribute the responses and have the students circulate around the room to find the person whose paper they have. Ask the students to give a report on their classmates' answers.

I prefer . . .

cool	stormy
hot	sunny
bright	brisk

. . . weather

I prefer . . .

Alpine	backpacking
Canadian	ski
European	seaside

. . . vacations

I prefer . . .

quiet	romantic
noisy	secluded
peaceful	crowded

. . . places

#3 This activity is a variation of one you came across earlier. Bring in a group of 15 to 20 common and not-so-common items to class (dictionary, tennis ball, safety pin, hair dryer, butterfly net, etc.). Spread them out on your desk and cover them up. Gather the students around your desk and uncover the items. Tell the students that they'll have a couple of minutes to study the items in detail. Cover the items back up and have the students return to their desks. Tell them they have five minutes to list and describe as many of the items as they can remember. After they've written down the items and their descriptions, check their responses. Give the students one point for each correctly remembered item and one point for each descriptive adjective they've used properly.

#4 Select colorful pictures of products or things from your picture file. Divide the class into pairs or small groups. Let the groups choose one of the pictures and have them write advertising copy for the product or item they've chosen. (If the students aren't familiar with advertising English, prepare a mini-lesson on the language of advertising before they begin the project.)

#5 Let the students select travel pictures from the picture file or have them bring in pictures of places that they've been to or are interested in. Have them work in small groups to prepare a travel brochure for the tourist industry about the place they've chosen. Be sure the students use ample adjectives to entice "prospective customers" to travel to these places.

#6 Help! You've lost your luggage and everything in it. Go to the Lost and Found Office of the nearest bus station, train station, or airport and make a report. First divide the class into two groups: the "Lost and Found agents" and the "unfortunate travelers." The agents will brainstorm questions that they need to ask the travelers and the travelers will make up the items in their suitcases. Remind the agents that they need to ask very specific questions about the lost luggage and that the travelers must have detailed descriptions of the suitcases and their contents. When the questions and details have been worked out, pair up an agent and a traveler and have them role play the encounter.

#7 Divide the class into small groups. Have the groups study one another carefully; they're going to need to remember as many precise details about the members of the other groups as they can. After a couple of minutes of studying the other groups, send the groups to different parts of the classroom and let them discuss what they've just observed . . . and . . . have them change something about themselves. One student may take off his glasses. Another may comb her hair in a different way. Two students may exchange sweaters. After a few minutes, have the groups face one another again and try to reconstruct the "original look" of the groups. Award points for correct reconstructions; the team with the most points is declared the "Best Lookers."

#8 This activity gives your students a chance to discuss astrology and prepare horoscopes for themselves and their classmates. First, find out if they know their own signs of the Zodiac. List them on the board; you should even include your own. Prepare a handout like the following one that lists the signs, dates, students' names, etc. (You can also draw one on the board.) If possible, get a copy of the actual constellations and their places in the sky and samples of real horoscopes to show the class. Have the students fill in the charts for one another and then write up horoscopes based on what they've learned.

CONSTELLATION	SIGN	DATES	TRAITS	STUDENT	STUDENT'S OWN TRAITS
	Virgo	Aug. 23 to Sept. 22	sensitive artistic in control	Patricia	
	Libra	Sept. 23 to Oct. 22	fair creative outgoing	Ricardo	

#9 Before class think of an imaginary crime (you only need to provide the most general details). Divide the class into two large groups, "police investigators" and "witnesses." Have the police investigators prepare as many questions to ask the witnesses as they can think of. And have the witnesses prepare a story of what actually happened (location of the crime, victims, etc.). When all the stories and questions have been prepared, divide the class into small groups and have them role play the investigation of the crime.

Mind Bogglers!

What's wrong with saying the following, and why?

1. Jim's enough old to vote.
2. It's such hot that I can't sleep.
3. He makes much money.
4. I ate too many chickens.
5. That's the expensivest car I've ever bought.
6. You can say both of these:
   "The woman is sleeping." / "the sleeping woman"
   So why can't you say both of these:
   "The woman is asleep." / "the asleep woman"?

Chapter 6

The Futures

"Qué será, será."

> **A:** **Are** you **taking** Jacques to the airport tomorrow?
> **B:** Yes, I **am**. His flight **leaves** at 6:15.
> **A:** **Will** you **have** enough time to get there after work?
> **B:** I**'m taking** off early so I **won't have to rush.**
> **A:** **Are** you **going to call** him so he knows what time to be ready?
> **B:** Yes. In fact, I**'m about to call** him now.
> **A:** The traffic's awful at that time of day.
> **B:** Don't worry. By the time I meet you for dinner tomorrow evening, I**'ll have dropped** Jacques off at the airport, and he**'ll be flying** somewhere over the Atlantic!

How many ways are there to express the future in English? There are lots of them! Actually, you've just gone over most of them in the dialog above. Let's see what kind of sleuth you are by having you identify as many of them as you can. See if you can explain why they're being used in their particular sentences. (Here's a hint: there are seven different forms of the future that you need to come up with.)

1. _____

_____

2. _____

_____

3. _____

_____

4. _____

_____

5. _____

_____

6. _____

_____

7. _____

_____

No doubt you recognized certain verb forms that we've already discussed at length in previous chapters, but there are some forms that appear here for the first time. Let's get into the forms that we've already dealt with in other contexts and then proceed to those new ones.

THE PRESENT PROGRESSIVE

"<u>Are</u> you <u>taking</u> Jacques to the airport tomorrow?"

This is one of the most commonly used forms to express the future in current spoken English, yet it's rarely introduced early on in most ESOL grammar books as a way to express the future, and it should be!

The reason that the speaker's asking this question in the present progressive is because he's referring to **a planned event in the near future.** We can also think of it as **something in the future that is being anticipated in the present.**

While we're on the subject of planned events in the near future, we should mention two alternative forms that can mean the same thing, and they are the simple present and the expression "be going to," both of which we'll discuss shortly.

Teaching Tips

Before class, prepare two detailed schedules that show activities and times that are similar but not identical. Make as many copies of the schedules as you have students. Pair up the students and give each student one half of a schedule. Tell the students that they need to find a time that will suit both of them to get together and, for example, study for a big test. The students must explain when they can and cannot meet by asking questions and giving responses using the present progressive forms.

Note

Students aren't permitted to see each other's schedules—they have to <u>ask</u> for the information. Your two schedules might look something like these, though yours will likely have many more details:

Student "A"	Monday	Tuesday	Wednesday	Thursday	Friday	Saturday	Sunday
8:00 A.M.	get up		go to class	post office		shopping	rest
noon	lunch	work	lunch	work	airport		

Student "B"	Monday	Tuesday	Wednesday	Thursday	Friday	Saturday	Sunday
8:00 A.M.	breakfast		go to class	get up	library	breakfast	cook
noon	dentist	lunch	lunch	study	lunch		party

Responses may be similar to the following: "What are you doing at 8:00 Tuesday morning?" "I'm not doing anything." "When are you having lunch on Thursday?" "I'm not eating on Monday; I'm going to the dentist instead."

THE SIMPLE PRESENT

"His flight <u>leaves</u> at 6:15."

It may seem strange, when you stop to think about it, that the verb form which normally represents general ideas or repeated actions should also be used to represent the future.

The question is, why would the speaker choose this verb form for something in the future? What nuance is communicated this way that isn't made if other future forms are used? The answer is that **we use the simple present to represent <u>formalized, scheduled</u> future events**. In this case, it's not that Jacques' flight will leave tomorrow at 6:15 and never do so again. The airlines schedule certain flights to leave at predetermined times, and even though we're referring to Jacques' flight, which is still in the future, we're also communicating that it's a scheduled flight, not just a unique event that will happen one time only in the future and never be repeated. This is the reason the speaker has chosen the simple present. Notice the neat connection to that basic concept of the simple present: repeated actions.

Teaching Tips

This activity focuses on the use of simple present in scheduled future events. Feel free to prepare this initially as a reading exercise because it's rather involved, and the students will have to refer to it to accomplish the activity. Pairs of students will set up travel plans for the president of an import/export company. They'll base the travel plans on the following information. The president, Mr. Watson, is going to Asia for his annual twelve-day buying trip and will visit the factories that he imports from in Tokyo, Singapore, Hong Kong, and Seoul. He always begins his trip in Tokyo and ends up in Singapore. As "administrative assistant" and "personal secretary" to Mr. Watson, the pairs of students must arrange the trip (arrival and departure times, meetings with factory managers, side trips) and any other details that seem appropriate for a business traveler.

Mr. Qing is the factory manager in Singapore, as are Mr. Wong in Hong Kong, Mr. Pak in Seoul, and Mr. Matsuo in Tokyo.

While in Tokyo, Mr. Watson wants to take a side trip to Mt. Fuji; in Seoul, he wants to visit the Temple of Heaven; in Hong Kong, he wants to eat at Jumbo's floating restaurant; and in Singapore, he wants to have high tea at Raffles Hotel.

(1) The pairs of students are to work together to plan out the details of Mr. Watson's itinerary, and both students should write them down. (2) Once they have prepared his itinerary, rearrange the pairs of students. (3) Have one member of each new pair be the administrative assistant and the other Mr. Watson's personal secretary. The administrative assistant needs to tell the secretary the exact details of the trip that he/she planned out with the <u>original</u> partner. (4) After the administrative assistant has done so and the secretary has copied it all down, the students should reverse roles and repeat this procedure. (5) When they finish, they are to read out what they wrote down while playing the role of secretary to check for accuracy.

"BE GOING TO"

"<u>Are</u> you <u>going to call</u> him . . . ?"

The expression "be going to" has two basic uses. Our dialog features one use, namely, **future plans** or **intentions**. In this case, instead of asking "*Are you taking Jacques to the airport tomorrow?*" the speaker could just as easily have asked, "*Are you going to take Jacques to the airport tomorrow?*" Both the present progressive and "be going to" mean the same thing here, but in other situations they're not interchangeable. We'll get back to this point and discuss "be going to" more in depth a little later.

What, then, is the other use of this expression? Look at this sentence and see if you can figure it out:

A worldwide oil shortage <u>is going to</u> be
a very big problem for future generations.

"Be going to" is used for _____.

If you've written a prediction, you've got it right.

A Note on Pronunciation

Many ESOL teachers fail to teach the typical pronunciation of "be going to" and inadvertently have their students practice sentences with this expression in its utterly pristine state without taking into account how native speakers normally say it. Although formal speech still dictates that we pronounce each word in the expression separately and clearly, "I'm going to" / aɪm goɪŋ tu /, the acceptable variation in conversational English is / aɪm / or / am gənə / or / gɔnə /, that is, the words "going to" are pronounced as if they were written "gunnuh" or "gawnuh"—and there's nothing wrong with it!

Troubleshooter

 Keep in mind that there is a distinct difference in the pronunciation of "going to" in the future expression "be going to" and in the case of the common verb "go" in its progressive form.

- Most native speakers of American English tend to say / gɔnə / ("gaw-nuh") or / gənə / ("gunnuh") in the expression "be going to."
- Most native speakers tend to say / gó-ɪn-tə / ("gó-in-tuh") or a variation of this pronunciation when they say such sentences as "He's going to the grocery store."

THE SIMPLE FUTURE (WILL)

"<u>Will</u> you <u>have</u> enough time to get there after work?"

Why has the speaker chosen to use "will" in his question rather than some alternative form? In this case, "will" represents what is referred to as the **pure future** or **simple future**. There's no extra meaning or nuance in his question; it's simply an inquiry about something in the future.

This doesn't mean that you couldn't hear someone say, "*Are* you *going to* have *enough time to get there after work*?" That's a possible form, too, with a bit of a change in our focus. We could be thinking of a planned future event or even a prediction, but by using "will," we're simply focusing on the future without any extras. We should mention, however, that many native speakers would find this area fuzzy and not worry much over which form to use.

Teaching Tips

Find or create paragraphs that use "will" to indicate the future. Have your students rewrite the paragraphs using "be going to." This technique is one that can be adapted for almost any grammar point and is similar to those activities found in *10 Steps* and *26 Steps* by Alemany Press.

More Teaching Tips

Divide the class into pairs or small groups. Have the students plan the trip of a lifetime ("The Perfect Honeymoon," "The Anniversary Trip," etc.). Have the pairs/groups report their underlined itineraries to the class, making sure that they use "will" where appropriate. "The trip will begin at the airport where Romeo and I will board the Concorde for Paris. We'll arrive there a short time later and take a private limo to the George V Hotel. We'll have a private suite reserved for us for the three weeks we'll be there. . ."

The "pure future" concept of "will" can also deal with future **predictions**. In our introductory dialog, one of the speakers says, "*I'm taking off (from work) early so I won't have to rush.*" Why do you think he switches from the present progressive in the first verb to "will" with the second?

He's using the present progressive in the first verb because _____

_____

He's using "will" with the second verb because _____

_____

Let's see how good a linguistic sleuth you're becoming. The speaker has chosen the present progressive for the first verb because it communicates that this is his plan of action for the future. He's used "will" with the second verb to show that he's making a prediction.

Another example of using "will" to make a prediction can be found in a sentence like:

"My car isn't working. When I turn the ignition key, it <u>won't</u> start."

Teaching Tips

Select several pictures from your picture file or even have your students bring pictures that they like to class. They can be actual photos or pictures from magazines, books, etc. Have the students brainstorm as many predictions about what "will occur" next in the various photos as they can.

Variation

After brainstorming what comes next, have the students develop a complete storyline for their pictures. They can tell their stories as groups or individually, in writing or orally.

More Teaching Tips

Divide the class into small groups. Give the students a small, blank city map, one that has only the streets and blocks indicated on it. Ask them to design their "ideal city" or "city of the future" by indicating where the following kinds of places or buildings will be: government offices, water treatment plant, shopping centers, hospital, zoo, etc. Then have the students give a report on what they have come up with. Make sure that they use the various futures in their reports.

Are we finished with "will"? Not by a long shot! There are more cases in which "will" has various nuances. Take a look at the following examples and see if you can categorize the way that "will" is used in each situation:

1. I**'ll** call you tonight.   _____

2. **Will** you give me a hand?   _____

3. You**'ll** be sorry you did that!   _____

4. He**'ll** often forget the time.   _____

In the first three examples, it's clear that we're referring to things in the future even though there are differences in usage. In Sentence 1, the person is making **a promise**; in Sentence 2, someone's making **a request**; in Sentence 3, someone's making **a threat**.

In Sentence 4, however, something very different is happening. In this case, "will" doesn't carry future meaning at all; it's used here to mean what is **apt to happen** or to show **a tendency** for something to happen on a regular basis. Another example of this unusual use is in the saying "Boys will be boys," which parents might say after their sons have gotten into some sort of mischief, played too roughly, or gotten too dirty.

There's no doubt that "will" can be a very tricky word. In many ways, it's unfortunate that the word is taught as a form of the future in beginning ESOL grammar books. What happens is that the students latch on to this word and think it can be applied to every situation in the future—and how wrong that assumption is! In fact, it's just possible that "will" is used less frequently than other forms to express the future.

Moreover, the simple fact is that forms like the present progressive, "be going to" and "will" are sometimes interchangeable, but at other times they aren't. Look at the following sets of sentences. Compare the sentences in each set and check off if you are comfortable that <u>all three are interchangeable</u> or if you're not so comfortable with that prospect.

1. **They're meeting us at 3 o'clock.**
   They're going to meet us at 3 o'clock.
   They'll meet us at 3 o'clock.

   ☐ comfortable ☐ not comfortable

2. **A:** **Any plans for today?**
   B: **I'm going to the beach.**
   I'm going to go to the beach.
   I will go to the beach.

   ☐ comfortable ☐ not comfortable

3. **He's dying if he finds out the truth!**
   He's going to die if he finds out the truth!
   He'll die if he finds out the truth!

   ☐ comfortable ☐ not comfortable

4. **It's raining later tonight.**
   It's going to rain later tonight.
   It will rain later tonight.

   ☐ comfortable ☐ not comfortable

In the first set of sentences, we're comfortable that all three versions are interchangeable. The reason is that all three communicate variations of the same common futurity without many nuances getting in the way. The present progressive tells us that we're anticipating a near future event; "be going to" predicts that future event; "will" can also predict a future event. So all three variations share commonalities and seem all right to us.

With the remaining sets, we're <u>not</u> comfortable with the prospect of interchanging all the variations in the three sentences. Let's look each set over and discover why we're not comfortable with it.

All three sentences in the second set are grammatical, so that's not our problem. *I'm going* and *I'm going to go* are both acceptable because they overlap in meaning: they can both represent intentions or plans for the future. *I will go*, on the other hand, is more commonly used for predictions or for the pure future with no nuances. This sentence is certainly not a prediction, so "will" just doesn't work, and the sentence seems to be missing something without the idea that this is my intention or plan. Therefore, even though all three are grammatical, most native speakers would tend to use either of the first two forms and not "will."

In the third set, we have more clear-cut problems. These are variations of a real conditional sentence, that is, a sentence which states that one circumstance will happen depending on whether or not the other one does. The form most native speakers would choose is the one containing "will" because this is traditionally the way most people form one part of a real conditional sentence to mean prediction. Using "be going to" is a variation, but one that most native speakers wouldn't choose as their first option. The first sentence in the set, *He's dying if he finds out the truth* doesn't work for anybody because it's ungrammatical. **We cannot use the present progressive in a real conditional sentence to mean prediction**. So in this case, the present progressive is not interchangeable with the other forms.

In the last set, the present progressive is once again our culprit. We're comfortable with interchanging *It's going to rain* and *It will rain* because both share a commonality: they can both be used for predictions. Once again, **the present progressive cannot be used for predictions; it's used for certainties**.

Before we leave this topic, let's take a look at one more set of sentences. Are you comfortable with the present progressive in this set?

> **If it rains tonight, I'll stay home.**
> **If it rains tonight, I'm going to stay home.**
> **If it rains tonight, I'm staying home.**
>
> ☐   comfortable   ☐   not comfortable

We're sure you've checked off the box that means you're comfortable with all three sentences—and so are we. This time, the present progressive works well because we're not making a prediction, but rather stating a future fact.

If you remember, we said that we weren't done with "will" by a long shot—and we're still not! Because there's so much to say about this word and its counterpart, "would," we're going to get back to it in Chapter 11. We think you can wait till then!

Troubleshooter

 <u>A word about "shall"</u>: There is a certain degree of controversy over this modal auxiliary, and that probably won't end with this book. Except in certain circumstances, "shall" is not the word of choice in American English for the pure or simple future; we let "will" do that job for us.

- In formal language, "shall" can be used to make suggestions: Shall we leave now?
- Again, in formal speech, "shall" can be used to introduce an offer: Shall I do that for you?

 Even when "shall" is used as a pure future form, it is restricted in its use with the pronouns "I" and "we" and is rarely used with the combined phrase "you and I."

 It's interesting to note that "will" is the preferred modal auxiliary in every English-speaking country, and that "shall" is losing ground even in the British Isles.

"BE ABOUT TO"

"I'm about to call him now."

For a change, we've got something with no ambiguity and no nuances. The semi-modal "be about to" has just one meaning: **the subject is on the verge of doing something**. In other words, it's the nearest that the future can be to the present.

Teaching Tips

Before class, record a TV or radio program that has lots of action and a strong storyline. Note points in the program where you can stop the tape and get the students to predict what's about to happen, what's apt to happen, and what will happen next. Present the program to the class, stopping at each point you've noted and ask the students to use the various futures to interpret the drama. Don't play them the end of the program. Have the students brainstorm various endings in small groups and have them act out their endings for the entire class to enjoy.

THE FUTURE PERFECT

"By the time I meet you . . . <u>I'll have dropped</u> Jacques off at the airport . . ."

Once again we've hit upon a verb form that leaves no ambiguity for us to wonder about. Why does the speaker use this form in our dialog? Think about the sentence from the dialog which we've quoted above and come up with a description of what the underlined portion means in this time frame. Write your idea on the following lines.

_____

_____

The future perfect is an odd way for us to look at the past by way of the future. **We project ourselves to some point in the future, stop, turn around, and look back at what's already in the past for us at <u>that</u> moment**. In a way, it's a form of hindsight. There are two uses of this verb form, but in short, the future perfect tells us what will already be finished by the time we arrive at a certain point in the future.

In the sentence quoted from our dialog, the speaker is saying that at the point in the future when he meets the other person, the action of his dropping Jacques off at the airport will already be completed. This represents the first use of the future perfect.

The second use has to do with something that's happening currently. When the speaker in our dialog says he'll drop Jacques off at the airport before the two people meet that evening, he's referring to a short-term action that has its whole beginning and end in the future. But the future perfect can also refer to another time frame. Look at the following example and see if you can come up with an explanation of what the future perfect represents in this case. Write down your thoughts on the following lines:

Midori <u>will have been</u> a nurse for twenty years by the year 2000.

_____

_____

We can view an action or state of being at some point in the future even though it's already happening now. Midori is a nurse now; in fact, she's been a nurse since 1980. If we want to project Midori's career status into the future from the time she first became a nurse and see what her total years in the profession will be at the turn of the century, the future perfect is our vehicle for doing so. What we're really doing is jumping from the past into the future and bypassing the present.

We do have another aspect of this verb form, **the future perfect progressive**. Let's go back to our subject, Midori, and project something else about her professional life. Let's say that Midori began working as an operating room nurse in 1985 and she has no intention of changing her specialization. If we want to project what she'll be doing in the year 2000, we can say:

**By the turn of the century, Midori <u>will have been working</u>
as an operating room nurse for fifteen years.**

Of course, we can also say that Midori _will have worked_ as an operating room nurse for fifteen years; in other words, we can use the simple form or the progressive form of the future perfect in this idea. Remember the discussion about these two versions for the present perfect in Chapter 2? The same basic rule we applied then holds true now, too: **if a verb can be used only in the simple present, use only the simple form of the future perfect; if the verb can be used in the present progressive form, you can opt to use the progressive form in the future perfect.**

Teaching Tips

Have your students imagine themselves ten, twenty, or thirty years from now. Ask them to predict what they think their lives will be like then. Typical answers are: By the year 2001, I will have learned English well enough to get a good job. By the same year, I'll have been living and working for this company for fifteen years. By then, all my children will have grown up and left home.

Variation

Give your students the name of a famous person and have them do some research on that person's life. Then have the students give reports on their subject. Start off the reports with the following to encourage the future perfect and future perfect progressive: "It's _____ (date) and _____ (person) has just been born. By _____ , he/she will have _____ .

THE FUTURE PROGRESSIVE

". . . he'<u>ll be flying</u> somewhere over the Atlantic!"

For a while now, we've had the good fortune to deal with a future expression ("be about to") and a verb form (future perfect) that offered us simplicity of meaning and a respite from some of the more complicated topics that we've braved so far in this book. Well, the respite is over and we're back into the thick of it!

First of all, we'll deal with the most common use of the future progressive which reflects the basic concept of the present and past progressive forms. Let's go back to our original dialog and take another look at the sentence we've just quoted and compare it to the same sentence with the simple future form instead of the progressive form:

1. **By the time I meet you for dinner tomorrow evening, Jacques <u>will be flying</u> somewhere over the Atlantic!**

2.   **By the time I meet you for dinner tomorrow evening,
Jacques <u>will fly</u> somewhere over the Atlantic!**

One of these sentences is ungrammatical—any native speaker would sense this immediately. Explaining why one just doesn't work is another matter. What's your guess? Draw a circle around the number of the sentence you think is ungrammatical.

We're sure that you didn't hesitate at all in deciding that the ungrammatical sentence is the **second one**. But why? Think of the whole idea that the sentence conveys (especially the information supplied in the first part). Then think about the basic concept of the progressive forms which we discussed in previous chapters. Now come up with a reason that makes the future progressive work in this sentence and write your conclusion on these lines:

_____

_____

_____

Just as its name implies, and just as is the case with the past and present progressive forms, the future progressive deals with an action that's in progress at a specific moment which we're pinpointing, this time, in the future. The opening part of the sentence says "By the time I meet you for dinner," which means <u>during that period in the future when I meet you and we are having dinner</u>. The opening part of the sentence sets up the idea. It means that **something else will be in progress in that same time period, and we use the future progressive to show which action will be in progress at that time**.

Here's another example which clearly shows how this verb form communicates that the underlined action will be in progress at that future time we're pinpointing:

**I know that Jacques <u>will be working</u> on that import/export
deal we discussed when I get to see him in Paris next week.**

Let's return to the sentence "By the time I meet you for dinner tomorrow evening, Jacques will be flying somewhere over the Atlantic." Now we need to discover why using the simple future form doesn't work in the context of this sentence. Think about what type of verb "fly" is. Then think about what meaning you get from this action in the isolated phrase *he will fly over the Atlantic*. Now come up with an explanation to show why the simple future form is ungrammatical with this verb and in this context. Write your conclusion on these following lines:

_____

_____

_____

Because "fly" is an action verb, not a stative one, it conjures up a definite beginning and end. When we say *he will fly over the Atlantic*, we get the impression that it's a completed future event. Perhaps in your mind's eye, you can picture him leaving New York and arriving in Paris. In other words, the idea is too complete and sabotages the very essence of what our original thought was. We don't want to focus on a completed act; quite the contrary, we want to focus on an act <u>in progress</u>, and that's why "By the time I meet you for dinner tomorrow evening, Jacques will fly over the Atlantic" doesn't work.

Here's a sentence that does work with the simple future form because we're using a stative verb instead of an active one:

> **By the time I meet you for dinner tomorrow evening,**
> **Jacques <u>will be</u> home in Paris.**

 **Troubleshooter**

In the example on page 148, note the part of the sentence which says ". . . when I get to see him." In some other languages, it would be grammatical to use the equivalent of the future form of *get*. After all, we are referring to a future time, aren't we? Many of your students will more than likely put a verb after "when" in the future if that's the time of the sentence. Be prepared to explain the following:

- If we are referring to some point in the future, we don't need to use a future form after the following words or phrases:

  when / while / as soon as / just as / before / after / until

  Here are some more examples:

  - As soon as he <u>wakes</u> up, I'll make him breakfast.
  - Before I <u>leave</u> work, he'll have the report ready.
  - They won't offer more scholarships until the proper funds <u>are</u> allocated.

- Another thing to note and point out to your students is that it's the <u>other</u> part of the sentence which contains the future verb form, <u>not</u> the one with one of the above expressions!

There are certain situations in which using the simple future form or the future progressive form can make quite a difference. Look at the following pairs of sentences. Decide if you feel there's no big difference in meaning between the sentences in each pair or if their meanings are definitely different:

1. **Will you see Mr. Chang before you leave work today?**
   Will you be seeing Mr. Chang before you leave work today?
   ☐ no big difference ☐ big difference

2. **The Grants won't sue their neighbors.**
   The Grants won't be suing their neighbors.
   ☐ no big difference ☐ big difference

3. **Will you come to our party on Sunday?**
   Will you be coming to our party on Sunday?
   ☐ no big difference ☐ big difference

4. **I'll spend next summer in the mountains.**
   I'll be spending next summer in the mountains.
   ☐ no big difference ☐ big difference

It's hard to predict whether your students will ever develop the language sensitivity needed to get a "feel" for the differences that can be found in Pairs 2 and 3, but not in Pairs 1 and 4. However, it certainly will be nice if a student asks you one day to explain the differences, and you can! Let's go over each pair of sentences and find out why there are or aren't big differences in meaning.

To "see someone" can mean two basic ideas in English. It can mean to have someone in your view, or it can mean to have an appointment or date with someone. In the first pair of sentences, it can even mean just to check in with someone before leaving work for the day. In this context, it seems obvious that we're talking about either meeting Mr. Chang for an appointment or checking in with him before leaving work. For this reason, we don't perceive any real difference in meaning between the two forms "Will you see" and "Will you be seeing."

In the fourth pair of sentences, the same principle applies. There are really no shifts in meaning which are carried in one form or the other, so there's really no difference perceived between saying "I'll spend" and "I'll be spending" in this context.

The second pair, however, is a different matter. The first sentence tells us that the Grants refuse to sue their neighbors. It's an idea we can even apply to a hypothetical situation that might come up in a discussion about suing. The second sentence makes us believe that a real situation has arisen in which the Grants could be considering a law suit. The sentence tells us that, at least on this occasion, the Grants aren't going to sue their neighbors, but it doesn't imply that they would never consider doing so.

The sentences in the third pair are also very different. The first sentence is an invitation in the form of a question. The second sentence is not an invitation but a way of asking for a confirmation from a person who has already been invited.

Teaching Tips

Find a picture of a wedding or other event which permits speculation about it. Have the students brainstorm vocabulary and questions that they want answered about the event. (Who are the people? How old are they? What are they wearing? What will they promise in their vows? What's he about to do? Where will they be spending their honeymoon? Where do people in your culture go on a honeymoon? Where will they live after the wedding? How many children are they going to have? etc.) Write any vocabulary or information on the board that will help students with the rest of the assignment. Divide the class into small groups and have them write various versions of the picture: a newspaper report, a letter from the bride-to-be to someone who can't come to the ceremony or an invited guest describing the event to someone over the phone, etc. Have the class share the various versions of the event with their classmates.

TWO MARGINAL FUTURE EXPRESSIONS

There are two more expressions which show futurity although their main focus isn't necessarily on time so much as it is on other ideas. Let's take a look at the following dialog which includes these two expressions:

A: When is Mr. Aziz arriving in town?
B: His flight **is due** in at noon, I believe.
A: Fine. He**'s to see** Mr. Craig as soon as he gets here.
B: All right. I'll make a note of it.

"BE DUE" (+ INFINITIVE VERB / ADVERBIAL PHRASE)

Can you think of other ways to express the phrase "His flight <u>is due in</u> . . ." as it appears in our dialog? See if you can come up with at least two phrases that mean the same idea, and write them on the lines below:

_____

_____

_____

Chances are you've come up with phrases such as:

- *His flight is expected in / is expected to arrive*
- *We anticipate his flight to get in / to arrive*
- *His flight should be in / should arrive*

All of these synonymous phrases clearly show that their focus is on expectations about Mr. Aziz's flight; the secondary consideration is that we're dealing with a future event.

We can use "be due" with an infinitive verb (He's due <u>to arrive</u> at any moment) or with an adverbial phrase (He's due <u>in town</u> / He's due <u>here</u> by 3 o'clock).

So when do we tend to use this expression? Think about the situation we've presented in the dialog and any other situations you can imagine when "be due" is appropriate. What would you say is its main use? Write your conclusion on the following lines:

_____

_____

To sum up, **we tend to use "be due" for events that are scheduled in the future.** Actually, "be due" accomplishes the same thing that the simple present accomplishes in this use, but the difference is that **"be due" carries the extra nuance which tells us what is expected.** Compare these two sentences:

They appear in court tomorrow at 3 P.M.
(They're scheduled to appear in court tomorrow at 3 P.M.)

They're due to appear in court tomorrow at 3 P.M.
(We expect them to appear in court tomorrow at 3 P.M.)

"BE TO" (+ BASE VERB)

Let's approach this expression the same way we looked at "be due." Can you think of at least two ways to express the same idea as in our dialog? Remember, the sentence is: "He's to see Mr. Craig as soon as he gets here." Write your phrases down on the following lines:

_____

_____

_____

Here are some possible synonymous phrases:

- *He's supposed to see Mr. Craig*
- *He should see Mr. Craig*
- *He has to see Mr. Craig*

What would you say is the focus or the main intent of this expression? Just as you did for "be due," think about the situation in our dialog and come up with other situations in which "be to" would be appropriate. When you've formed a conclusion, write it down on the lines below:

_____

_____

The overriding focus of this expression deals with **instructions, orders, arrangements, or planned events**. There's also something very formal sounding about this expression. And then, of course, there's the idea of futurity, too.

If we expand the dialog we've already presented to you, something interesting happens to the expression "be to." Take a look at this and figure out what's happened:

A: Be sure you do make a note of it. Oh, and by the way, he **isn't to speak** to anyone until he's seen Mr. Craig. Have you got that?

B: Don't worry. I'll make sure he doesn't.

An interesting development, right? What other phrases would you think of that could substitute for "he <u>isn't to speak</u> to anyone"? Think of at least two, and write them down on these lines:

_____

_____

_____

Once again, here are some of the possibilities you could have chosen as synonymous phrases:

- *Don't let him speak to anyone*
- *He mustn't speak to anyone*
- *He isn't allowed to speak to anyone*

Even though we can still make a case for the element of futurity in this expression when it's used in the negative, we have to concede that the main focus is on some sort of prohibition. It's interesting how making this a negative expression changes the meaning so much.

Teaching Tips

Before class, think up as many situations as you can where orders are issued (what you say to a child; what a sergeant says to recruits; what a chef says to the kitchen personnel; what a father says to his teenage son or daughter; what new home owners say to their furniture movers, etc.). Have students brainstorm as many different instructions, orders, arrangements, etc. as they can using "be to" in the affirmative and negative.

The Futures in a Nutshell

Present Progressive
- **a planned event in the near future:**
  I'm visiting some friends tonight.
- **present anticipation of a future event:**
  They're moving some time next spring.

Simple Present
- **scheduled future events:**
  The next semester begins on May 28.

Simple Future (WILL)
- **a basic future idea with no nuances:**
  We'll see you later.
- **making predictions:**
  I think they'll be successful.
- **making promises:**
  I'll do it before I leave the office.
- **making requests:**
  Will you help me move this furniture?
- **making threats:**
  You'll regret the day you were born!
- **what is apt to happen:**
  It will usually rain here every day between June and November.

"Be Going To"
- **showing future plans or intentions:**
  We're going to have a party next weekend.

"Be About To"
- **on the verge of doing something:**
  Quiet, please! The guest speaker's about to begin.

Future Perfect
- **project ourselves to some point in the future, stop, turn around, and look back at what is already in the past for us at <u>that</u> moment:**
  The next time you see me, I'll have finished the last chapter of my manuscript.

Future Perfect Progressive

works the same way as the present perfect progressive does in relation to the present perfect, and shows something in progress:

I'll have been working on that manuscript for over six months by the time I see you again.

Future Progressive

can be used at times as an alternative to the simple future:

I'll be giving you this report by the end of the week.

can show an action in progress at some future point:

When we arrive at my folks' house, I'm sure Mom will be getting dinner ready.

"Be Due"

scheduled future events with the nuance of expectation:

The baby is due the middle of October.

"Be To"

in the affirmative, used for future instructions, orders, arrangements, planned events:

You're to fill out this application form and then set up an appointment for an interview.

in the negative, used for (future) prohibition:

You aren't to take this medicine on an empty stomach.

Mind Bogglers!

1. Why does Person B's response to the following question sound odd?

    A: What are you doing on your vacation?
    B: I'm coming back to my country.

2. And what about what Person B says this time? It doesn't seem right either.

    A: (knock! knock! knock!) Let me in!
    B: Who is it? Who's here?

Chapter 7

Compound Nouns and Adjectives

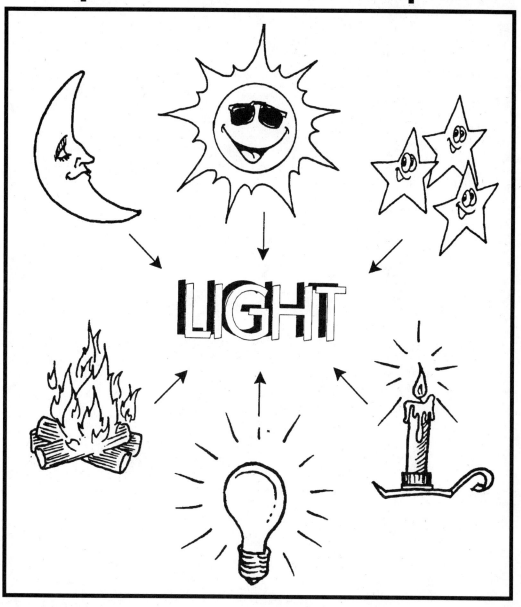

"It was a one-eyed, one-horned flying purple people eater."

A: You know, I just bought a rubber baby buggy bumper.

B: A what?

A: A rubber baby buggy bumper.

B: What on earth is that?

A: Well, the baby buggy, or stroller, that I put my baby in when I go out for a walk used to have a metal bumper on it.

B: Yeah, so?

A: Well, this new bumper's made of rubber to cushion any shocks if I bump the baby buggy into something.

B: Oh, now I get it! It's a bumper made of rubber that protects your baby buggy—better known as a stroller.

A: Exactly! It's a rubber baby buggy bumper!

B: Of course.

The dialog you've just read deals with an interesting and yet perplexing phenomenon of English for ESOL teachers, namely, making compound forms. In this chapter, we're going to deal first with compound nouns and then look at compound adjectives. We dealt briefly with one type of compound noun in the section of Chapter 5 entitled "When Nouns are Adjectives," so some of the introductory material in this chapter should sound familiar.

Before we get going, we want to let you know that this chapter is going to be handled differently from what you've seen up to now. The subject of compounding can be treated in two ways, and we can describe those ways best by drawing the following analogy: picture a large body of water. There's the surface area which is relatively uncomplicated. The water is clear, a good deal of light can penetrate it, and that makes it easy to see your way round. This is where people go snorkeling. Then there's the deep water. Less light can penetrate these depths. There are rocky outcroppings to avoid and a good deal of muck on the bottom. These elements make the going somewhat hazardous and make seeing difficult. This is where people go scuba diving. You can enjoy certain things while snorkeling, but a real feeling for what can be found in the waters can only be experienced through scuba diving.

So it is with compounding. The introductory sections of the two major parts of this chapter will be like snorkeling. They'll offer you a basic investigation into the material that will prove immediately useful in the ESOL classroom. Then will come a deeper look, like scuba diving, which will offer you more detailed exposure to the material if you'd like to dive a little more. At first glance, you may wonder why we've included such complex information. To anticipate your reaction, we want to explain the reasons for approaching the topic in this way. Simply put, if you've got a clearer picture of the rules and combinations that English has for creating compound nouns and adjectives, you'll be able to help your students in two main ways.

First, you'll be able to show them how they can understand compound forms when they come across them for the first time; if they understand how they're constructed, they'll understand their meanings more easily. Second, if they understand how these forms are put together, that is, which combinations are and are not possible, they'll be able to create their own compound forms whenever the situation arises—and it will arise. Even if they create a compound form that the listener has never heard before, he/she will instantly understand what they're talking about if they put it together the right way.

Here's one example to demonstrate how this works. We have a bathroom telephone in our house. More than likely you've had no trouble understanding what we said. Had we said that we have "a telephone bathroom," you'd be looking at us with a very confused expression on your face. The reason it works when we say "a bathroom telephone" even if you've never heard that phrase before is that all of us understand the basic rule we've used to construct this compound form, and so it has meaning.

COMPOUND NOUNS

To begin with, let's see if we can come up with a simple definition of what a compound noun is. In our dialog, one of the speakers talked about a stroller, using its colloquial name "baby buggy." "Baby buggy" is a good example of a compound noun. The part of the baby buggy discussed was a buggy bumper, another good example of a compound noun. What, then, would you say a compound noun is? See if you can write a simple recipe for making a compound noun on the lines that follow:

_____

_____

You've probably come up with something like this: take two nouns, put them together, and you've got a compound noun. Okay, that's certainly the basic idea, but rarely are things that simple in language. One observation we'd like to reiterate from Chapter 5 is that language is so marvelous that it allows us to take words which really have no connection with each other, put them together, and create a brand new word.

Teaching Tips

"Disappearing Dialogs" are excellent for practicing any written or oral grammar point. Before class, prepare a dialog that contains several examples of the grammar point you want to deal with—in this case, compounds. Prepare an overhead transparency of the dialog or write it on the board. Give the various roles in your dialog to different groups in your class. Model the dialog for your students and have them repeat after you. Go through the dialog two or three times to get them comfortable with it and then begin your "disappearing act" by placing pieces of paper on the overhead or erasing small bits of the dialog. Cue the "actors" to start the dialog again, repeating it completely, even those parts of it which are now obscured or erased. Go through the dialog several times more, each time removing more and more until it's completely gone; by that time, students will have no doubt learned their parts by heart.

Getting back to the issue at hand, the first question we should ask ourselves is, which noun do we place first, and which one second? Is it possible to say "bumper rubber" instead of "rubber bumper"? And if it is possible, do they mean the same thing? Well, the answer to the first question is YES, we can say "bumper rubber," but the answer to the second question is NO, they don't mean the same thing. Let's see why.

To start, we have to understand the order that the nouns are placed in. **The last noun is the head noun**, the noun being described. Therefore, **the noun before the head noun is a descriptive element**, one that tells us some detail about the head noun. With this information, let's see if you can interpret what it means when we say "rubber bumper" or "bumper rubber."

A rubber bumper is _____

Bumper rubber is _____

The interpretation of "a rubber bumper" is a bumper that's made of rubber, and in this case, we're using "rubber" as an adjective. This phrase is *not* a compound noun, but simply a head noun with another noun being used adjectivally (see Chapter 5). It's important to understand that it's still a bumper, whether it be a rubber or a metal bumper or even a plastic bumper—it's still a bumper! Since we haven't created a new entity, but have only described what the bumper is made of, we know it's not a compound noun.

The interpretation of "bumper rubber," on the other hand, is that it's some sort of rubber specially formulated to be made into bumpers—a totally different thing. In this case, the word "bumper" is not just being used as an adjective; rather, together with the head noun, "rubber," it represents a totally new entity, a specific material ("bumper rubber"), and is indeed a compound noun.

Another example of this linguistic juggling act is "housework" vs. "workhouse." "Housework," of course, is all of the cleaning and washing, etc., that goes on in and around the house. A "workhouse," however, is something totally different. It was a place like a prison during the 19th century (made familiar to us by Charles Dickens) where debtors were forced to stay and work. What a difference word order can make!

What else is important for our recipe? Here are a few more compound nouns. See if you can describe the head noun in each case by paraphrasing. We've done the first one as an example.

1. A knife sharpener is *a tool or appliance that sharpens knives.*
2. Star light is _____
3. A toy store is _____
4. A coin slot is _____

If you've followed our example, you've probably written that star light is the light from the stars, a toy store is a store that sells toys, and a coin slot is a slot where you insert coins (like part of a vending machine). What slight but important change do you notice in the descriptive nouns as they appear in the compound form compared to their appearance in your paraphrases? Write your observation on the following line:

_____

We're sure you're becoming a very good linguistic sleuth by this point in the book! The observation is that **the descriptive nouns usually appear only in the <u>singular</u> when used to make compound nouns** even if they refer to more than one thing. So, even though it's the light coming from many, many star**s**, it's called star light. There are exceptions to this rule, though, such as "the appropriations committee," "a sports car," and "the arms race." These exceptions arise when words that usually appear only in the plural become the descriptive elements. The majority of descriptive elements in a compound noun, however, do appear in their singular form.

The next logical question is, why should the descriptive noun stay in the singular form even if it represents a plural? Any idea? If you've got one, state it here:

_____

_____

We can answer this question about why descriptive nouns normally stay singular by analogy with one of the basic rules in English about adjectives. We know that adjectives aren't pluralized in English, and since these descriptive nouns work just like adjectives, they follow that same basic rule. That's why the descriptive nouns aren't usually found in the plural.

Teaching Tips

Because students often have trouble with the interpretation and actual construction (what part goes where) of compounds, one effective way to get your students more comfortable with them is to take them apart and have the class reconstruct them. Before class, decide which words you want to use and put them on an overhead transparency, a handout, or the board. Put the first element of each compound in Column A and the second element in Column B. Make sure that you mix up the elements. Have the students reconnect the compounds and provide a definition.

A	B
1. bird	a. day
2. rail	b. bath
3. farm	c. sting
4. bee	d. road
5. school	e. animal

There's one more ingredient needed in our recipe. We're only going to treat it briefly here because we'll be dealing with it in detail in Volume 2. It has to do with stress. In short, **the stress** (some people call it **the accent**) **falls on the descriptive element in a compound noun**, <u>not</u> on the head noun: a knífe sharpener; stár light; a tóy store; a cóin slot.

We've already discussed the fact that the descriptive element in a compound noun is placed before the head noun, and that's assuming that we're dealing with just one element, but what happens if there are two descriptive elements before the head noun? Is there a special order that they should be placed in? Here are a couple of examples that you can use to refresh your memory about the rule for ordering these descriptive elements which we covered in Chapter 5:

a steel fishing rod

a ceramic flower pot

The order is _____

If your memory has served you well, you've written that the order is **material + purpose + head noun**.

A Deeper Look

We've now covered the basic recipe for a compound noun, but we're not done yet. So far, we've looked into a compound noun that's formed from two nouns, but there are other combinations that we can use to make compound nouns—nine others, actually, for a total of ten.

Let's do some more sleuthing. Following are compound nouns which represent all the combinations we can make. Look them over and figure out what those ten combinations are. (You know that the first one is **noun + noun**.) Write down the combinations on the blanks directly below the list. You'll notice short blanks after each word, but don't worry about them for now. To give you some help, we'll tell you that you're going to find combinations with **gerunds** (-ing forms), **particles** (similar to prepositions; you'll read more about them later), **adjectives, verbs**, and the word **self.**

railroad **n+n**	ice skating _____	sleeping bag _____
self-esteem _____	gun-for-hire _____	Bigfoot _____
washing machine _____	passerby _____	girlfriend _____
sundown _____	insight _____	throughway _____
put-down _____	self-defense _____	downpour _____
skin diving _____	blackmail _____	shoe-in _____
upswing _____	cleaning fluid _____	maid-of-honor _____
funny bone _____	pin-up _____	duck hunting _____
by-law _____	lighthouse _____	breakthrough _____
mother-in-law _____	overkill _____	self-control _____

1. _____   *noun + noun*   _____
2. _____
3. _____
4. _____
5. _____
6. _____
7. _____
8. _____
9. _____
10. _____

Now that you've decided what the other nine combinations are, go back and label them in abbreviated forms in the short blanks that we've provided after each compound noun. We've already done the first one for you.

Here are all ten combinations that you'll find represented in our list. Understanding which elements can go together and how they go together will help your students figure out new vocabulary items they're bound to come across, and will also give them the skills necessary to build their own compound nouns when the case arises.

noun + noun (railroad, lighthouse, girlfriend)
noun + gerund (skin diving, ice skating, duck hunting)
noun + particle* (sundown, passerby, shoe-in)
noun + phrase (mother-in-law, gun-for-hire, maid-of-honor)
gerund + noun (washing machine, cleaning fluid, sleeping bag)
adjective + noun (funny bone, blackmail, Bigfoot)
self + noun (self-esteem, self-defense, self-control)
particle + noun (by-law, insight, throughway)
verb + particle (put-down, pin-up, breakthrough)
particle + verb (upswing, overkill, downpour)

Teaching Tips

Pictures from your picture file, or even the pictures introducing the various chapters of both the main text and workbook, can be used to stim-

---

*Don't worry if you wrote "preposition" instead of "particle" for words like *up, down, by, in, through,* and *over.* There's a slight difference between a preposition and a particle. A preposition must always have an object either mentioned or implied (up the stairs / by the door / in the house), but a particle has no object following it (Look up! / Come in! / pass by). Although there are some prepositions that can't be used as particles and vice versa, most are interchangeable.

ulate compound recognition and formation. Take a look at the picture introducing Chapter 6 of the workbook. Can you find things that relate to these compounds (newspaper, curtain rod, table top, outfit, passerby, Bigfoot, break-in, far-fetched, hook-nosed, wide-eyed)? Are there any others?

One last word we'd like to say about compound nouns is that the ten combinations we've gone over in this chapter don't account for every compound noun in English. There are other possibilities—we might call them "fringe combinations"—which don't seem to follow any commonly used pattern. Examples of these are **comeuppance, wherewithal,** and **do-gooder.**

 # Troubleshooter

 Students may ask you why some forms are written as one word, but others as two words. The only help we can offer is that the tendency is to write commonly used, easily recognizable words as one word, but there is no rule to explain this phenomenon of the written language.

 Another question that often comes up deals with hyphenation. Again, there is no set rule for this, but here are some observations which may help:

- Compounds formed with a noun + particle tend to be hyphenated (sun-up, runner-up)
- Compounds formed with a verb + particle tend to be written the same way (make-up, sit-in)
- Compounds beginning with "self" are always hyphenated (self-respect, self-evaluation)

COMPOUND ADJECTIVES

The most typical kind of compound adjective, and the kind that ESOL teachers need to deal with quite early on, is the **hyphenated form**. In the dialog on the next page, all but one of the examples are hyphenated compound adjectives. Happily, most of these adjective forms are not so wordy. Let's take a look at some common ones by doing another paraphrasing activity. Complete the following

A: Darn it! It's time to get my garden ready for planting.
B: You don't seem too thrilled with the idea.
A: I'm not. It's a **backbreaking** job.
B: Maybe that's because you use **old-fashioned** methods.
A: What do you mean "old-fashioned"?
B: You still use those **twenty-year-old** handtools of yours and nothing else, right?
A: Right. So what?
B: Go out and buy some **up-to-date** equipment like a **gas-powered** tiller and a **state-of-the-art**

mulcher. They'll save you all that toil. And they'll save your back, too!
A: Mmmm. That's a **work-saving** idea. Thanks!

sentences by rewording what their initial parts tell you. We've done the first one as an example.

1. A note that's worth five pounds is *a five-pound note.* _____

2. A snake that's six feet long is _____

3. Watermelons that weigh five kilos are _____

4. A wall that's two meters thick is _____

5. Children who are six years old are _____

   Reworking the descriptions of these head nouns (note, snake, watermelons, wall, children) is really quite straightforward. The paraphrases you should have are: **a six-foot-long snake / five-kilo watermelons / a two-meter-thick wall / six-year-old children**.

What's the one major internal change you had to make in order to create these hyphenated compound adjectives? Write your answer on the following line:

_____

The one major internal change was that you had to make the plural items singular in each case: "feet" became "foot" / "kilos" became "kilo" / "meters" became "meter" / "years" became "year." So why the need for this change? By now you should have that answer down pat! Write it on the following lines:

_____

_____

Even though these phrases contain plural elements when they appear after the subjects they're describing, once they've been turned into the components of compound adjectives, they're rarely pluralized in English. It's as simple as that!

Let's take a moment to discuss what we can explain to students about when and why we tend to hyphenate compound adjectives. It seems to be the case that the vast majority of compound adjectives are indeed hyphenated, most assuredly ones that contain numbers (a two-year-old filly / a 100-acre farm / a 1,000-rupee check). What's very important for students to understand is that there is a reason for this convention in the written language. In short, it's to show that even though we may be using two, three, four, or even more descriptive words before the head noun, **these words are being linked together as if they were one word representing one idea**. The hyphens act as the links; they're a visual aid on the written page to let the reader know that these descriptive phrases are to be treated as whole units.

As we mentioned earlier, what we've gone over so far is the basic compound adjective form that's most commonly taught in ESOL classes. It's a bit tricky for students to know when to hyphenate the appropriate phrase, make any plural element singular, and then front the whole thing before the head noun. In many languages, genitive or possessive forms are used to do what we accomplish in English with compound adjectives. In Spanish, for example, it would be typical to say "a stamp of thirty cents" (*una estampilla de treinta centavos*) instead of "a thirty-cent stamp," so you can see how much adjusting your students may have to make when they learn this English form. As an example of how bizarre their phrases could be if they didn't use the English form, think about how your students might try to say "my mother tongue" by following the rules of their language. They'd probably end up saying *"the tongue of my mother"!*

A DEEPER LOOK

Unlike the ten combinations we found for compound nouns, compound adjectives (besides the hyphenated form we've already covered) don't have so many combinations—only eight, to be precise! Three of these are combinations containing **nouns**, three contain **adjectives**, and two have **adverbs**. Look at the following list of compound adjectives and repeat the procedures you used for the identical kind of exercise that dealt with compound nouns. We've used "dovetailed" as an example; it's composed of **noun + noun + ed**. You'll find these combinations also include **present participles** (another -ing form) and **past participles**.

dove-tailed **n+n+ed**	low-flying _____	hard-hitting _____
light-hearted _____	well preserved _____	moonstruck _____
fast-growing _____	flea-ridden _____	foul-smelling _____
good-looking _____	bow-legged _____	badly built _____
ear-splitting _____	narrow-minded _____	far-fetched _____
short-lived _____	fresh baked _____	thought-provoking _____
ill-conceived _____	easy-going _____	pig-headed _____
fuel-injected _____	backbreaking _____	short-sighted _____

1. _____ *noun + noun + ed* _____
2. _____
3. _____
4. _____
5. _____
6. _____
7. _____
8. _____

Now that you've identified the other seven combinations for compound adjectives (not including the hyphenated forms), and now that you've gone back and labeled each one with an abbreviation to identify it, here are the eight combinations you should have found:

noun + noun + ed (dove-tailed, bow-legged, pig-headed)
noun + present participle (ear-splitting, backbreaking, thought-provoking)
noun + past participle (fuel-injected, flea-ridden, moonstruck)
adjective + noun + ed (light-hearted, narrow-minded, short-sighted)

adjective + present participle (good-looking, easy-going, foul-smelling)
adjective + past participle (short-lived, fresh baked, far-fetched)
adverb + present participle (fast-growing, low-flying, hard-hitting)
adverb + past participle (ill-conceived, well preserved, badly built)

The last thing we'd like to say about compound adjectives is that the eight combinations we've gone over in this chapter don't account for every compound adjective in English. There are other possibilities, just as there are the "fringe combinations" with compound nouns which don't follow any commonly used pattern. Examples are **brand-new** and **stir-fry**.

Teaching Tips

"Password" is a game based on the American television quiz show of the same name. The object is to get your team/partner to guess a word before another team/partner guesses it. Before class, write up a list containing a wide variety of compounds that the students will work with. In class, divide the students into groups of at least four. Two students become "Team A" and the other two, "Team B." ("Password" is especially good for large classes because it's quite easy to have several games going on at the same time if you walk around the class and referee.) One person on each team becomes the "giver" and gets one of the pre-selected vocabulary items (e.g., highway). The other person becomes the "guesser."

Flip a coin to see which team goes first; in this case, let's say it's Team A. Giver A gives his/her partner a <u>one-word clue</u> ("road"). The givers have to be very careful with their clues. If the clue contains any part of the targeted word, they lose their turn (Giver A says, for example, "roadway" as his/her clue). Guesser A has one chance to come up with the word. If he/she guesses wrong, it's Team B's chance to try. Giver B gives his/her partner a different one-word clue for the same word ("tolls"). If Guesser B gives a wrong guess, play returns to Team A.

Continue like this for five or six clues. (You don't want to frustrate the givers or guessers by beating a word to death, and any more than six clues is likely to be beating it to death.) If Guesser B gives the correct word, play is over and Team B gets a point. Givers and guessers change roles and start with a new word. The first clue for the new word is given by the team that won the previous point. The game continues until all the words have been played or time is called. To play "Password" with larger teams, rotate guessers each time a new clue is given.

Once again, we'd like to emphasize the reason for presenting you with what some might consider an overwhelming amount of information that may make your head spin. Understanding the possible combinations for the formation of compound adjectives can only go to help your students recognize the meanings of new words they come across or give them the tools to make their own compound forms. Of course, what's most important is that they master the basic ideas of compounding (especially concerning hyphenated forms) and develop the skill to use this construction at will. Should they learn the other possible combinations of compound adjectives just listed, you can consider that a bonus.

There's one other category for us to examine. The adjectives in this group are **hyphenated pat phrases** which have become standard vocabulary items and should be learned as such. Here are some examples:

do-it-yourself	**run-of-the-mill**
devil-may-care	**holier-than-thou**
up-and-coming	**down-and-out**
fly-by-night	**would-be**
middle-of-the-road	**catch-all**

Teaching Tips

Find pictures of objects that you think are unusual or unknown to your students. Divide the class into small groups and have them decide what the items are. Students then write up ads for their items making sure that they use several compounds in their descriptions. (Suggest appropriate compounds if your students need help.)

More Teaching Tips

A "cinquain" is a five-line poem that's excellent for practicing compounds. (Cinquain comes from the French word for "five"-"cinq"). Here's one way to compose a cinquain. On line 1, state the topic in one word. On line 2, describe the topic in two words (an adjective and noun or two adjectives/nouns). On line 3, list actions that describe the topic in three words (three verbs, three gerunds, or even a three-word sentence). Line 4 is for a description of the topic in four words. Line 5 restates the topic in five words. Don't forget to have your students give their cinquains a title! Feel free to adapt your cinquains to the needs of your particular class as there's no one way or best way to create them. Show your students a couple of examples of cinquains and divide the class into small groups. Have the groups compose their own cinquains, making sure that they include at least one compound adjective and one compound noun in their poems.

Title:	"Poetry"
Topic:	Poems.
Adjectives:	Up-lifting, thought-provoking.
Action:	Don't always rhyme.
Description:	Truth about our world.
Restatement:	They provide insight into life.

More Teaching Tips

In Appendix 1 and the workbook, we discuss the inventor, Rube Goldberg. He invented whimsical, though thoroughly complicated machines for performing simple actions. These machines are excellent for practicing compounds. Show your students pictures of these machines and have them come up with as many compounds as they can. (Because Goldberg's machines have such great language potential, we've included two of them in Appendix 1 and one in the workbook). In reference to those machines, here are some possible compounds that students might come up with: ashtray, signboard, watering can, window washing, deadbeat, oversight, slip-up, outcry, self-propelled, and all-purpose. Encourage the students to use a variety of different forms (n + n, -ing + noun, prep. + verb, etc.); have them also create both noun and adjective compounds.

Variation

If you have low-level students with limited vocabularies, you can provide the various parts of the compounds, scrambled. Students then put the parts back together to form logical and correct compounds. Then have them describe the machine using the vocabulary they've been working with.

 Troubleshooter

 One area of compounding that's often overlooked deals with adverbial forms. These tend to be pat phrases that students should learn just as they are. Here's a short list of some typical ones:

upside down	side by side
back-to-front	inside out
above-board	top-to-bottom

Make it a point to incorporate adverbial compound forms like these in your lessons on compounding.

Mind Bogglers!

What's the difference between:

say and **tell**

talk and **speak**

hear and **listen (to)**

Chapter 8

Genitives

OF OF OF S' of OF S'
of OF of of of OF S'
of of of S' of
's 'S of of of 's OF
Of of of of 's 's OF
of of S' of 's of 'S
of S' of s' of S'
of of of of
of Of of 's
Of of 's of of's
of

Mice's and men's best laid plans?
The best laid plans of mice and men?

We're about to investigate one of the most deceptive topics of English grammar. The reason it's so deceptive is that what appears to be quite straightforward and relatively uncomplicated on the surface (after all, aren't we just talking about -'s and **of** ?) is really somewhat perplexing when you get below the surface. As with other topics covered in this book, we're going to focus our attention on those points which tend to be troublesome to understand and explain. Although many ESOL grammars refer to -'s and **of** as "possessives," we prefer to use the broader term "genitives" which includes any and all of their uses. We're sure you'll understand why we don't want to limit ourselves to the term "possessives" as you read on.

Teaching Tips

Even though possessive adjectives aren't covered in this book, we wanted to include this very energetic activity here. Most students are first introduced to genitives as possessive adjectives (my, your, his, her, its, our, and their). A fun way to practice these forms is with the game "Simon Says." The object of "Simon Says" is to find out who the best listener in class is. The best listener is the student who makes no mistakes carrying out what the teacher tells him/her to do. To play the game, the teacher asks all the students to stand up and follow his/her directions **exactly.** This doesn't sound like such a hard thing to do, and indeed it wouldn't be but for the fact that you yourself don't have to do what you've ordered the students to do. You might say, "Put a finger on the end of your nose" as you put your finger on the end of your nose. You might just as well put your finger on your chin. But any student who's put a finger on his/her chin is out of the game and has to sit down. Hearing one thing and doing another is reason for expulsion. Any directions that you give should have a genitive form in them. (Touch the leg of your chair.) The game continues until there's only one student left standing.

THE -S GENITIVE

To begin, let's examine the most typical uses of what we refer to as the **-s genitive** because we add **-'s** to the noun. Of course, if the **-s** is already present, we only need to add the apostrophe. Take a look at the following dialog and note how the -s genitive is used:

A: Phyllis' daughter just joined a girls' football team.
B: Really? Was it the school's idea to create a football team for girls?
A: I think so. Anyway, she was great in yesterday's game. One funny thing: the team insists on having their mascot at every game. It's the cutest white dog.
B: Ah, that's nice.
A: Yeah. They say the dog's presence brings them luck.

Teaching Tips

Give each student a fairly uncomplicated picture, one that doesn't have too many details in it. Divide the class into groups of approximately ten. One by one, each student shows his/her picture to all the members of the group and briefly says what it contains ("There's a green sofa in my picture." / "There are two kids in mine." / "There's a beautiful queen in my picture." etc.). After all the pictures have been described, ask the students to write down as much information as they can remember about each of their group's pictures. Model example sentences, highlighting the various genitive forms. ("Charlie's sofa is green. One of the legs of the sofa is broken." / "The children in Hugo's picture had red hair. I think the tips of their shoes were dirty." / "Jean Claude's picture had a queen in it. I think she's the Queen of Sheba.").

As we've already mentioned, most ESOL grammar books refer to **-'s** as the possessive ending. Remember that **-'s** is attached to singular nouns (clerk**'s**) and irregular plural nouns (children**'s**), but only the apostrophe is added onto singular nouns ending in -s (boss') and regular plural nouns (boys'). Even though that's often the case, it's not the only reason that **-'s** is used. In the dialog you've just read, which examples of the -s genitive would you say clearly demonstrate possession or belonging? Write your observation on the following line:

_____

The answer is that there are just two times when the -s genitive clearly shows possession or belonging in our dialog, and that's with the name "Phyllis" and in talking about the dog. We can definitely say that Phyllis has a daughter, so she's "Phyllis' daughter," and that the dog has presence, so it's "the dog's presence." This way of thinking about the -s genitive leads us to the first use of the **-'s**: we tend to use the -s genitive as a marker of possession or belonging on words that represent people. We tend to use it the same way for animals (a dog's bark; an alligator's stealth; a canary's song). In fact, we can make a general observation that **we can use the -s genitive for possession or belonging on words which represent living things (people and animals)**.

 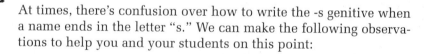

Troubleshooter

At times, there's confusion over how to write the -s genitive when a name ends in the letter "s." We can make the following observations to help you and your students on this point:

- In the rules of such countries as Great Britain, the -'s is added to a name even if it ends in -s: Phyllis → Phyllis's
- In the rules of such countries as the U.S., only the apostrophe is added to a name that ends in -s: Phyllis → Phyllis'

Keep in mind that there is no difference in pronunciation whether the genitive is written one way or the other.

What, now, are we going to do with the rest of the cases of the -s genitive in our dialog? For instance, how can we explain the **-s'** in the phrase "a girls' football team"? It's not that the team is a possession of the girls or that it belongs to the girls; similarly, we can't say that "the idea" is a possession of the school. We can say, however, that the presence does belong to the dog. Is there a simple way to paraphrase all of these phrases to see them in another light? If you were going to paraphrase them, what common way could you come up with? Write down your idea on this line:

_____

We've used paraphrasing before to find the essence of a grammatical construction, and we can use it in this situation, too. Another way to say each of these phrases is: "The girls have a football team." / "The school had an idea." / "The dog has presence." The verb **have** is a common element in these sentences, and that's an easy way to explain this to your students. In fact, many teachers find this paraphrasing quite useful in teaching their students how to form -s genitive phrases as well as how to use the possessive adjectives (my, your, his, etc.). **We can use the concept of "have" to understand and teach how we use certain -s genitive forms.**

Let's pursue the use of "have" as it appears in the previous paraphrases for just a moment. Take another look at the paraphrases we've made:

Phyllis' daughter	= **Phyllis has a daughter**
a girls' football team	= **the girls have a football team**
the school's idea	= **the school had an idea**
the dog's presence	= **the dog has presence**

Do you get the impression that "have" means different things in some of these phrases? Can you figure out what "have" really means in each one? Consider another way to express what "have" means in each case just listed and write your interpretations on the following blank lines:

Phyllis has a daughter _____

the girls have a football team _____

the school had an idea _____

the dog has presence _____

The way we see it, the first "have" really means **belonging** (the daughter belongs to Phyllis); the next "have" means it's a football team **for** girls; the third "have" actually tells us that the school (meaning the administrators) **came up**

with, or **thought of**, an idea; the last "have" is like the first one, meaning that the presence belongs to the dog.

We can think of this paraphrasing with "have" as an *umbrella category* under which there are different subcategories that depend on interpretation. Many times, the interpretation depends on what the head noun is. For example, with the head noun "idea," we've interpreted "have" to mean "come up with" or "think of"; if the head noun were "party," we could interpret "have" to mean "throw" or "give." Keep in mind that although using "have" is a good way to paraphrase almost all -s genitive phrases, its meaning can vary greatly depending on the head noun.

Getting back on track by returning to the examples in our dialog, we still have to account for the **-'s** on the end of "yesterday." First of all, let's take a look at some similar words and phrases and see if the -s genitive can be added to them as well. How about choices like *today / this week / Monday / next month?* Yes, the **-'s** works nicely with these, too: *today's newspaper / this week's stock reports / Monday's weather forecast / next month's tournament.* What observation can you make about these words and phrases?

If you've written that we can use the -s genitive with words and phrases that denote **periods of time**, you've got it right.

Let's move on by comparing the following two phrases. Decide if they're grammatical or not, and check the boxes appropriately:

the school's idea	grammatical ☐	ungrammatical ☐
the school's wall	grammatical ☐	ungrammatical ☐

We already know that "the school's idea" is grammatical, but what about "the school's wall"? The answer is that it's **ungrammatical**. Why is there a difference? We're not going to answer this question just yet, but we'll get back to it very soon.

Troubleshooter

Be prepared for an inevitable occurrence: your students may tend to drop the -s genitive when you're not drilling them on it and produce phrases such as "my mother house" and "the teacher pen." Don't get too exasperated over this—and don't stop correcting them either!

Another problem you'll have to deal with concerns the pronunciation of the -s genitive. Interestingly enough, the rules are identical for pronouncing the regular plural -s on nouns.

- If the noun ends in a voiceless sound, pronounce the -s genitive as /s/:

    Jeff's /jɛfs/   Scot's /skats/

- If the noun ends in a voiced sound, pronounce the -s genitive as /z/:

    Brenda's /brɛndəz/   Ann's /ænz/

- If the noun ends in /s/, /z/, /č/, or /j/, pronounce the -s genitive as /ɪz/ or /əz/:

    Bess' /bɛsɪz/   Mitch's /mɪčɪz/

- In some dialects of English, the /ɪz/ sound for the possessive marker is dropped on nouns that end in /z/. In other dialects, however, it's kept:

    Charles' /čarlz/   /čarlzɪz/

Let's observe some other ways we use the -s genitive when possession is <u>not</u> the meaning by taking a look at another dialog:

A: Let's have some coffee.

B: Okay. Oh! Don't use the large, white mug. That's Mom's mug.

A: All right. So what's happening with that law suit between the paper mill and us over dumping pollutants into the bay?

B: I'm happy to say the committee's trip to the capital was a success and they've persuaded the government to step in.

A: That's great! Who's on our side in the government?

B: Tess Hyman. I really like her. She's a politician's politician.

A: Terrific! You know, I bet we used at least a thousand dollars' worth of stamps mailing out all of those flyers.

B: I guess so. Well, with Tess behind us, getting anti-pollution regulations enforced should be child's play.

A: I hope so. Wouldn't it be wonderful to be able to swim in that water again to your heart's content and not worry about pollution?

In order to zero in on the uses of the -s genitive in this dialog, let's take each item separately and add some other examples to it. Perhaps that will help you figure out how to categorize each kind of -s genitive we've used. When you think you've got a category for each set of phrases, identify it on the line we've provided for you.

1. **Mom's coffee mug** / Dad's easy chair / the cat's rug
   (Note: think of a category other than possession or belonging)

   _____

2. **the committee's trip** / the enemy's retreat / Ali's promotion

   _____

3. **a politician's politician** / a man's man / a poet's poet

   _____

4. **100 dollars' worth** / 500 pesos' worth / 6,000 liras' worth

   _____

5.   **child's play** / everyone's dream / men's clothing / lovers' lane

_____

6.   **to your heart's content** / at journey's end / at death's door

_____

Granted, this is one of the more difficult tasks we've asked you to do, but even if you've only come up with two or three of the categories, you're doing fine. Here's the way we see these categorizations of the -s genitive. You might have used different wording, but if the concepts are the same, that's all that counts:

1.   **a preferred thing:**
     - that's the coffee mug that Mom is partial to; all the other coffee mugs may belong to her, too, but that one is her favorite mug and she doesn't like others using it
     - that's the easy chair that Dad likes the most
     - that's the rug that the cat loves to nap on
2.   **actions that the head noun has done or received:**
     - the committee took that trip (they're the "doers")
     - the enemy retreated (they're the "doers")
     - Ali got that promotion (he's the "receiver")
3.   **the best; the epitome:**
     - a politician that other politicians would like to emulate
     - a man who other men can admire for his manly qualities
     - a poet who is held in esteem by all other poets
4.   **an amount of money equal to** (used with ". . . worth of . . .")
5.   **things that seem appropriate** (paraphrased with "for"):
     - play that is appropriate for a child
     - a dream for everyone
     - clothing for men
     - a place that seems appropriate for lovers to meet at
6.   **pat phrases (formulaic phrases):**
     - tend to be idiomatic (and disregard rules for using **-'s**)

Now let's go back to answer that question we gave you about why it's grammatical to say "the school's idea," but it isn't to say "the school's wall." **The -s genitive is normally <u>not</u> used with nonliving things. However, when one noun has two different meanings (i.e., a living and a nonliving thing), we use the -s genitive for the living thing.** There's a definite difference in the meaning of "school" in the previous two phrases. In the phrase "the school's idea," we're really talking about the administration, in other words, the <u>people</u> who run the school; therefore, it's proper to use **-'s**. In the phrase "the school's wall," we're not talking about the administration, but the actual physical structure, which is a nonliving thing, so we don't normally use the **-'s** in that case. Instead, we'd say "a wall **of** the school" (and we'll discuss the word **of** in the next part of this chapter).

One exception to using **of** instead of **-'s** for nonliving things can be found in newspaper headlines. You could very easily see a headline like this splashed across the front page of your daily newspaper: **SCHOOL'S WALL COLLAPSES! NO ONE HURT!** This convention in "newspaper talk" may simply have come about in order to save space, but whatever its reason for being, it doesn't seem to be the norm in standard English.

When "school" represents a living thing, i.e., "people," it's being used as a collective noun. Can you think of other collective nouns, this time representing groups of people, that we can add the **-'s** to? Here are a few examples: **New York's** skyscrapers / **Chile's** coastline / our **club's** next meeting / their **church's** annual bazaar.

Other collective nouns represent animals, and we can use **-'s** on such words as "herd" and "pride": the herd's migration patterns / the pride's hunting females / a wolf pack's territory.

Here are other examples of things which can take the **-'s**. They're things which we perceive as performing actions: our **ship's** first mate / the **plane's** departure / an **ICBM's** range / the **earth's** orbit.

So are we done with the -s genitive? Not quite; we still have two important areas to talk about, and one of them can be seen in this next dialog:

A: What are you doing tomorrow?

B: Well, first I'm going to the doctor's and then I'm meeting my sister for lunch at Murphy's. I've got nothing special planned after lunch, though.

A: Well, that's not far from St. Jerome's. How about meeting me there in the afternoon to help me with my daughter's wedding arrangements?

B: Sure, I'd love to. My son's wedding there a year ago was just beautiful, and I'm sure your daughter's will be, too.

Unlike all the other forms of the -s genitive that we've looked at up to now, this time we have the form standing on its own without any accompanying nouns. Take a look back at the words we've boxed in and guess which nouns you could add after them through the help of context:

the doctor's_____

Murphy's_____

St. Jerome's _____

your daughter's _____

We're sure you've filled in the blanks with *office (surgery), restaurant (pub/ tavern), Church,* and *wedding.* This wasn't such a hard task because the context of the dialog helped you figure out what these words with **-'s** stood for. **We can use the -s genitive on its own when it's clear what it refers to.**

Now we're coming to the last point we should discuss about the -s genitive in this section of the chapter. Look at the following phrases and decide if they mean the same thing or different things.

Gilbert and Sullivan's works

Gilbert's and Sullivan's works

☐ same   ☐ different

Even though these phrases may seem the same at a quick glance, they're really quite **different** in meaning. See if you can figure out what the difference is, and write your thoughts on the following lines:

_____

_____

_____

When we have two or more names, and all the people involved are connected to the head noun (in this case, "works"), only the final name, the one closest to the head noun, gets the **-'s** ("Gilbert and Sullivan's works," meaning the works that are connected jointly to Gilbert and Sullivan). However, if the head noun is distinct for each person mentioned, each name gets **-'s** ("Gilbert's [works] and Sullivan's works"; in other words, works that they didn't create as a team).

Another example of this phenomenon is **Juan and Olga's children** as compared to **Juan's and Olga's children**. How would you interpret the difference in meaning between the two phrases?

_____

_____

In the first example, Juan and Olga had some children together; in the second example, Juan has some children, and Olga has some children, but they didn't have them together!

Group Genitives

Another phenomenon that occurs with the -s genitive is called the group genitive. What happens is that the end of a compound noun or a phrase describing the head noun receives the suffixed **-'s**; in other words, the whole phrase is treated as a single unit. What follows are four examples of typical group genitives:

an hour and a half's wait / the notary public's office

my sister-in-law's boss / a man-about-town's wardrobe

Here's a curious observation about such phrases as "sister-in-law" and "man-about-town." In Chapter 7, we discussed how such compounds as these are pluralized; that the plural form (whether it's regular or irregular) normally appears with the noun it pluralizes: *sisters-in-law/ men-about-town*. The -s genitive form for these plural compound nouns will still be attached to the end of the phrase: *sisters-in-law's* and *men-about-town's*. As for "notary public," even though the traditional plural form is "nota**ries** public," you'll remember we mentioned in Chapter 7 that there's a tendency nowadays to pluralize the second element in such phrases and say "notary public**s**." That's how people generally add the -s genitive: they simply attach the apostrophe to the **-s** and produce *notary publics'*.

These next three group genitives are rather unusual but possible. They're likely to be found in colloquial speech—not in formal writing—and can be a lot of fun. We'll be discussing a more formalized way of dealing with such awkward phrases later on:

the guy who works in the mailroom's wife

the neighbor whose wife won the lottery's house

the woman who I spoke to's son

Teaching Tips

People in the same family often resemble one another. Have the students use genitives to describe themselves and their family members. "I have my mother's disposition and my father's eyes. I also have my grandmother's shape," etc.

The -S Genitive in a Nutshell

 used for people and animals:
- **possession/ belonging:**
  Myrlande's skirt / the parakeet's feathers
- **paraphrasing with "have":**
  Yuri's fever (Yuri has a fever.)
  the dog's fleas (The dog has fleas.)

> **- a preferred thing:**
>   Kurt's place at the dinner table
>   the dog's spot for burying things
> **- head noun does/receives action:**
>   Bill's resignation / the lion's kill (doers)
>   the thief's arrest / the zebra's capture (receivers)
> **- showing esteem:**
>   a surgeon's surgeon
> **- appropriateness (can be paraphrased with "for"):**
>   soldiers' uniforms (uniforms for soldiers)
>   a tiger's habitat (the habitat for a tiger)
> **- collective nouns (groups of people or animals):**
>   the committee's members / the flock's lead ram

used with words representing periods of time:
this month's gas bill / tomorrow's weather / a day's wages

amount of money equal to (always with "worth"):
thirty francs' worth of gasoline / 100 rubles' worth of cheese

on words representing periods of time with "worth":
three weeks' worth of work done in five days

sometimes for nonliving things which are perceived as performing actions:
my car's special features / the train's dining car / the sun's rays

formulaic phrases (pat phrases):
a hair's breadth / a stone's throw / at arm's length
a doctor's appointment / a dentist's appointment

on its own when the reference is clear:
The family reunion is going to be at my cousin's.

when two or more names share the head noun:
Bill and Ted's Excellent Adventure

group genitives:
The Out-of-Towners' Guide to Auckland
the man who got shot in the leg's medical bills

THE *OF*-GENITIVE

A: Magda, did you know the brother **of** that boy you're dating has been arrested?

B: Anton**'s** brother? Arrested?

A: He's been charged with stealing the car **of** that nice old couple who live right next door to his parents.

B: The Nagys**'** car? I don't believe it!

A: Believe it! I never did like him.

The dialog you've just read offers us a convenient transition from the -s genitive to the of-genitive. According to what we stated in the first part of this chapter, the -s genitive should be the proper form when we focus on living things, but we can clearly see the of-genitive used for some of the people mentioned in our dialog. Why is that? In fact, not only have we used both forms of the genitive in this dialog, but we've even used them at different times for the same people. Isn't that strange! Or is it? After you take another look at the way **-'s** and **of** are used in this dialog, can you come up with an explanation to defend both uses? If you can, write your ideas on the following lines:

_____

_____

_____

Although the -s genitive is the more typical form we use for possession or belonging when living things are involved, **we tend to use the of-genitive if there is an adjectival clause present which describes the head noun:** the brother of that boy <u>you're dating</u> / the car of that nice old couple <u>who live right next door to his parents</u>. True, in colloquial speech (see page 187), we might hear group genitives used in these two cases: *that boy you're dating's brother / that nice old couple who live right next door to his parents' car*. Even though all group genitives are slightly bizarre, this first one seems more plausible than the second one simply because it's shorter and easier to deal with. Using the of-genitive in these cases certainly saves us a lot of trouble. Let's take a look at one more dialog that demonstrates the of-genitive in this way:

A: Remember that song "Scarborough Fair"?
B: Yeah, sure. In fact, I remember it was on an album that was a birthday gift to me from the parents **of** a high school friend I tutored in algebra.
A: So what ever happened to your friend?
B: I hear he married the daughter **of** some math genius who's always winning awards!

Now that we've discussed how **of** can be used in place of **-'s** under certain circumstances, we should restate the most typical use for the of-genitive which we mentioned a few pages back when discussing those phrases "the school's idea" and "a wall of the school." Whereas the -s genitive seems to be used primarily with living things, **the of-genitive seems to be used primarily with non-living things (both concrete and abstract).** Here are some examples for you to look at. Note that you probably wouldn't interchange them with the -s genitive:

the color of that <u>shirt</u> / the cost of a <u>computer</u> (concrete things)

the taste of <u>lamb</u> / the price of <u>fish</u> (food items = nonliving things)

a line of <u>defense</u> / a standard of <u>conduct</u> (abstract things)

 Troubleshooter

 Genitive forms are not used the same way in every language. A case in point is how the *of*-genitive is used in some languages where we use the preposition "in":

> Spanish: El desierto más grande del mundo. (del = of the)
>
> English: The largest desert in the world.

Expect some of your students to demonstrate this bit of interference from their first languages.

Partitive Genitives

A very common use for the of-genitive deals with a category which we can place under the umbrella of **partitives**, concrete and abstract words that represent a part of the whole. Take a look at this dialog which demonstrates this use:

A: Have you seen that new **pair of gloves** I just bought?
B: Weren't they on **the top of the dresser**?
A: I thought so, but they're not there now!
B: I have **a piece of advice** for you. Don't leave things lying around.
A: And here I am ready to go to the store, and I was going to wear them. Where can they be?
B: What do we need at the store?
A: Oh, let's see—**a can of coffee, half a kilo of butter, two loaves of bread**, and some other things as well.
B: Coffee? There's a can of coffee on the kitchen counter.
A: What you see is a coffee can, but it's empty. Well, gloves or no gloves, I'm on my way.

Just as we've done before, let's list the various highlighted phrases that appear in this dialog and see if we can identify categories for the partitive genitives they represent. Where there aren't many examples, we've given you some more to look at. Write your categories on the blank lines.

a pair of gloves / a pair of scissors / a set of dishes / a set of knives

_____

the top of the dresser / the back of the chair / the leg of the table

_____

a piece of advice / a time of plenty / a heap of trouble

_____

a can of coffee / half a kilo of butter / two loaves of bread

_____

So what would you call these categories under the umbrella heading of partitives? As we see it, the first category is simple—it's just anything which comes in **pairs or sets**. The next category deals with **parts of things**; the third category deals with **abstracts** which can't be counted but which we feel the need to think of as if they could be. Finally, our fourth category deals with **measures**, and, although these three examples all have to do with food, the category isn't limited to this: _a pound of nails / a ball of twine / a ream of paper._

By the way, did you notice that curious twist on words at the end of the last dialog? Person B says that she saw a can of coffee sitting on the kitchen counter, but Person A explains that what she saw was a coffee can—an empty one at that. What's going on here? How would you explain this? Here are a few more examples just to help you out. When you've got an idea, write it down on the lines below:

a cup of tea / a tea cup

a jar of mayonnaise / a mayonnaise jar

a barrel of oil / an oil barrel

_____

_____

Knowing that you're quickly becoming such a good linguistic sleuth, we bet that you've been able to explain the difference in the previous phrases. What it comes down to is that when we describe the specific uses for these containers, we make compound nouns: *a coffee can / a tea cup / a mayonnaise jar / an oil barrel*. But when we speak about what's inside the containers (amounts, in these cases), we use the partitive genitive: *a can of coffee / a cup of tea / a jar of mayonnaise / a barrel of oil*.

Appositives

Finally, we have one more use for the of-genitive that can seem a bit perplexing. Look at the next dialog and see if you can figure out what the reason for this use is:

A: Why are you so excited today?

B: Because **the President of Fulania** is going to be the guest speaker at our graduation exercises.

A: That's terrific! I hear he's **a jewel of a speaker**.

B: That's what I've heard, too. It's amazing to think that he comes from such a humble background.

A: Oh, really?

B: Yes. He comes from **the little village of Abadoo** in the desert part of the country, but he spent quite a few years in **the city of Leicester**, you know, in England.

A: Do you know what his speech is going to be on?

B: Uh-huh. "**The Art of Active Listening**," whatever that is.

What role do you think the of-genitive is playing in all these phrases? Here's a little hint: all of them except one deal with literal usage, and the other one is idiomatic. After you've given this some thought, write your conclusions on the following lines:

_____

_____

_____

In all of the phrases we've highlighted (except for "a jewel of a speaker"), there's one basic purpose for using the of-genitive and that is **to explain or give more information about the preceding noun.** All these phrases answer the question *which?* or *what?* The president of what? Fulania. Which little village? Abadoo. What city? Leicester. Which art? Active listening. This use for the of-genitive is called the **appositive use.**

As for the other phrase, "a jewel of a speaker," this is an idiomatic use of the appositive construction meaning *a very good speaker.* Other examples of this usage are *a beast of a night/ a prince of a man/ a nightmare of a flight.*

Teaching Tips

Students whose languages don't have as wide a variety of genitive forms as English does often have a difficult time trying to decide which English form to use. To help them get a better feel for the -s and of-genitives, create a group of sentences or a modified cloze activity before class (see Appendix 2). Be sure that the sentences or cloze contains a variety of the different genitive forms. Here's a brief sample.

_____ (books / $50 million)

Last month, the English-speaking world was stunned to learn that two old-looking texts discovered in _____ (basement / castles / one / Queen Elizabeth / a trunk) were actually written by William Shakespeare and Geoffrey Chaucer. _____ (Shakespeare and Chaucer / works) were in almost perfect condition even though they'd been in the trunk for _____ (hundreds / years). The texts, a play, and _____ (Bible / copy), were immediately sold, earning a _____ (king / ransom).

More Teaching Tips

Before class, find or create pairs of pictures that are similar but not identical in details. Have two students work together and give them one of the pairs of pictures. Get them to discover the differences in their pictures by asking questions about the various items. To get the specific information that the students need, tell them to use a variety of genitives in their questions and answers. Some typical questions and answers are: "Is there anything over the back of the chair?" "No, but there's a sweater on the seat of the chair." / "What is in the dog's mouth?" "There is nothing in the dog's mouth."

 Troubleshooter

It's a good idea to keep in mind that there are many languages which don't have genitives such as we have in English. In many languages, the genitive is expressed simply by the syntax of the phrase, that is, where the words are placed. Let's look at some disparate languages and see how they do fine without a true genitive form. To demonstrate our point, we'll use the phrase "the boy's book."

Haitian Creole:	liv-aa the book	ptigason-an the boy
Arabic:	kitab book	alwalad the boy
Amharic:	yɛliju the boy	mæʒhæf book
Cantonese:	nam-haɪji boy	dɛk sɪ the book

So if you find your students having a lot of trouble with the English genitive forms, it might be because their languages simply don't have the equivalents of our -'s or of.

The *Of*-Genitive in a Nutshell

 used to focus on some aspect of most nonliving things (concrete and abstract):
the texture of the snow / the roll of the waves
the heart of the matter / the depth of his anguish

 **used as a partitive for concrete and abstract things:**
  - **pairs or sets:** a pair of glasses / a set of rollers
  - **parts of things:** the limbs of a tree / the pages of a book
  - **measures:** 4 litres of gasoline / 10 yards of cloth
  - **abstracts:** a bit of pleasure / a moment of silence

 **with head nouns that are followed by adjectival clauses:**
the son of the lady <u>I introduced you to at the party</u>

 **used as an appositive to explain or describe the preceding noun:**
the Book of Kells / the Cliffs of Dover

THE DOUBLE GENITIVE

We've covered the -s genitive and the of-genitive separately, but there are occasions when the two are used together—that's why we call this the double genitive. It's really quite an odd-looking form, especially to ESOL students, but one that's quite commonly used. Let's take a look at a couple of these:

a friend of the priest's / a son of the teacher's

To the ESOL student, this may be a very confusing construction. Most likely, the student would say that it's the **-'s** on the end of each phrase that makes it so odd. Isn't it enough to say "a friend of the priest" or "a son of the teacher" and leave it at that? It might be, except for the fact that we normally use the -s genitive for living things. No, something else is going on here. The student might be more comfortable with the construction "the priest's friend" and "the teacher's son" (assuming he or she has already learned this basic genitive form), but are these accurate paraphrases of our original phrases? What's your opinion?

_____

_____

_____

The answer is that the paraphrases we've come up with <u>don't</u> accurately reflect the meaning of our original phrases. The reason is that they inadvertently mislead us. Saying "the priest's friend" leads us to believe that the priest has only one friend or that one specific friend whom we've already mentioned is being cited; likewise, saying "the teacher's son" makes us think that the teacher has only one son or, once again, he's the son we've already mentioned—and that's not the case. The truth is that this person is just one friend out of several that the priest has (a friend of the priest's), and the other person is just one of at least two sons that the teacher has (a son of the teacher's). There's nothing intrinsically wrong with saying "the priest's friend" and "the teacher's son" as long as it's true that the priest does only have one friend and the teacher only one son or that we've already mentioned these people. If, however, that isn't the case, we have to find another way to express our ideas, and this is where the double genitive helps out.

Let's focus for a moment on the indefinite article that's used in the double genitive construction. What if a student of yours says "He's **the** friend of the priest's"? Is this acceptable? Think about what you'd say to your student, and write it on the following lines:

_____

_____

_____

It turns out that you can't say a sentence like the one the student created because "the" reflects exclusivity. The whole purpose of this odd construction is to communicate that the person is just <u>one</u> of several friends, so if your student uses "the," he defeats this purpose. Of course, there's an easy way to circumvent this whole problem and that's by paraphrasing once again. Instead of saying "a friend of the priest's," we can say "one of the priest's friends," and instead of saying "a son of the teacher's," we can say "one of the teacher's sons."

Getting back to that student for a moment, let's say he wasn't finished after he said "He's the friend of the priest's . . ." but wanted to say something about this person. Could saying **the** end up being grammatical after all? See if you can figure this out:

_____

_____

_____

It so happens that your student can definitely make the phrase perfectly grammatical by adding adjectival information which will then give exclusivity to that person. For example, he could say "He's the friend of the priest's <u>who appeared on that TV game show</u>." If there's exclusivity, it's all right to use "the."

There's one more thing to be said about the double genitive. It's quite common to use possessive pronouns (mine, yours, his, etc.) as the second element in this construction. Here are two examples:

a friend of mine / a neighbor of theirs

This use of possessive pronouns goes hand in hand with the use of the **-'s** in the double genitive that we've just finished discussing. On a final note, there's one aspect of this form which ESOL instructors rarely teach. Here are four examples of it. Try to identify what's going on:

This dog of yours has been digging holes in my yard again!

Those kids of hers always manage to get into mischief.

That nose of his is quite aristocratic.

These cats of mine are lovable, aren't they?

_____

_____

If you've written that this **double genitive plus the addition of the demonstratives** *this, that, these,* or *those* shows some sort of extra emotion or feeling, you've hit on it exactly. Among other things, this special phrase can communicate **affection or disdain, approval or disapproval.**

Teaching Tips

Write a group of sentences with non-restrictive relative clauses using "whose" before class (e.g., The most popular Civil War film is *Gone With the Wind,* whose heroine lives on a plantation called Tara.). Have the students rewrite the sentences using appropriate genitive forms. **Note:** This activity can also be done in the reverse; give the students sentences with genitives and have them create the non-restrictive relative clauses. Here are some examples of the types of sentences you would write and answers your students might come up with. "The most popular Civil War film is *Gone With the Wind,* whose heroine lives on a plantation called Tara." (". . . film is *GWTW. GWTW's* heroine lives on a plantation called Tara.") "The ideas for air conditioning and helicopters were first thought of by Leonardo DaVinci, whose later years were spent in France." (". . . by Leonardo DaVinci. DaVinci's later years were spent in France.") "The long cold spell devastated the economy in Florida, whose revenue is based on tourism and agricultural products." (". . . economy in Florida. Florida's revenue / The revenue of Florida is based on tourism and agricultural products.")

-'S VERSUS *OF*: THE GRAY AREAS

We've finally arrived at the last topic concerning the genitives. It's a problematic topic which perhaps deals more with style than grammar. Read the following items and choose the genitive form which seems <u>more appropriate to each situation</u> and check it off. (Here's a tip: go by your first impressions; don't think about them too much!)

1. "My lords and ladies, ladies and gentlemen, it is my distinct honor to present to you His Royal Highness, Juan Carlos de Borbón,

   ☐ **Spain's King** ☐ **the King of Spain."**

2. "Our next story on the *Evening News* has to do with

   ☐ **Spain's plans** for the upcoming summer Olympics."

   ☐ **the plans of Spain** for the upcoming summer Olympics."

3. A: Are you taking any literature courses next semester?
   B: Yes. I'm going to take a course called

   ☐ **"Hemingway's Novels"** ☐ **"The Novels of Hemingway."**

4.   "Welcome to my class, ladies and gentlemen. I'm glad that you've signed up for this course, and I hope you enjoy the subject as much as I do.

☐   **Hemingway's novels** have greatly contributed to international literature."

☐   **The novels of Hemingway** have greatly contributed to international literature."

5.   "Good evening. My name's Tom, and I'll be your waiter this evening. Besides the seafood listed on our menu,

☐   **the catch of the day** is sea bass. Just let me know when you're ready to order."

☐   **the day's catch** is sea bass. Just let me know when you're ready to order."

6.   A: Hi, Joe! How did the fishing go today?
     B: Not bad at all, Frank. How about you?
     A: We did just fine, I'm glad to say. So what are you planning to do with

☐   **the catch of the day**   ☐   **the day's catch?**

     B: We'll be selling it to some of those restaurants along the beach.

Style in language can be a difficult thing to pin down. There really are no hard-and-fast rules that cover every given situation concerning style and which option (**-'s** or **of**) to choose, but there are some conclusions we can draw from observing how a great many native speakers handle phrases like the six items you've just dealt with. We'll wait to give you our conclusions a little later; right now, let's go over the items.

First of all, here's what the majority of native speakers would choose:

1.   Juan Carlos de Borbón, *the King of Spain*
2.   *Spain's plans* for the upcoming summer Olympics
3.   A course called *"The Novels of Hemingway"*
4.   *Hemingway's novels* have greatly contributed. . .
5.   *The catch of the day* is sea bass.
6.   What are you planning to do with *the day's catch?*

Compare your choices to these. Then see if you can figure out what seems to be the underlying factor that accounts for the choices that were favored. When you've come up with an idea, write it down on the following lines:

_____

_____

The answer may lie in what we refer to as **formulaic phrases,** that is, certain traditional usages in a language which may or may not go along with the usual conventions. Sometimes it's quite easy for us to decide why one of these formulaic phrases is used in a given situation, but sometimes it's not so clear.

We probably all agreed that saying "the King **of Spain**" in Item 1 *sounded* more appropriate in that situation than saying "**Spain's** King" even though **Spain's** seems perfectly appropriate when the newscaster says it as he refers to that country's plans for the summer Olympic games. Pretending a little, we can imagine hearing Item 1 during the formal presentation of a visiting monarch to the Court of St. James's—or is it St. James's Court?

As we've said, there are no hard-and-fast rules on this subject, but there does seem to be a tendency we can discern. **It appears that the formulaic phrases which employ the of-genitive tend to sound more formal to us than the -s genitive and give the phrase an air of importance or dramatic effect**. This "feel" that native speakers have seems to govern which genitive they choose, but we want to stress that there are probably exceptions to our observation.

Now let's talk about Items 2 through 6. Because university course titles are usually presented in formal catalogs, most people would choose "The Novels **of** Hemingway" even though entitling the course "Hemingway**'s** Novels" works just as well, grammatically speaking. Conversely, most people would feel it's appropriate for the professor to use the -s genitive in his introductory remarks to the class (Hemingway**'s** novels), perhaps because there's no need for him to *sound* more formal or dramatic in his opening comments.

People are of the opinion that by saying "the catch of the day," our waiter seems to give the phrase that extra dramatic or important air which he might want to impart to his customers. The fisherman, on the other hand, is just making small talk with another fisherman, so people feel he has no need to give the phrase any special effect ("the day's catch").

By the way, let's go back for a moment to that question we whimsically posed about whether to say "the Court of St. James's" or "St. James's Court." Once again, both phrases are perfectly grammatical; it may just depend on how "formal" or "dramatic" we want the title to sound. It therefore goes back to what kind of situation we're going to use the phrase in or who the speaker is, and it also takes into account what seems to be customary, or formulaic, to say.

There's one more troublesome issue we'd like to address concerning the gray areas of the genitives. In many scholarly, traditional works on English grammar, mention is made that the -s genitive is used with "higher" animals, and the of-genitive with "lower" animals. We find these rules to be questionable; after all, where is the line to be drawn between what is a "higher" animal and what is a "lower" animal? Is it *wrong* to say "my turtle's food" or "a mosquito's wings"? Or is it that those two creatures are too *low* on the scale for the -s genitive? Many—if not most—native speakers, would not flinch either way if they heard someone say "a mosquito's wings" or "the wings of a mosquito." Likewise, would you cringe if you heard someone say "the song of a canary" instead of "a canary's song"? We doubt it. We think it best to leave well enough alone and simply say that there are certain gray areas concerning **-'s** and **of** where both forms are probably more acceptable than not, and the use of one or the other may best be left up to the individual speaker.

Mind Bogglers!

See if you can figure out the differences between the pairs presented below. What you may arrive at is really quite interesting!

a bee's sting / a bee sting

a dog's kennel / a dog kennel

a sheep's skin / a sheep skin

a cow's hide / a cow hide

Chapter 9

Prepositions

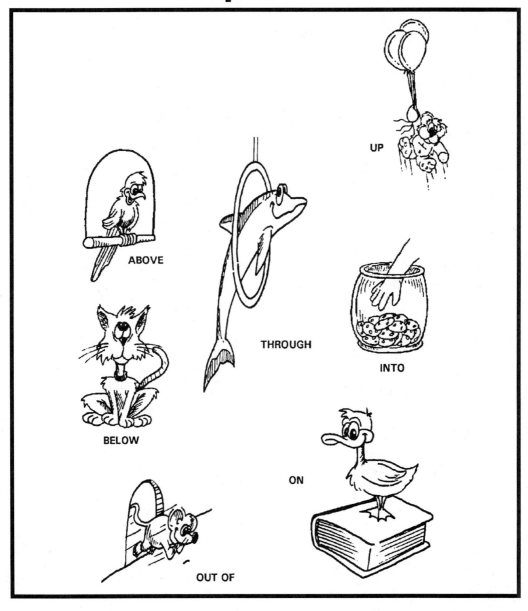

UP

ABOVE

THROUGH

INTO

BELOW

ON

OUT OF

"There's a frog on a log in a hole at the bottom of the sea."

What are prepositions? In general, they're **words which show some sort of relationship or connection between two things.** In addition, **prepositions can help to answer such questions as *where? when? why?* and *how?*** They can be **simple** (one word: *behind*), or **complex** (two or more words: *ahead of, in front of*). In this chapter, we're going to deal mostly with simple prepositions and focus on the troublesome aspects of teaching them. If you want complete lists of prepositions, you'll be able to find them easily in all ESOL student grammar books. So what are prepositions? What they really are is the bane of all ESOL teachers!

Why is it that ESOL students always have so much trouble with prepositions? After all, don't they have them in their languages, too? Of course they do, but it isn't just a simple matter of translating a preposition from one language to another. To add to the difficulty, some languages (like English) have more prepositions than others. At any rate, English prepositions do cause a great deal of frustration and annoyance to ESOL students and their teachers.

There are three basic sections to this chapter. First, we'll deal with the meanings of some of the most commonly used prepositions. Along with this, we'll give you ideas on how to demonstrate them in vivid ways so your students start developing a "feel" for the little beasts. We'll also deal with their idiomatic uses, and how choosing one preposition over another can change meaning in very important ways. In addition, we'll offer insights on how to handle the teaching of prepositions in the classroom and how to present them more meaningfully and interestingly to your students.

A look at the chapters on prepositions in most scholarly grammar books can be quite unnerving; the array of uses and meanings the reader is presented with can be intimidating, not to mention overwhelming. We don't intend to cover every single preposition, but we'll break some of them down into their basic meanings. Our main goal is to help you clarify some prepositions for yourself so that you'll be better prepared to deal with them in your classes. You can continue where we leave off and delve into the basic meanings of those we don't cover.

In many ways, the choice of which preposition to use depends on the viewpoint of the speaker or writer, especially when dealing with spatial relationships. Teaching the spatial, or literal, uses of prepositions comes early on in any ESOL curriculum, and visualizing them both on the board and with a little physical reinforcement has always proven to be an effective teaching technique.

LITERAL (PHYSICAL) MEANINGS

Let's see how astute you are at graphically visualizing the spatial meanings of some commonly used prepositions. Below, you'll find an assortment of them, each one followed by a box. Draw **an arrow (for movement)** or **a dot (for stationary location)** wherever you think it will best demonstrate the literal meaning of the preposition in relation to its accompanying box. For the sake of this exercise, let's say that the orientation of the boxes is just like this page you're reading; in other words, <u>the top of each box is in the same location as the top of this page</u>. Also, let's have <u>all movements going from left to right</u>. You'll find that it's easier to visualize some prepositions graphically than it is to depict others. We've done the first one to get you started. (By the way, we know you're going to cover up the section that follows with all the answers until you've finished, aren't you!)

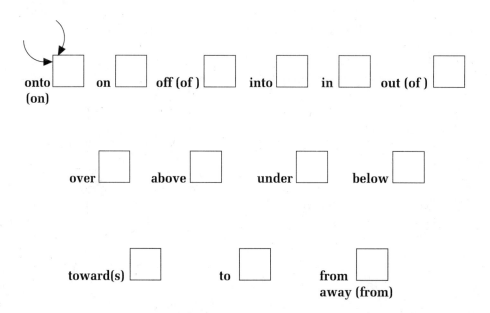

before ☐   after ☐   near ☐   next to ☐

past ☐   through ☐   around ☐

It's interesting to visualize just what each of these prepositions looks like on paper, isn't it? Well, here are the answers we've come up with. Compare yours to ours. You may be surprised to find some answers that you didn't think of. You may also be surprised to see that it's not always very clear-cut when it comes to showing a visual representation of some of these prepositions. Remember: the arrow represents movement; the dot represents stationary location.

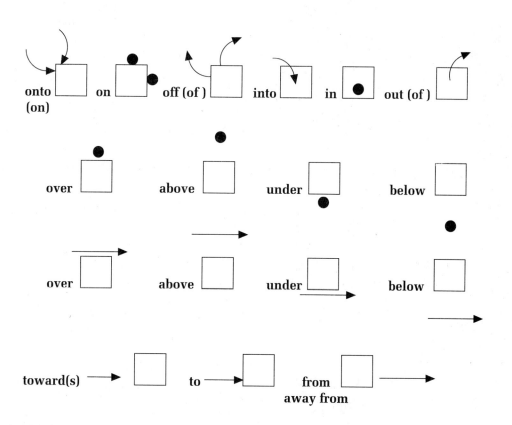

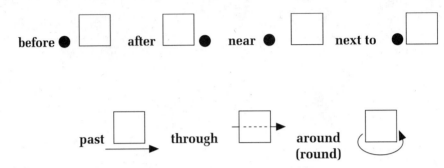

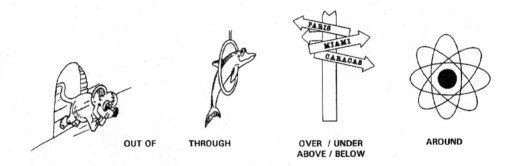

Teaching Tips

Because so many prepositions are spatial, a good way for students to practice them is to draw pictures to show the meanings of these prepositions. The pictures need not be detailed or elaborate; they only need to be clear enough to represent the meanings. This activity can be done individually, in pairs, or in small groups. Once the pictures are drawn, have the class compare and contrast the ways that they chose to depict the prepositions. Then have the class choose the drawings that best visualize the prepositions or draw a class composite that synthesizes the best representations. Put these pictures on a wall chart and leave it up for students to look at and refer to later.

More Teaching Tips

Before class, find a text that has a variety of spatial prepositions in it. Copy the text leaving blanks where the prepositions should be. Have the students fill in the blanks with pictures to represent the prepositions.

Exchange papers and have students read their classmates' papers aloud, interpreting the visualizations with words. You can also do this activity in the reverse. Have the students write stories (individually, in pairs, or in small groups) with the prepositions in them. Have them exchange their papers and let the new partners/pairs/groups visualize the prepositions. (Sami goes → _____ school _____ 8 every morning. He walks ⌢ the freeway and ⊢---⊣ a long tunnel.).

Variation

Use the same text as you used in the previous *Tip*, only this time, leave the prepositions in. Put blanks after each preposition and have the students draw what the prepositions represent in the blanks. When all the students are finished drawing their prepositions, let them compare and contrast their visualizations.

Now that you've had a chance to compare your art work to ours, let's see if you can come up with <u>literal</u> definitions for these prepositions. If their meanings are clear in your mind, it will be much easier to communicate them to your students. Use the visualizations we've created and the example sentences we've provided to help you. **Among other things, state whether they're prepositions of <u>location</u> or <u>movement</u> or <u>both</u>.**

ONTO / ON: *He placed the star **onto/on** the top of the Christmas tree.*

_____

_____

ON: *His family loved all the ornaments **on** the Christmas tree.*

_____

_____

OFF (OF)*:   *During the holidays, some of the ornaments fell **off** (of) the tree.*

_____

_____

INTO / IN: *As the guests arrived, they came **into/in** the house.*

_____

_____

IN: *When the guests were seated **in** the living room, their host served them some refreshments.*

_____

_____

OUT (OF):   *The hostess came **out of** the kitchen carrying a basket of bread and rolls.*

_____

_____

A: Hello. This is Mrs. Porter. May I speak to your mother, please?
*B: I'm sorry, but she's **out** right now. Can I take a message?*

_____

_____

---

*We'll explain why we've put secondary prepositions in parentheses later on in the chapter.

OVER: *If you're feeling a little chilly, wear this sweater **over** your shoulders.*

_____

_____

*While out in the woods on a fall day, we noticed a flock of geese flying **over** us on their way south for the winter.*

_____

_____

ABOVE: *The helicopter hovered **above** the field for a few minutes before flying off.*

*During the storm, the dark clouds passed **above** us at incredible speed.*

_____

_____

UNDER: *Our dog likes to sleep **under** the dining room table.*

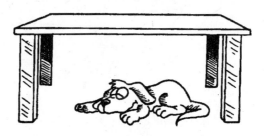

_____

_____

*Did you feel all that vibration and hear the rumbling? It was the subway passing **under** this building.*

_____

_____

BELOW: *In this part of the country, the water table is a great many meters* ***below*** *the surface of the land.*

_____

_____

Believe it or not, there are places on this planet where the water travels ***below*** *the surface of the land in subterranean rivers.*

_____

_____

TOWARD(S):   *The explorers continued traveling west* ***towards*** *the mountains.*

_____

_____

TO: *I'm sending this postcard **to** my relatives in the States.*

_____

_____

*When he got **to** the office, he gave some candy and flowers **to** his secretary for all her hard work.*

_____

_____

FROM: *He comes **from** Cairo, Egypt. I just got a letter **from** him.*

_____

_____

AWAY (FROM)*:   *He went **away from** home at the age of eighteen.*

_____

_____

*Technically speaking, "away" is an adverb, but we've included it here because it fits in so conveniently.

BEFORE: *When it was time for him to be sentenced for his crime, the convicted man was made to stand **before** the judge.*

---

*If you want the all-night coffee shop, it's the red brick building **before** the movie theater down this street.*

AFTER: *Looking for the bank? It's the building **after** that gas station.*

NEAR: *Don't you know that our house is **near** the stadium?*

---

*Don't be afraid to come **near** me, little boy.*

NEXT TO: *You'll recognize our house when you see it. It's the yellow one **next to** the florist's shop.*

PAST: *We drove **past** your house last night, but we couldn't stop to say hello.*

_____

_____

THROUGH: *Last summer, we took a car trip **through** the Canadian province of British Columbia.*

_____

_____

AROUND /   *Before the tunnel was built, our trip was a lot longer because we*
ROUND: *had to drive **around** the mountain.*

_____

_____

*I like that arrangement of daffodils with the flowers all **around** the tree.*

_____

_____

*On Sunday afternoons, they used to like driving **around** in the country and taking in the beautiful scenery.*

_____

_____

Without any ado, let's get right to our interpretations of the literal meanings of these prepositions. We're sure you're anxious to see how close you've come to the meanings we see them having.

ONTO / ON:

A preposition of movement which means something lands or is placed so that it touches the surface of an object. In the case of a three-dimensional object, this could include the top or sides:

*He placed the star **onto/on** the top of the Christmas tree.*

Note that "onto" clearly relates to movement, whereas it's short form, "on," can be ambiguous: *He jumped **onto** the desk.* vs. *He jumped **on** the desk.* (Did he jump from the floor and land on top of the desk, or did he jump while standing on the desk?)

ON:

A preposition which shows that something has contact with the surface of something else. If it's a three-dimensional object, it could be the top or sides:

*His family loved all the ornaments **on** the Christmas tree.*

*That dress looks just beautiful **on** you!*

OFF (OF):

The opposite of "onto," this preposition shows the movement of one object leaving a surface of another:

*During the holidays, some of the ornaments fell **off (of)** the tree.*

INTO / IN:

Another preposition of movement which refers to something entering the interior of an object:

*As the guests arrived, they came **into/in** the house.*

IN:

A preposition showing stationary location. It means that something is encompassed or enclosed by something else:

*When the guests were seated **in** the living room,
their host served them some refreshments.*

OUT (OF):

The opposite of "into" or "in," this preposition involves movement or stationary location. It can mean one thing leaving the object that has encompassed or enclosed it:

*The hostess came **out of** her kitchen carrying a basket of bread and rolls.*

"Out (of)" can also mean stationary location showing the converse of "inside":

A: Hello. This is Mrs. Porter. May I speak to your mother, please?

*B: I'm sorry, but she's **out** right now. Can I take a message?*

OVER:

In this first use, it's a preposition of stationary location. To many native speakers, "over" may mean that something is <u>slightly</u> at a higher elevation than the top of some other thing:

*During the final judging of the contestants, the master of ceremonies
held his hand **over** the head of each finalist for the voting.*

"Over" can include the idea of one thing being in proximity to or even touching or covering the other:

*If you're feeling a little chilly, wear this sweater **over** your shoulders.*

In another use, "over" is a preposition of movement. In this use it means one thing moving horizontally at a higher elevation than the top of another thing. In the case of movement, how much distance there is between the two objects is not an issue:

*While out in the woods on a fall day, we noticed a flock of geese
flying **over** us on their way south for the winter.*

ABOVE:

As with our first definition for "over," this preposition means that one thing is at a higher elevation than the top of another thing. The difference between "above" and "over" is that, for many native speakers, "above" implies there's a greater distance between the two objects than "over." In the example we've cited, the preposition is used with stationary location:

*The helicopter hovered **above** the field for a few minutes*
before flying off.

"Above" can also be used for movement:

*During the storm, the dark clouds passed **above** us*
at incredible speed.

UNDER:

This preposition is the opposite of "over" and is used for stationary location. It carries the same meaning as "over" in reverse:

*Our dog likes to sleep **under** the dining room table.*

Likewise, "under" is the opposite of "over" for movement and carries the same meaning as that preposition in reverse:

Did you feel all that vibration and hear that rumbling?
*It was the subway passing **under** this building.*

BELOW:

Here we have the opposite meaning of "above." It has the same definition as "above," but in reverse, and can be used for stationary location:

In this part of the country, the water table is a great many meters
***below** the surface of the land.*

"Below" can also be used for movement:

Believe it or not, there are places on this planet where
*the water travels **below** the surface of the land in subterranean rivers.*

TOWARD(S):

A preposition of movement meaning that an object is going in the (general) direction of another, but it doesn't imply that the moving object reaches any destination:

*The explorers continued traveling west **towards** the mountains.*

TO:

This preposition of movement, whose opposite is "from," means one thing going in the direction of and reaching or arriving at a destination of one kind or another:

*I'm sending this postcard **to** my relatives in the States.*

*When he got **to** the office, he gave some candy and flowers*
***to** his secretary as a sign of his appreciation for all her hard work.*

FROM:

This preposition, the opposite of "to," refers to the starting point or source of something:

*He comes **from** Cairo, Egypt. I just got a letter **from** him.*

AWAY (FROM):

Here we have another preposition whose opposite meaning is "to" or "toward(s)." Instead of reaching a destination or other object, or going in its direction, this preposition of movement means leaving a destination or other object:

*He went **away from** his home at the age of eighteen.*

BEFORE:

This stationary preposition is a synonym for "in front of" (which is an example of the complex prepositions we mentioned earlier in this chapter):

When it was time for him to be sentenced for his crime,
*the convicted man was made to stand **before** the judge.*

"Before" can also mean something you'll come upon immediately <u>preceding</u> another thing mentioned as a reference point:

If you want the all-night cafeteria, it's the red brick building
***before** the movie theater down this street.*

AFTER:

This stationary preposition means that the object you're looking for is the <u>next</u> place you'll come upon as soon as you pass another object mentioned as a reference point:

*You're looking for the bank? It's the building **after** that gas station.*

NEAR:

The meaning of this preposition has to do with proximity. It means one thing is in the general area of another thing with a relatively short distance between them. The opposite is "far (from)," which, strictly speaking, is an adverbial phrase. This preposition can be stationary:

*Don't you know that our house is **near** the stadium?*

"Near" can also be used for movement:

*Don't be afraid to come **near** me, little boy.*

NEXT TO:

Synonyms for this stationary preposition are "beside" or "alongside (of)," or the adverbial phrase "side by side." It carries the idea of very close proximity, that is, with very little or no distance between two objects and, as its synonyms say, the reference points are the sides of two objects:

> *You'll recognize our house when you see it.*
> *It's the yellow one **next to** the florist's shop.*

PAST:

This preposition carries the idea of one thing moving in front of another thing and not stopping as it approaches. In other words, it passes the object:

> *We drove **past** your house last night, but we couldn't stop to say hello.*

THROUGH:

The meaning of this preposition of movement carries with it the idea that one thing enters one end or side of another thing, traverses its interior, and comes out or reaches the opposite end or side:

> *It was pitch black in our compartment*
> *as the train went **through** the tunnel.*

> *Last summer, we took a car trip **through** the*
> *Canadian province of British Columbia.*

AROUND / ROUND:

This can be a preposition of movement meaning one thing partially or completely encircling another:

> *Before the tunnel was built, our trip was a lot longer*
> *because we had to drive **around** the mountain.*

"Around" can also be a preposition of stationary location:

> *I like that arrangement of daffodils all **around** the tree.*

In its idiomatic use, it can also have the idea of movement with no specific destination:

> *On Sunday afternoons, they used to like to drive **around***
> *in the country and take in the beautiful scenery.*

Of course, the definitions we've given you for these prepositions are ones that you might like to have for clarification, but it's probably inadvisable to give them to your students in this way. However, as we mentioned earlier, if their meanings are clear in your mind, it will be a much simpler job for you to demonstrate them for your classes. One further note: remember that not all English speakers use every preposition in the same way; there's room for debate on some of these.

Teaching Tips

Before class, find a picture that has prepositions represented in the various things and activities. Make copies for <u>half</u> of your students. Prepare a second handout for the other half of the class. This handout should have one or two features from the original picture on it which will serve as starting points or points of perspective for drawing the rest of the picture. For example, if the complete picture has one particular landmark in it, draw just that on the handout. If the picture has a building in the middle, draw that. You decide how much needs to be put on this handout.

Pair off the students and sit them back to back. Then give each student in the pair a different picture. The students who have the complete picture will describe what's in it so that their partners can draw a faithful copy of the original. Encourage the "describers" to be as accurate as possible, but the "artists" are permitted to ask as many questions as is necessary to get the drawing right.

Variation #1

If providing photocopies is a problem, you can draw a picture or put one up on the board and have all the "describers" face the board and all the "artists" face the other way.

Variation #2

For students with very limited vocabularies, provide a handout that's ready to fill in or just a blank piece of paper for them to draw and/or color in. Give directions yourself about how you want your students to complete the pictures (e.g., Draw a (brown) easy chair in the upper left corner. Put an oriental rug in front of it. Hang (blue and white) curtains in the window. Place a table next to the (brown) chair and put a table lamp on top of it, etc.).

Variation #3

Divide a sheet of paper into boxes. The boxes can be as large as half a sheet or as small as a square inch (2 1/2 cm.). Have the students fill in the different boxes according to directions given by you or another student. To make the exercise more interesting, don't have the students fill in the box in the upper left corner and then the one next to it and then the one next to that. Jump from corner to corner, from top to bottom, from center to side.

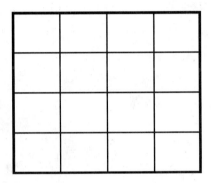

FIGURATIVE (IDIOMATIC) MEANINGS

Notice that we've concentrated on the literal meanings of these prepositions; that is, we've focused on their physical nature. Many of them also have figurative (idiomatic) meanings. Some can stand alone, while others are used together with verbs or other words to take on their idiomatic qualities. Some examples are *dress up, get through,* and *catch on.*

At this point, let's go over the prepositions we've been discussing and see if you can come up with any <u>figurative</u> uses for them. Remember that some can stand alone, while others are used in conjunction with verbs (*think over*) or adjectives (*mad at*). On the blank line that follows each preposition, write down any figurative uses and idiomatic expressions that come to mind which incorporate the preposition. We've done the first one for you to show you what we mean:

ONTO: *be onto someone (not be fooled by someone),*

ON:

OFF:

INTO:

IN: _____

OUT: _____

OVER: _____

ABOVE: _____

UNDER: _____

BELOW: _____

TOWARD(S): _____

TO: _____

FROM: _____

AWAY (FROM): _____

BEFORE: _____

AFTER: _____

NEAR: _____

NEXT TO: _____

PAST: _____

THROUGH: _____

AROUND: _____

Here are our entries for figurative uses and idiomatic expressions. These are just examples; you've probably come up with other examples that are equally good. (**Fig.** = figurative use; **Id.** = idiomatic expression):

ONTO*:   **(Id.)** be onto somebody (not be fooled by someone)
ON: **(Fig.)** about; concerning
                (Id.) be on (performing); be on something (medication or other drugs)

*You may have come up with something like the idiom "Go on to (the next topic for discussion.)" If you did, you've confused the preposition "onto" with the preposition "on" which is allied with the verb "go." In other words, it's really "go on" and there's a secondary preposition needed before you can state the object, in this case, "the next topic for discussion." We'll deal with this in more detail later on in the chapter.

OFF:	**(Id.)** be off (leaving / spoiled, as with food); go/be off one's rocker (crazy); be off the record (not for public knowledge)
INTO:	**(Fig.)** into the night; get into trouble / into mischief
	(Id.) be into something (interested)
IN:	**(Fig.)** be in trouble / in love / in jeopardy / in some business
	(Id.) be "in" (stylish / accepted); the "in" crowd (those who receive some sort of prestigious position in a social context)
OUT (OF):	**(Fig.)** be out of trouble / out of danger / out of touch
	(Id.) be out of one's mind; run out of / be out of (have no more of something)
OVER:	**(Fig.)** more than; by means of (a telephone, telegraph, intercom, etc.); over the holidays / over the weekend
	(Id.) be over the hill (too old); be/get over an illness / bad news, etc. (recovered)
ABOVE:	**(Fig.)** be above the law (not following the laws meant for everyone) / be above someone (in social status or at work)
	(Id.) above it all (not bothered by mundane concerns)
UNDER:	**(Fig.)** less than / fewer than
	(Id.) under the circumstances; be under arrest / the weather (feeling poorly)
BELOW:	**(Fig.)** be below one's dignity / below wholesale (prices)
TOWARDS:	**(Fig.)** toward a better tomorrow; be hostile / antagonistic toward(s) someone
TO:	**(Id.)** look to someone (for help, advice); do something to someone (a bad act, nasty deed)
FROM:	**(Fig.)** from the start; from the very first
	(Id.) be from hunger (not any good / not any use); from nowhere (appeared suddenly); from now on
AWAY (FROM):	**(Id.)** be away (out of town); fire away (discharge a gun multiple times)
BEFORE:	**(Fig.)** before leaving; before it gets dark; before two o'clock; before the public
AFTER:	**(Fig.)** after dinner; after six o'clock; after the fact
NEAR:	**(Fig.)** be near someone's age / the truth / the end (of a story)
	(Id.) be near the end (dying)
NEXT TO:	**(Fig.)** besides (Next to me, he's your best choice for the job.)
PAST:	**(Fig.)** be past one's prime (getting older)
	(Id.) past caring (apathetic)
THROUGH:	**(Fig.)** through the years (spanning time)
	(Id.) get through (survive / recuperate / recover / finish); be through (be finished)
AROUND:	**(Fig.)** approximately
	(Id.) beat around the bush (not coming to the main point of one's thought or idea); get around someone (arrange it so that a certain person doesn't interfere)
(ROUND):	**(Id.)** go round the bend (go crazy); go round and round (not reaching a conclusion or solution)

Teaching Tips

In general, idioms are difficult for ESOL students; idioms that contain allied prepositions are especially difficult. This *Tip* has two levels to it, a serious one and one with tongue in cheek. When it's possible to represent these idioms as drawings, do so. Before class, select group of idioms that can be "translated" into drawings. Pair the students up or have them work in small groups. Show them how to "draw an idiom" and then let them do the artwork for several of the idioms you prepared before class. Put the finished products up around the room and compare and contrast the various ways the students chose to represent their idioms.

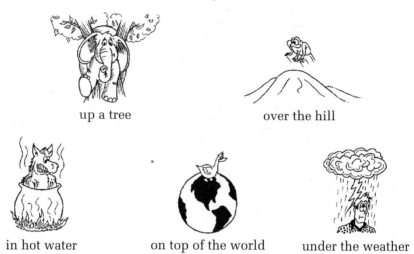

up a tree   over the hill

in hot water   on top of the world   under the weather

Variation

Before class, prepare a list of idioms with allied prepositions. Make absolutely sure that these idioms can be visually represented. Show the students what a "pictogram" is—a way to represent idioms verbatim; they show **exactly** what the idiom is. Once the students understand how pictograms work, let them make their own versions of the idioms that you've given them to work on in pairs or small groups. Here are a couple of examples to show you how pictograms work.

1. **ALL AFTER** ("after all")

2. **I N B ET O** ("be into")

3. **the bl**$^{\text{out of}}$**ue** ("out of the blue")

4. $\overset{\text{above}}{\text{**all else**}}$ ("above all else")

5. $\overset{\text{R}}{\underset{\text{N U}}{\text{**D O**}}} \quad \overset{\text{R}}{\underset{\text{N U}}{\text{**D O**}}}$ ("round and round")

6. **thought th**$\overset{\text{on}}{\text{ought}}$ ("on second thought")

More Teaching Tips

Before class, create an obstacle course with things that you have in your classroom. The obstacles can be as large as a desk or as small as a piece of paper on the floor. Blindfold one student and appoint another as guide. Have the guide give directions to the blindfolded student to get him/her through the course. It's often useful for the guide to follow along closely with the blindfolded student as he/she negotiates the course. This activity is particularly good for developing trust among students, precision in directions, and careful listening skills.

More Teaching Tips

This activity is a version of the game "Hide and Seek." Before class, hide something in the classroom. Students need to find the object by asking yes/no questions that pinpoint the location of the hidden item. When the students ask a question, you respond "hot" if the answer to the question points to a location which is very close to where the object is hidden, "warm" if relatively close, and "cold" if far away from the hidden object. Students keep asking questions until the object is found. This activity is also excellent for practicing question formation.

More Teaching Tips

Before class, prepare a dialog in which the participants discuss the layout of a room belonging to an imaginary person named Adele. If you have a tape recorder, record the dialog. If not, you can read it to your class. Give the students a bare-bones layout of a room and tell them that they'll "furnish" it after they listen to a discussion of the layout. Read the dialog or play the tape and have the students fix up the room.

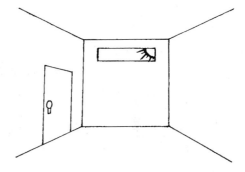

Variation

Instead of Adele's room, you can do the same activity with a building plan, a city map, a supermarket or supermarket shelf, a library, a shopping center, a tool box, a factory, or a workshop.

More Teaching Tips

Bring to class a set of children's blocks or "Legos" (multi-colored plastic building blocks). Make sure you have enough blocks for each of your students to have several of their own.

Pair the students up and have them sit back to back. Have one student in each pair create a design or pattern with his/her blocks. Limit the time to one or two minutes so that the partners don't get restless while they wait. Have the "designer" get his/her partner to recreate the same design or pattern by giving verbal instructions. When the students are done, have them compare their designs. Go over the differences in the patterns with the students to show them how to be more accurate in giving their instructions.

THE PREPOSITIONAL BANE OF BANES

There's one more preposition—a troublesome one—that we should look at in the same way we've looked at the others. It's troublesome because many people have a hard time putting their finger on just what it means. The preposition we're thinking of is *at*. We're giving you four boxes, so you'll have four chances to place a dot at whatever spot you think will graphically visualize the meaning of "at":

Truth is, you can place a dot practically anywhere outside each box (relatively close to each one, that is) and be quite accurate about how to visualize this preposition graphically. In its literal sense, **"at" means in the general area of something, and because it does refer to a general area, the dimensions of this something are really unimportant and the location isn't pinpointed.** (Keep these ideas in mind as we go on exploring this troublesome preposition.)

These ideas are especially useful for English speakers when they get into differences concerning location which have a literal or idiomatic meaning. Using the vague word "at" or the more specific words "in" or "on" can sometimes make a great difference in meaning, but quite often that difference depends on more than just the choice of preposition. Below you'll find some sentences with this interesting twist. Check the box after each pair of sentences which you agree with:

Fatima's at the hospital.
Fatima's in (the) hospital.   ☐ a difference   ☐ no difference

They're waiting at the ship.
They're waiting on the ship.   ☐ a difference   ☐ no difference

Meet us at the bookstore.
Meet us in the bookstore.   ☐ a difference   ☐ no difference

Most native speakers would agree that there's a definite difference in meaning between the sentences in each pair, so if you've checked **a difference** for all three pairs, you're in the majority.

People tend to interpret "Fatima's **at** the hospital" to mean that she's either visiting some patient or doctor there, whereas "Fatima's **in** (the) hospital" seems to mean that she herself is a patient there.

In the next pair of sentences, if you expect to find those people standing somewhere in the general area of the ship (**at** the ship), you're right; if you hear "They're waiting **on** the ship," you imagine them actually aboard the vessel.

As for the last two examples we've given you, "Meet me **at** the bookstore" probably makes you think you should be outside (perhaps in front of) the store or in the general area and wait for us there if you show up first, while "Meet us **in** the bookstore" leads you to understand that you should be waiting inside if you get there first.

We can clearly see that there are important differences between "at" or "in"/"on" in the previous sentences. Now let's look at some more sentences and play the same game:

I work at the bank.
I work in the bank.   ☐ a difference   ☐ no difference

We bought it at that bookstore.
We bought it in that bookstore.   ☐ a difference   ☐ no difference

I spent the day at the park.
I spent the day in the park.   ☐ a difference   ☐ no difference

That last statement we made, that there clearly are differences between "at" and the other two prepositions, isn't always the case as the sentences you've just looked over show us. If you checked **no difference** for all three pairs this time, you're once again going along with the majority opinion. Most people would say that they don't discern any real difference in these sentences between "at the bank" or "in the bank" or "at" or "in" the bookstore or park.

So now the question arises: Why do we easily perceive a difference in meaning between the two sentences in each of the first three pairs, but not in the second three pairs? Give it some thought and write your ideas on the following lines:

_____

_____

_____

What we have here is an amazing quirk in the language. Of course it's true that "at" and "in" and "on" can have very different meanings, but since we've now seen occasions when they really don't have such different ideas, we know that something else is at work—and that something else involves the verb and the object of the preposition in the context of each sentence.

In the first three pairs, we used the following combinations of verb + object of the preposition: be/hospital, wait/ship, and meet/bookstore. With these combinations, the prepositions show a marked difference in location and meaning. In the other pairs of sentences, we used the combinations work/bank, buy/bookstore, and spend/park. With such combinations as these, there doesn't seem to be any real difference in location or meaning. So what's the bottom line? It's simply that **the meaning comes from the context**. It also sends us teachers a very good message: we can't expect our students to learn how to use prepositions based solely upon simple rules which they can memorize and activate like mathematical formulas or that they can learn in a vacuum. Language just isn't that clear-cut!

We should admit that our sentence about Fatima being **in** (the) hospital as opposed to **at** the hospital carries an idiomatic meaning. Once again, it's the context that will often determine meaning and whether the sentence is literal or idiomatic. Now let's look at two pairs of sentences, one in each pair with a literal meaning, the other, idiomatic. Meanings will depend on the combination of verb and preposition used. Note that we're dealing here with **to** vs. **at**:

    1a.   The little girl threw the ball to the boy.

    1b.   The little girl threw the ball at the boy.

    2a.   The little boy shouted to the girl.

    2b.   The little boy shouted at the girl.

How would you interpret the two sentences in each pair, and how would you explain them to your students? Try it out on the following lines:

_____

_____

_____

_____

Sentence 1a has a literal meaning. It simply tells us that the girl tossed the ball to the boy intending for him to catch it. 1b is idiomatic and means that she didn't intend for him to catch the ball. It could even communicate that she was angry with the boy and meant to hit him with it.

Sentence 2a is literal and simply tells us the direction that his shouting was going in. 2b is idiomatic and could mean that he was angry with the girl or meant to send her a warning. The difference in communication is amazing!

Here are two more sentences. One of them is grammatical, but the other one isn't. After you've decided which is which, write an explanation showing why you think Sentence 1 or Sentence 2 is ungrammatical:

1. **She was so angry that she hurled a vase to the wall.**
   ☐ grammatical   ☐ ungrammatical
2. **She was so angry that she hurled a vase at the wall.**
   ☐ grammatical   ☐ ungrammatical

_____

_____

_____

_____

It turns out that **Sentence 1** is **ungrammatical**, and in order to understand the reason, we need to remember what the difference is between "to" and "at" in the sentences about the girl throwing that ball. With verbs like *throw* and *hurl* the preposition "to" means that the doer intends for the object of the preposition to catch something. This idea works fine if the object of the preposition happens to be a person, or perhaps a chimpanzee or dog, but it won't work at all if the object of the preposition is a nonliving thing—in this case, a wall! Therefore, when the object is a thing, we use the preposition "at."

Let's turn our attention to another difference between "at" and some other preposition. How would you explain the following corrections that invariably have to be made by probably all ESOL teachers from time to time?

A: You look tired today, Ali.
B: I am tired, Mrs. Klein. I was in a party almost all night. What a party!
A: You mean you were ***at*** a party, Ali.
B: "At"? Why "at"?
A: Uh, well, uh . . . Where was the party?
B: In my friend's house.
A: That should be ***at*** your friend's house, Ali.
B: Again "at"? Why "at"??
A: Well, you see, uh . . .

How would you rescue poor Mrs. Klein, who's obviously stalling because she doesn't have an answer ready for Ali? What would <u>you</u> say to Ali? Write your explanations on the following lines:

_____

_____

_____

_____

_____

If we keep in mind that "in" usually deals with one thing being <u>encompassed</u> or <u>enclosed</u> by another thing and that "at" refers to <u>general location</u>, we should be able to deal with Ali's questions. As for why native speakers would say "<u>at</u> my friend's house," it's because we don't want to limit ourselves in this context to one specific, enclosed area or room; we're keeping it *open* to take in the whole, general area.

For similar reasons, we say "<u>at</u> a party" because a party isn't any specific area that can encompass or enclose us; it's **an event** that takes place from room to room and even perhaps outside of the house, as in the backyard, for example. Because of this, "at" works much better since it simply places us in the general area of the event. Compare it with the use of "in" in this little dialog:

A: Where's Jack? I thought he was out here weeding the flower beds as I'd asked him to.

B: Nope. He's **in** the house watching *Batman*.

Here are a couple of examples that will bring this point about a specific, enclosed area versus a general area in even sharper focus. Fill in these blanks with **in** or **at**:

He works _____ the security office _____ the annex _____ the airport.

Most people would say that this person works *in* the security office *in* the annex *at* the airport. Why do we use "in" for the office and the annex? And why do we use "at" for the airport? Write your thoughts on these lines:

_____

_____

_____

We have a hunch that you had no trouble at all with your explanations. The person works inside the office (he's enclosed by it), and the office is a room inside the annex (the building encompasses the office), so he works **in** them. On the other hand, the building is located in the general area that we call the airport; that's why we say **at** the airport.

But we're not through with "at." Let's get back to some other idiomatic uses for this little devil of a preposition. Keep your mind in its "interpreting mode." Here are some prepositional phrases, dealing with both literal and idiomatic aspects of "at" which we'd like you to explain as you would to your students. Be brief, but clear!

at five o'clock _____

by five o'clock _____

on Maple Street _____

at 223 Maple St. _____

on Christmas _____

at Christmas _____

These are the kinds of phrases that drive ESOL students mad—and who could blame them? Native English speakers can appreciate the exactness of these prepositions, but our students just cringe when confronted with such exactness of meaning. Let's go over them now and see how closely your interpretations match ours.

At five o'clock means exactly when that hour arrives; *by* five o'clock means that something can occur before that hour or at that hour, but not after that hour.

On Maple Street gives us only a general idea of location; something is somewhere along that street. We use "at," however, when we have the actual house/building number to help us pinpoint the location. Does this strike you as a contradiction of one of the first meanings we gave "at," that it means in the general area and not a specific point? Initially, you might think so, but we have to look deeper. True, mentioning the number of the place does pinpoint the location for us, but "at" simply tells us that it's somewhere on those premises. For example, the real location of the person we're looking for could be *in* apartment 12 *at* 223 Maple Street, or *in* Suite 100 *at* 223 Maple. And even though it might border on the silly, we can take this a step further and say that if this is a private house, the person we're looking for could be *in* the kitchen *at* 223 Maple Street! So, all in all, there really isn't a big contradiction when "at" is used this way.

As for the last two phrases, we think of *on* Christmas as meaning during that one specific day, whereas we tend to think of *at* Christmas as something taking place during the general time of that holiday, not just on that one day.

Before leaving the prepositional bane of banes, let's explore other uses we have for "at" besides the ones we've covered so far. Since we've done it for the other prepositions cited in the chapter, it's only fair that we do it for this one, too. This time, though, we're going to carry out our investigation in a different way. You'll notice below that we've set up this activity as a matching exercise. Match up the examples we've given you with the uses they represent by filling in the appropriate corresponding number in front of each example.

Use #1:	conditions / states
Use #2:	rates / scales / ages
Use #3:	in the direction of
Use #4:	reactions
Use #5:	abilities

_____ Is he going to retire at 65?   _____ We seem to be at odds.
_____ They were at a turning point.   _____ I didn't shoot at the birds.
_____ She cried at the bad news.   _____ Are you good at math?
_____ She's a genius at bridge.   _____ We laughed at her joke.
_____ He aimed at the target.   _____ Water boils at 212° F.

Of course you understand now that the different uses we've found for "at" depend on the context in which the preposition is used. Here are the answers to this matching exercise for you to check your choices against: on the **LEFT—2, 1, 4, 5, 3**; on the **RIGHT—1, 3, 5, 4, 2**.

Here are other examples that fit into the different uses for "at":

Use #1:   be at ease, at an end, at play, at loggerheads, at rest
Use #2:   at 29,000,000 shares (stock market), at a fair price, at age 70

Use #3:   yell at, look at, glance at, grab at, lunge at, wave at
Use #4:   balk at, cringe at, frown at, weep at, recoil at, sneer at
Use #5:   be smart at / a whiz at / bad at / poor at / slow at

Teaching Tips

Before class, find a picture or pictures with enough prepositional phrases for a narration. Let's say you found a picture with the following: The sun is shining, but there are a few white, puffy clouds in the sky. A bird is in its nest. A chipmunk is arranging nuts in a tunnel, etc. (See Chapter 9 in Workbook 1 for this specific picture.) Prepare a narration which is based on the picture but which contains factual errors. (It's a beautiful day today. See? The sun is peeking out behind the tree. A bird is next to its nest. A frisky chipmunk is taking nuts out of the tunnel., etc.) **Note:** Don't change every preposition; it'll be far more challenging if some of the prepositional phrases are left correct. Tell the students that they're going to hear a narration which contains errors and that they'll be asked to write down as many of the errors as they can. Present the narration to the class several times so they can find all the errors. Go back and check to see that they've caught them all.

SOME TEACHING STRATEGIES

Before we go on to another topic, let's discuss some basic advice we can offer you for teaching prepositions. To begin, one technique we've always found useful and efficient is to teach pairs of prepositions that are opposite in meaning. For example, don't let your students learn "up" without learning "down"; don't let them learn "over" without learning "under" at the same time. When we've asked high intermediate ESOL students to give us the opposites of certain prepositions, many of them couldn't think of the right ones—in fact, many times they came up with bizarre answers. One reason that it's important to teach prepositions in this way when possible is that it will come in handy as the students get into two-word and three-word verbs (what some people refer to as phrasal verbs). By learning at an early stage of their English that "off" is the opposite of "on," your students will find it easier to learn converse phrasal verbs such as "put on" and "take off" or "turn on" and "turn off."

Another bit of advice we can offer is a grammar rule which many teachers avoid until the higher levels of ESOL. It's really unnecessary to put it off, as we've proven in practice, because this rule is very straightforward and has <u>no</u> exceptions: **when a verb follows a preposition, add -ing to it** (before leav<u>ing</u>, after eat<u>ing</u>, for mak<u>ing</u>, by heat<u>ing</u>).

Some people might want to take exception to this rule and say that it doesn't hold up if you consider examples like *used to* or *be able to*. After all, they'd say, verbs don't have the -ing stuck on the end if they come after these expressions which end in a preposition (*I used to <u>like</u> spinach. / They aren't able to <u>fly</u>*). The reason we don't consider these examples exceptions to the rule is that they belong to a category called **periphrastic modals** or **semi-auxiliaries**. Since they can substitute for modal auxiliaries (see Chapter 11), the verb that follows remains untouched just as it does after a modal:

He	**can**	go =	He	**[is able to]**	go
			He	**[is allowed to]**	go
She	**will**	go =	She	**[is going to]**	go
			She	**[is about to]**	go
He	**would**	go =	He	**[used to]**	go

Other expressions that fall into this category are *have to, have got to, be to, be about to,* and *be supposed to.* In short, the preposition "to" is an integral part of each of these semi-auxiliaries, not just a preposition on its own. Compare these to something like *be used to* which is an expression with an allied preposition that doesn't substitute for a modal auxiliary. Because this isn't a modal substitute, the verb that follows the preposition will have the -ing stuck onto it (*He's used to eating at 7 P.M.*) just as any other verb would.

We're sure you'll see that the rule for putting -ing on a verb that follows a preposition isn't difficult for students to master once they understand what prepositions are.

An additional idea we'd like to give you is that nothing works better for teaching prepositions than physical demonstrations. If you've decided, let's say, to teach "in/out" and "on/off," actually showing the class many different examples of these prepositions at work and then letting them go through the physical paces themselves will be your best bet for getting them to develop a feel for the concepts being taught. You should demonstrate many different examples for each preposition; if you're going to teach "on/off" in their literal uses, show them examples with a box, a desk, a chalkboard, a wall, a bulletin board, an article of clothing, etc. In order for the students to develop a real feel for these words, they must be exposed to enough varied examples for the message to hit home.

One last bit of advice we'd like to pass along at this point is that you're bound to come across times when your students overuse the secondary prepositions in the complex forms (those prepositions we listed earlier in this chapter with secondary prepositions in parentheses). For example, the reason we've shown you "out (of)" is that "of" isn't always going to be used. However, there are times when you may hear students say such oddities as "The dog is out of" instead of "The dog is out" or "The dog is outside." Another example is if you hear a student say "I put it into" instead of "I put it in." Why do you suppose the student sentences we've just cited are ungrammatical? Can you figure this out of—we mean, out?

_____

_____

_____

The reason is that **we only require the secondary preposition when the complex form is followed <u>by its object</u>**. It's perfectly all right to say "The dog is out of <u>the house</u>" and "I put it into <u>the drawer</u>," but when we omit the objects, we omit the secondary prepositions as well (The dog is out. / I put it in.) Note that "into," although written as one word, is really a combination of the primary preposition "in" and the secondary preposition "to." If there's no object with the preposition "into," the "to" gets dropped just as our rule says.

While we're on the subject of prepositions and their objects, we should mention a mistake made by many native English speakers. Unfortunately, it's quite common to hear people say such phrases as "You can go to the show *with Charlie and I*" or "*Just between you and I,* he's really not such a nice guy." Why should we say *with Charlie and <u>me</u>* and *between you and <u>me</u>*? Come up with an answer and write it on the lines that follow:

_____

_____

The answer is that you can't have a pronoun in the subject form (I, he, she, we, they) when it follows a preposition. You must use the object form (me, him, her, us, them), even when there are two pronouns separated by the word "and." Note that this mistake occurs most commonly in a phrase with the first person singular pronoun (*with so-and-so and I*).

POSTPOSED PREPOSITIONS

One very typical feature of English which has gone from being considered not so acceptable to acceptable is the final topic of this chapter. Its fancy name is the postposed preposition, and many a native English speaker will remember being corrected in primary or secondary school for this infraction of old-style, traditional grammar. What was that infraction? It was ending a clause or a sentence with a preposition! Most traditional English teachers of days gone by didn't consider it "proper" to say sentences like:

The play (which/that) **I was speaking about had a great plot.**

Which play were you speaking <u>about</u>?

Those teachers used to insist that we say:

The play <u>about which</u> I was speaking . . .

<u>About which play</u> were you speaking?

Most native speakers consider it very formal language to place the preposition at the beginning of the clause—but they themselves would rarely speak that way. It must be said, though, that things have changed considerably in the last few decades, especially in regard to the spoken idiom. As modern ESOL teachers, it should be our responsibility to teach the language as it's <u>really</u> spoken and written, and not hold on to some idealized, traditional form which no one would normally use in everyday language. Not only would it sound odd for a native speaker to say those two sentences above which the old-fashioned English teachers preferred, but, in some situations, it would also sound affected and out of place. Actually, that syntax, called a **preposed preposition**, would now seem *marked* in everyday speech, that is, it would be noticed in a negative way by most of us, whereas the postposed position wouldn't attract the least bit of unwanted attention and is referred to as *unmarked*.

Let's try an experiment. Decide which one of the following sentences contains a marked word and which one doesn't:

How tall are you?	☐	marked	☐ unmarked
How short are you?	☐	marked	☐ unmarked

If you understand that a marked word is one that creates a reaction in you which the unmarked word wouldn't, you'll know that the sentence with the marked item is *How short are you?* It's marked because we normally don't use the adjective "short" in this question and there's a pejorative connotation here that draws unnecessary attention to itself. In addition, it would probably end up embarrassing whoever the question was addressed to.

It's basically the same for questions and clauses that don't have the preposition postposed. In the most typical ESOL setting, whether in an English-speaking or non-English-speaking country, we should make the students aware of the more formal style (especially for writing and/or reading formal text), but we should stress that they learn to use postposed prepositions for everyday speaking and writing.

Before we go into detail about postposed prepositions, we'd like to mention our viewpoint about this term. If you know some basic Latin root words, you know that "postposed" literally means "put after," and we have to disagree with that term. To be "put after" gives you the idea that something is deliberately being moved and placed after something else—and that's not the case at all with this phenomenon so peculiar to English. To understand what postposed prepositions are all about, you have to realize that the preposition isn't being moved and placed after anything; it's simply staying right where it is in the original idea/sentence. Take a look at the following diagram which demonstrates how the preposition isn't moving anywhere—although other things are:

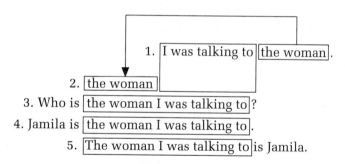

1. I was talking to the woman.
2. the woman
3. Who is the woman I was talking to?
4. Jamila is the woman I was talking to.
5. The woman I was talking to is Jamila.

So what's happened? (**1**) We're looking at the basic idea. In fact, we can say that there are actually two basic ideas at our starting point: Jamila is the woman. / I was talking to the woman. (**2**) What we've moved to another position is "the woman" (the object of the preposition) and <u>not</u> the preposition! Note that we've moved it to the front of the clause. Now we have the clause "the woman I was talking to," and this newly formed clause is going to serve many purposes as we can see. (**3**) We can add a question phrase before our new clause, or (**4**) some information, or (**5**) we can add information after our clause. Now we think you can see how the preposition hasn't been moved and placed anywhere new; it's actually right where it's been all along. Let's look at one more example of these changes at work:

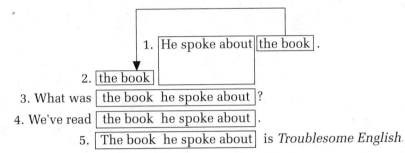

3. What was | the book he spoke about |?

4. We've read | the book he spoke about |.

5. | The book he spoke about | is *Troublesome English*.

(**1**) Here we have our basic idea. (**2**) We've moved the object of the preposition (the book) to the front of the clause so that we now have "the book he spoke about." (**3**) We've chosen to add a question phrase to the front so that we have a complete question. (**4**) Instead, we can choose to add some information to the front of the clause so that we now have a declarative sentence. And finally (**5**), we've added some information after the clause to form another declarative sentence. It's a very slick operation!

There's one more thing we need to mention when these changes are made with our basic idea. We can add the words **whom/who** or **that** after the initial noun phrase if the noun is a person:

The woman **who(m)** I was talking to . . .

The woman **that** I was talking to . . .

These two variations are considered more formal by most native speakers, especially if "whom," the object form of "who," is used. It's considered a more conversational style to omit "who" or "that" in this construction, but we'll go into detail about these forms in Volume 2.

As for our sentences about the book, we can choose to add **which** or **that** after the initial noun phrase if the noun is an animal or a thing, and the effect is again to make the sentence somewhat more formal:

The book **which** he spoke about . . .

The book **that** he spoke about . . .

Let's take a look at one more diagram that shows how we get another so-called postposed preposition:

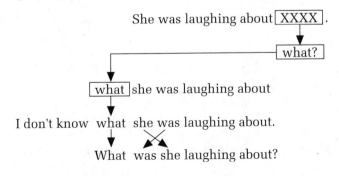

In this diagram, you can see that the operations in this case are just about the same as in our other diagrams. Here, however, there are two slight differences. The first one has to do with the fact that we have an unknown as the object of the preposition, so we use the word "what" to signify that unknown object and move it to the front of the clause. The other difference is that, in order to form the question, we need to invert "she" and "was," which is the normal way to make a question with the verb "be" anyway. Again, notice that the preposition hasn't moved at all!

As we come towards the end of this chapter, there's a peculiar—though traditional—teaching tactic that we'd like to discuss. In many traditionally conceived English grammar books, you'll find the following order given when postposed prepositions are dealt with:

1. The woman is my neighbor. I was talking **to the woman**.
2. The woman **to whom** I was talking is my neighbor.
3. The woman **who(m)/that** I was talking **to** is my neighbor.
4. The woman I was talking **to** is my neighbor.

We think this a very odd way indeed to demonstrate the changes that take place in order to arrive at a so-called postposed preposition. Notice how the preposition in Step 1 is in its *rightful* place together with its object (to the woman). Suddenly, in Step 2, it's been thrust in front of the clause and in Step 3, it's been moved down the line again back to its original spot after the clause! Isn't this peculiar? All that these traditional grammar books need to do is leave well enough alone. The only reason the preposition has been finally **post**posed is because it was **pre**posed in Step 2!

For some strange reason, these traditional grammarians feel that the preposed preposition is somehow a more basic construction and should therefore be Step 2; we feel, on the contrary, that the preposed construction is not so basic as it is affected and doesn't seem to go along with the way English constructs this kind of sentence. By the way, an interesting note about this preposed arrangement is that you can't use the word **that** any longer in place of "who" or "which":

1a. The woman to whom I was talking . . .
1b. The woman to **that** I was talking . . . (ungrammatical)
2a. The book about which he spoke . . .
2b. The book about **that** he spoke . . . (ungrammatical)

Before we close this chapter, we'd like to offer you a list of the clauses and sentences that you'll find postposed prepositions in, or if you prefer, in which you'll find postposed prepositions:

Wh-questions: What are you thinking **about**?
Wh-clauses: [Who I associate **with**] is none of your business.
Relative clauses: The person [I was talking **to**] is my boss.

Indirect speech:	He didn't tell me who he'd gotten the gift **from**.
Infinitive forms:	I can't find the right pot to cook this **in**.
Exclamations:	Here's another nice mess you've gotten me **into**!

Mind Bogglers!

You've really got your work cut out for you this time! First, see if you can figure out what's different about *Star Trek* in these two sentences:

Isn't Mr. Spock a character on *Star Trek*?

Isn't Mr. Spock a character in *Star Trek*?

Now see if you can figure out why we have this variety of prepositions with the verb *make*:

Almost all paper is made from wood pulp.

That old dresser is made out of knotty pine.

This paint is made with latex.

Chapter 10

Troublesome Plurals

Hippopotami or Hippopotamuses?

This is not going to be a chapter which contains nothing but lists of nouns with their singular and plural forms. As we've mentioned in previous chapters, you can always get information like that in any good English grammar book, ESOL or otherwise. Instead, we're going to focus our attention on the so-called irregular plurals of nouns which cause trouble among native English speakers as well as ESOL teachers and students. Parts of this chapter will explore some odd facts about some odd nouns and clarify some misconceptions that many people have regarding their meaning and usage. Other parts will consist of activities which ask you to produce the plural forms of certain nouns.

To begin, let's talk about this term "irregular." We don't really care for the term because it can be a hard word to pin down and it can be misleading, too. Actually, within their small spheres of influence, the rules that apply to troublesome plurals are really quite regular in their own right. That's why we've called this chapter "Troublesome Plurals," not "Irregular Plurals."

A PRONUNCIATION PHENOMENON

Let's start off the chapter with an eye-opener that's an unusual occurrence not dealt with by many ESOL teachers. To get into it, here's a little experiment. Slowly say the following words <u>out loud</u> pair by pair, first the singular form and then the plural form:

path, paths / mouth, mouths / house, houses

Notice any unusual change between the way you've pronounced the singular forms and the plural forms? Most native speakers would. If you didn't, try saying the pairs one more time and then write down what you perceive is going on phonologically on the following lines:

_____

_____

_____

What's happening is that the final sound in "pa**th**," "mou**th**," and "hou**se**" has gone from the voiceless / θ / and / s / to the voiced / ð / and / z /. The phonological rules for pronouncing the regular plural -s are the same rules that we've already discussed for pronouncing the -s genitive. Since the rule states that the -s will be voiceless when following a voiceless sound, but voiced when following a voiced sound, this accounts for the -s becoming voiced in the plural of "path" and "mouth." And even though the plural for "house" would still be pronounced / ɪz / regardless of whether the final sound in "house" (/ s /) becomes voiced or not, it's interesting that most of us do voice that final sound.

Why do the final sounds in the singular forms of those words become voiced when most of us pronounce the plural forms? It's not really important except to say that there are times in language teaching when you come upon phenomena that don't have any so-called _logical_ explanations—and this is one of them. If the words are written out phonetically the way you've probably enunciated them, this is how they'll appear:

/ **pæθ, pæðz** / / **mauθ, mauðz** / / **haus, hauzɪz** /

There's another group of words like the three just listed, but they have one difference: speakers have a choice of pronouncing their plural forms in the regular, voiceless way or in this unusual, voiced way. Which way you pronounce them can depend on the region of the English-speaking country that you come from, or it can depend on who taught you English. Among the words we're talking about are:

bath, baths / truth, truths / youth, youths / wreath, wreaths /

oath, oaths / roof, roofs / handkerchief, handkerchiefs

In all of these words, speakers can choose to pronounce the final sound on the singular word as voiceless or voiced before pluralizing it; if they leave the sound voiceless, the plural -s will be voiceless, but if they voice it, the plural -s will be voiced, too. One note about "handkerchief": if the speaker chooses to voice the final consonant (/ f / becoming / v /) which forces the use of the plural marker / z /, the previous vowel sound, / ɪ /, changes to / i /, so we have / hæŋkər-čivz / instead of / hæŋkərčɪfs /.

What about these next four words? Is there only one pronunciation in the plural, or are there two possibilities? After you've considered this, write your thoughts on the lines that follow:

dwarf   scarf   hoof   wharf

_____

_____

The fact is these four words can also be pronounced two ways in the plural. The one difference between these words and the words in the preceding group is that there will be a change of spelling to show the phonological change if the pronunciation of the final sound is voiced in the plural:

dwarf   →   **dwarfs / dwarves**

scarf   →   **scarfs / scarves**

hoof   →   **hoofs / hooves**

wharf   →   **wharfs / wharves**

SINGULAR NOUNS THAT ARE PLURAL; PLURAL NOUNS THAT ARE SINGULAR

Turning our attention to another matter now, let's consider whether the following nouns represent something singular or plural or both. Check off the appropriate box after each item on our list:

the French	☐	singular	☐	plural	☐	both
statistics	☐	singular	☐	plural	☐	both
the news	☐	singular	☐	plural	☐	both
fish	☐	singular	☐	plural	☐	both
billiards	☐	singular	☐	plural	☐	both
people	☐	singular	☐	plural	☐	both
the aged	☐	singular	☐	plural	☐	both
acoustics	☐	singular	☐	plural	☐	both
physics	☐	singular	☐	plural	☐	both
vermin	☐	singular	☐	plural	☐	both

Let's compare your answers to ours. We listed three nouns that represent something **singular** (**the news / billiards / physics**). We listed three that represent something **plural** (**the French / the aged / vermin**). And we listed four nouns that can represent **both** something **singular or plural** (**statistics / fish / people / acoustics**).

English has quite a few nouns or names that look **plural but are usually singular** in meaning like *news, physics, the United States, measles, mumps,* and *billiards.* And speaking of billiards, some other games that fall into this category are *checkers/drafts, dominoes, jacks,* and *darts.*

The next category we've featured in our list contains those words that **look singular but really represent something plural**. We refer to them as **collective nouns**. Besides *the French, the aged,* and *vermin,* we can also cite words like *the police, the poor, the rich, the military, the clergy,* and *cattle.* And speaking of cattle, there are other nouns that represent animals which belong to the next category we're going to discuss. (By the way, even though *people* is technically a collective noun, we're going to deal with it a bit differently a little further on in this chapter.)

The third category—perhaps the most deceptive—deals with **words that can represent either singular or plural** things, and there are three groups within this category. The first one is comprised of nouns whose endings appear to be plural but may in fact be singular or plural depending on their meaning. Let's see if your sleuthing skills are still intact. Here are two nouns that are in this category. On the blank line next to each one write down your interpretation of its meaning when it stands for something singular or what it means when it stands for something plural:

statistics (sing.)_____

statistics (pl.)_____

acoustics (sing.)_____

acoustics (pl.)_____

When we use words like *statistics* and *acoustics* as singular concepts, we refer to a science or subject that can be studied in school:

Statistics <u>is</u> being offered next trimester.

Acoustics <u>is</u> a complex branch of physics.

When *statistics* is a plural concept, we mean tables of numbers:

The statistics in this report <u>are</u> quite revealing.

When *acoustics* is a plural concept, it means the quality of sound in some specific place:

The acoustics in ancient Greek theaters <u>are</u> wonderful.

The second group of nouns in this category deals for the most part with animals. The difference between these nouns and the ones we've just reviewed is that **these nouns never add the -s as a plural marker**, so the plural form looks like the singular. Some typical ones are: *moose, deer, sheep, salmon,* and *trout.* Whether you count one of them or more of them, these nouns take no plural marker.

The third group in this category, comprised of collective nouns which may represent singular or plural concepts, can prove quite troublesome to ESOL teachers and students if they happen to be in countries where British English predominates. This group is interesting for another reason as well: the nouns within this group are one of the ways that differentiate British varieties of English from American varieties. British English tends to concern itself more than American English does with whether or not we should view a collective noun by focusing on it as an impersonal whole or focusing on the individuals involved in a group. Because of this, British English contains much greater double usage of these nouns as singular or plural concepts. Let's look at some examples from British English. In these examples, the British plural concepts will be examined since that's what appears so unusual to speakers of American English varieties:

The committee <u>are</u> looking into ways to reduce the budget.

The plane was delayed because the crew <u>were</u> late in arriving.

The jury <u>have</u> some questions for the judge.

In the three sentences cited, these British versions are focusing on the individuals in each group and therefore use the plural concept (the group = <u>all</u> the individual<u>s</u>). The verbs that follow reflect the idea of "they." The American versions, on the other hand, normally keep the singular concept in these sentences (the group = <u>one</u> body of people) and the verbs that follow reflect the idea of "it": "The committee <u>is</u> looking into . . ." / ". . . the crew <u>was</u> late in arriving." / "The jury <u>has</u> some questions . . ." In British varieties, however, if nouns like *the committee, the crew,* and *the jury* are viewed as whole groups, the verbs that follow will appear the same as in the American versions. This is not to say that such double usages don't occur in American varieties of English—they do—but let's just say that in American English, nouns like these are not as complex as they are in the British varieties.

SINGULAR FORM VERSUS PLURAL FORM

Moving along to another odd feature of troublesome plurals, let's take a second look at the words *people* and *fish*. First of all, let's see if you can answer this question about *people.* In everyday English, we normally say *one* **person***, two* *people, 400 **people***, but we can also use the plural form of *person* and say *two **persons*** and *400 **persons***. What's the difference?

_____

_____

The oddities of English are manifold! For some reason, we perceive the plural of *person* to be more formal sounding than the word *people*, and because of this, we tend to find *persons* used on legal documents, regulatory signs, and the like. That's why notices in public places such as theaters and movie houses which state the maximum number of people allowed in by law usually include the word *persons*. Remember that the next time a student of yours asks you why you changed *persons* to *people* in his sentence when he said "There are five persons in my family"!

Another interesting point to note is that there are times when both *people* and *fish* can end with the regular plural -s and -es even though they already seem to be plural concepts. When this happens, though, it reflects changes in their meanings. Can you figure out the differences? Think about these oddities and write your ideas on the blank lines following the words:

peoples = _____

fishes = _____

The word *people* can mean an ethnic group, a nation, or a tribe. In this meaning, we can also say *a people*. It follows, then, that we can add the plural marker -s to the word and say *peoples:*

The world's nomadic peoples are dwindling in number.

When we use the word *fishes*, we usually mean various species:

The fishes in our city's aquarium come from all over the world.

Along similar lines, we should take a moment to mention some of the words which more commonly demonstrate this change in meaning between the singular and plural forms. For once, we really will give you a list. Keep it in mind and go back to check out the differences in meaning between the singular and plural words when you have the time. Sometimes these changes are minor, but at other times they make for completely different meanings. Sooner or later, this list will be a good resource for you when you teach vocabulary items like these:

ash / ashes	glass / glasses
custom / customs	look / looks
damage / damages	manner / manners
drawer / drawers	scale / scales
fund / funds	work / works

As we come upon one interesting occurrence after another in this chapter, there are more that we should bring to light. Look at the following dialog which deals with the first of these:

A: I'm starving! And you don't have to tell me what's for breakfast . . . I can smell it all over the house!

B: Well, your steak and eggs will be ready in a jiffy.

A: What a treat! Steak and eggs **is** without doubt my favorite!

B: Calm down! The steak and eggs **are** almost done cooking.

To paraphrase Alice as she explored Wonderland, things can get "curiouser and curiouser!" Here we have two nouns connected by "and," and the verb which follows them first appears in the singular form (is), but then in the very next sentence is in the plural form (are). Why do you think this is? See if you can come up with an explanation:

_____

_____

_____

There's an interesting phenomenon taking place here which, oddly enough, revolves around food. When two nouns are connected as in our dialog and they jointly refer to one thing (in this case, a prepared dish), we consider them as *it*, so the verb that follows will reflect this—that's why it's "steak and eggs <u>is</u>." On the flip side, when we think of the two nouns as separate items and consider them as *they*, the verb that follows will reflect this, too, and that's how we get "steak and eggs <u>are</u>." Other examples of this strange occurrence are: *bread and butter, peanut butter and jelly, oil and vinegar, chicken and rice,* and that world-famous staple of Great Britain, *fish and chips.* By the way, the two nouns involved always appear in the same order, probably because of custom.

QUANTITATIVE WORDS

Another occurrence we should examine has to do with numbers or quantities of things. First off, let's see if you can create a grammar rule that will explain the following:

A: I need a **dozen** eggs, please.
B: Here you are. Oh, check to make sure none of them is cracked. Lately I've found **dozens** of them that were.
A: Really? I hope you don't end up paying for the cracked ones.
B: No, thank goodness, but my delivery service does. I've told them a **hundred** times to be careful when they load and unload the egg crates.
A: What a waste! **Hundreds** of eggs ruined because of carelessness.

The problem, of course, is that the words "dozen" and "hundred" appear in both the singular and the plural. Can you account for this?

_____

_____

_____

We've got a curious little rule about when we can and when we can't pluralize words that represent quantities or numbers: **If a quantitative word is immediately followed by a plural noun, it never has the plural -s on it**. It follows, then, that **if a plural noun doesn't immediately follow a quantitative word, you need to add the plural -s**. Some examples of this are:

They broke eight dozen eggs the other day.

They broke dozens (of eggs) the other day.

He lost ten thousand dollars in the stock market.

He lost thousands in the stock market.

Other words that work this way are *million* and *head* (when counting animals such as cattle).

So what do we say about this next strange occurrence? Examine this dialog and figure out the problem:

A: Have you heard about what happened to Kinder?

B: Yes, I have. It's just terrible.

A: Well, I don't feel any sympathy for him. After all, $500,000 **is** a lot of money to embezzle from your company!

B: I know. There's no excuse. And frankly, I think that six years **is**n't a long enough sentence for him. The judge should have thrown the book at him!

A: Well, whatever, I just feel sorry for his wife and kids. You know, eighty miles **is** a heck of a long distance to travel to visit him at the penitentiary.

Once again, we find ourselves looking at plural nouns that are followed by the verb in the singular form. Your students would probably be ready to give up at this point—but we're sure you're not! What's responsible for this unusual grammatical combination? See if you can make it out and write your thoughts down on the following lines:

_____

_____

_____

Even though there are times when things like this can make you want to pull your hair out, the explanation is really not that unusual. It all comes down to one simple rule: **When we deal with money, time, or distance, and we're thinking about these things as whole amounts, we consider them single units and reflect this by using the singular form of the verb that follows.**

What about if we use the expression *a number* or a *large number*? Do we normally use the singular or the plural verb form with these phrases? Let's look at a couple of examples:

There are a number of people waiting to see you.

A large number were killed during the battle.

Even though the word "number" is obviously singular, we've used the plural forms of "be" in both cases ("are" / "were"). Why is this the case?

_____

_____

_____

The rule at work here is basically the same as the one we've just discussed—only in reverse. The phrases *a number* and *a large number* really equal the idea of *many*, so we think of them as plural ideas and reflect that by using the plural form of the verb.

FOREIGN LOAN WORDS: ORIGINAL VERSUS ANGLICIZED PLURALS

The last part of this chapter will deal with many of the words we have in English that have come to us from other languages. Originally, when loan words such as these were taken into English, their native plural forms frequently came along with them. Through the centuries, however, there's been a growing tendency to anglicize, or regularize, these plural forms. Let's see how good you are at pluralizing the loan words we've cited. After each noun, write its plural form(s) on the blank line provided. Keep in mind that each word may have only a foreign plural or only an anglicized plural, or it may have both:

stimulus   _____

bonus   _____

cactus   _____

hippopotamus   _____

virus   _____

arena   _____

larva   _____

formula   _____

album   _____

datum   _____

forum   _____

medium   _____

index   _____

appendix   _____

analysis   _____

basis   _____

metropolis   _____

demon _____

phenomenon _____

criterion _____

tableau _____

plateau _____

corps _____

chassis _____

soprano _____

paparazzo _____

tempo _____

virtuoso _____

cherub _____

kibbutz _____

Here are the plural forms of the words we've listed. If a word is followed by an asterisk, it means we've made some comment about it after this section:

from Latin:
stimulus, **stimuli*** / bonus, **bonuses** / cactus, **cacti** or **cactuses** / hippopotamus, **hippopotami** or **hippopotamuses** (or even **hippos** for short!) / virus, **viruses** / arena, **arenas** / datum, **data** / larva, **larvae** / formula, **formulae*** or **formulas** / album, **albums** / forum, **fora*** or **forums** / medium, **media*** or mediums / index, **indices*** or **indexes** / appendix, **appendices*** or **appendixes**

from Greek:
analysis, **analyses*** / basis, **bases*** / metropolis, **metropolises** / demon, **demons** / phenomenon, **phenomena*** / criterion, **criteria***

from French:
tableau, **tableaux*** or **tableaus** / plateau, **plateaux*** or **plateaus** / corps, **corps*** / chassis, **chassis***

from Italian:
soprano, **sopranos** / paparazzo, **paparazzi** / tempo, **tempi*** or **tempos** / virtuoso, **virtuosi**

from Hebrew:
cherub, **cherubim** or **cherubs** / kibbutz, **kibbutzim**

Comments:

stimulus:	With **stimuli**, the pronunciation of the final syllable is / aɪ /. Compare this pronunciation with the final syllable of the Italian words mentioned further on.
formula:	**Formulae** tends to be used more in science or mathematics. Its final vowel sound is pronounced / i /. **Formulas** is the more common plural form.
forum:	**Fora** is a formal plural. **Forums** is a more common plural form.
medium:	**Media** is used when speaking of TV, radio, newpaper, or magazine journalism. It's often misused as a singular noun, when in fact it's a plural. Because so many speakers get confused on this point, we have no doubt that "media" will become the accepted singular form eventually. **Mediums,** among other things, can refer to people who claim to be able to communicate with the spirits of the dead.
index:	The pronunciation of the **-ces** on words like **indices** and **appendices** is / siz /.
analysis:	The pronunciation of the **-ses** on words like **analyses** and **bases** is also / siz /.
phenomenon:	The plural form of this word, along with that of **criterion**, is frequently confused. People can often be heard mistakenly saying "This phenomena is" and "The criteria is" as if they were singular nouns when, in fact, they're plural forms.
tableau:	The plural endings of this word, **tableaux** or **tableaus**, along with other words that have the same endings like **plateaux** or **plateaus**, are normally pronounced using English phonology with the / z / sound: / tæbloz /; / plætoz /. Some people do keep the French pronunciation and pronounce the plural form the same as the singular.
corps:	In writing, this word and words like **chassis** are identical in the singular or plural form. The pronunciation, though, is different as the / z / sound is added when the plural is enunciated: / kɔr /, / kɔrz /; / č̌æsi /, / č̌æsiz /.

tempo: **Tempi** is the plural form you're likely to hear classical musicians use. The pronunciation of the plural ending of this word and other words from Italian which maintain the **-i** is / i /. Compare this with the way the ending **-i** is pronounced on words of Latin origin. **Tempos** is the more common plural form used.

We're putting all the *Teaching Tips* for Troublesome Plurals here instead of sprinkling them throughout the chapter; each tip works equally well for any and all troublesome plurals.

Teaching Tips

#1   Review the spelling of regular and irregular nouns with a Crossword Puzzle (Workbook 1, Chapter 10) or "Body Spelling" (page 48 of this text).

#2   A Spelling Bee is one of the most common ways to see if your students have learned the correct spelling of words. It's also a good way to check their pronunciation. Divide the class in half and have them stand on separate sides of the room. Ask the first person in one of the lines to say and spell the plural of an irregular noun you give them. (What's the plural of "child"? How do you spell it?) If the student says and spells it correctly, the student gets to stay in the spelling bee. Then ask the first person on the other team a second word. If an error is made, the student sits down, and the second person in line on the first team gets a chance to spell the word. (You can continue asking other students to spell the same word until someone gets it right, but if more than two or three students have made a mistake, you might want to put the word out of play. Give the correct spelling yourself and have the class repeat it after you. You don't want the entire class to be thrown out of play if no one knows the word. That's pretty discouraging!) Play continues until there's only one person left standing; he/she's the champion speller.

#3   This activity works best with small or medium-sized classes. Before class, put each letter of several irregular plural nouns on a separate slip of paper.

A	D	D	E	N	D	A

Take all the letters of each word and put them together in random order. Fasten them together with a paper clip. Divide the class into groups and make sure you have enough words for the groups to have two or three words each. Distribute these fastened words to each group and tell them to reconstruct the words. This exercise can be made into a timed activity; the group that finishes their words first is the winner.

#4   Before class, write the singular form of irregular plurals on small slips of paper. Make sure you have enough words for each of your students to have several. Mix the words up and distribute them to the students. Have them sort the words by separating them into groups that have the same plural ending. Don't worry about distributing the words evenly; however they fall, they fall.

#5   Before class, write the singular form of nouns that have irregular plurals on individual pieces of paper. Punch a hole at both the top and bottom of the piece of paper. Take a larger piece of cardboard and write an irregular plural ending on it. Punch a hole at the bottom of the cardboard. Unbend paper clips (so that they look like an "S"). Hang the pieces of cardboard from the ceiling or another appropriate place and distribute the individual singular nouns and paper clips to the students. Have the students hang their singular words under the proper plural heading. Keep the strings of nouns up for the class to review.

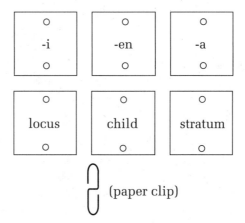

Mind Bogglers!

Here are some words that always confuse ESOL students. Let's see if you can figure out clear, easy explanations that will show their differences:

dirt / earth / ground / land / soil

Chapter 11

Modal Auxiliaries in the Present or Future

I would if I could, but I can't, so I won't.

One of the biggest challenges to an ESOL instructor is successfully teaching the uses of the surprisingly complex little words and phrases that we call modal auxiliaries. Modals are a real challenge because they have several meanings, they can vary in usage from one part of the English-speaking world to another, they have numerous "gray areas" where they overlap in meaning, and they may exhibit differences in meaning and usage from one speaker to another even in the same region. Because of all this, we'd like to give you some advice for the information you're about to discover in this chapter: Pick and choose among what we have to offer; there will be points that you feel can be useful to you in your teaching, but there will be other points that you may decide aren't appropriate or necessary for an ESOL lesson or should be reserved for more advanced students. That, of course, doesn't mean you shouldn't become sensitized to those points—you never know when an astute person in one of your classes may throw a question at you on one of those points, so it would be nice if you could answer the student with confidence!

Just exactly which words are we talking about? Here's a list of them: *can, could, will, would, shall* (which received a mention in Chapter 6), *should, ought to, may, might,* and *must.* Some grammarians also include *used to, would rather,* and *had better,* but we'll be dealing with these three and some others under a heading other than "modals."

We can explain what modals are by comparing them to verbs. (Note the asterisks before most examples; they mean the phrase is ungrammatical):

- Modals never take the infinitive "to" (*to can / *to may).
- They never add the -s to the 3rd person singular in the present or general time (*he mays / *it shoulds).
- They never take the -ed ending for the past (*we shoulded).
- They never have -ing attached to them (*by oughting).
- They never use forms of "do" or "be" to make negatives (*you don't can / *he isn't mighting); instead, they use the word "not" after them for the negative (you cannot / he might not).

We call them "auxiliaries" because their main function is to *help* a true verb by altering its meaning, that is, adding some extra meaning or nuance that the verb itself doesn't have alone.

265

There are some other general points we should mention about modals:

- In standard English, two modals can never be used together:
  *I think Pancho **might could** be at the office.*
- All modals can refer to the present or the future using the same form—even "will" can do this in a certain context as you'll see later on:
  *We **can** take samples of the lake water <u>now</u>.*
  *We **can** take samples of the lake water <u>tomorrow</u>.*
- What many commonly call the past form of modals (like "could," "would," and "might") isn't really the past at all the way we normally use these words:
  ***Could** you give me a lift downtown?*
  These forms are only truly the past when they're clarified with additional information or through context:
  *He **couldn't** come (<u>yesterday</u>).*

Because most grammar books created for ESOL students only give a superficial presentation of modals and usually fail to mention semi-modals such as "would rather," we're going to fill in the gaps and give you a more complete picture in this chapter.

Before we get under way, we should mention that this chapter will only deal with the modals in their present/future use. You'll find a detailed exploration of the modals in the past in Volume 2.

 Troubleshooter

   Be prepared for an inevitable occurrence: many of your students are going to use the word "to" after each and every modal auxiliary!

This may happen because they're accustomed to using "to" after so many verbs like *want, plan,* and *try.*

It may also happen because, in many languages, it's quite normal to use the infinitive form (our "to" with the verb) after their equivalents of our modals.

CAN / COULD

We're going to begin our exploration of the modal auxiliaries by taking a good look at the words "can" and "could." Read this first dialog and figure out what the exact uses of "can" are. You'll notice a number attached to the modal for each use that's being demonstrated in the dialog. This system will help us discuss the various uses of modals in all of the dialogs that follow, too.

When you think you've figured out what each use of "can" is in this dialog, write your idea on the following lines that numerically match them:

A: Did you know that different species of whales **can**[1] create different kinds of "songs" to communicate with?

B: Yes, I knew that. And I've met a famous marine biologist who **can**[1] tell one species of whale from another just by listening to their "songs."

A: You **can't**[2] be serious!

B: I am!

A: **Can**[3] that really be true?

B: Trust me. It is.

---

1. _____

2. _____

3. _____

Let's see how we interpret "can" in this dialog. **Can**[1] means **ability**. There's a slight difference, though, between the first modal labeled **1** and the second. In the first use, the modal means <u>innate</u> ability, but in the second it means <u>acquired</u> ability. Just as we don't distinguish between the two very much in real life, we don't bother differentiating these fine lines with the modal either.

Can't[2] has a different use. Here the modal in the negative expresses **disbelief** or **impossibility**. Person A is saying that he's having a hard time believing that Person B is serious about a marine biologist having that special skill. At this point, take a look at the following two sentences in which "can't" and "couldn't" represent disbelief or impossibility. See if you can perceive a difference between the two and write your idea on the following lines:

1. **You've been married how many years? You <u>can't</u> be!**

2. **You've been married how many years? You <u>couldn't</u> be.**

_____

_____

What many native speakers will perceive as the difference between these two sentences is that "can't" is a stronger form of disbelief or impossibility than "couldn't." In fact, using "couldn't" may actually soften the meaning enough so that it's used in a more tactful way communicating that something is "hard to believe" rather than "impossible."

Troubleshooter

There's a point concerning pronunciation that we'd like to bring to your attention. It may not seem like a major concern at first, but because it may interfere with accurate communication, we think it important enough to mention.

All the modal auxiliaries are <u>un</u>stressed in the context of a sentence when they're affirmative:

> He can GO with us on the trip.

> She can SPEAK three languages.

When the modals are negative, however, they're stressed along with their verbs:

> He CAN'T GO with us on the trip.

> She CAN'T SPEAK three languages.

With the modal "can," we have an important change in pronunciation between the affirmative and negative that truly affects communication:

- Unstressed "can" is really pronounced /kɪn/. In fact, there's practically no vowel sound at all.
- Stressed "can't," on the other hand, has a strongly pronounced vowel which in British English is /a/ and in American English is /æ/.

  Moreover, the final /t/ in "can't" is unreleased /t̥/ in many dialects when it comes before a verb, so for all intents and purposes, it's inaudible. These two phenomena, the added stress and the unreleased /t̥/, result in a modal which sounds negative simply because it has the stress on it and the strongly pronounced vowel: /kænt̥/.

Sensitizing your students to this change in communication brought on by these phonological changes will go a long way to stop any misunderstandings that could very well arise.

We have yet another meaning of "can" in our dialog. **Can³** expresses **hypothetical possibility**. What this means is that something is possible in theory. It doesn't mean, however, that this is a possibility that is likely to occur at any time soon; there's no reference to the near future as there can be with other modals as we'll soon see. In fact, we'll get back to this meaning of possibility shortly.

We should make it clear, moreover, that "can" is limited in its use as a modal of possibility. This is probably because it's easy to confuse it with the idea of *ability* in many sentences, and we try to avoid confusion whenever we can. Just look at the following little sentence, deliberately given to you here out of context, and see what we mean:

He can be rich.

Most native speakers are likely to consider this sentence ambiguous. They'll probably feel uncomfortable with it because they'll have trouble interpreting what "can" means. According to our definitions of "can," however, you really have the option to interpret the idea to mean "It's possible that he's rich," or "He has the ability to get rich." You can see why we normally avoid using "can" for possibility in ideas like this; it's much easier to use another modal which unambiguously conveys the idea of possibility.

Now let's look at another dialog and investigate these uses of "can" and "could" in the same way as we've just done:

A: So tell me, how was your year in Rio de Janeiro?
B: Just wonderful! But you know, it **can¹** get quite chilly in the hills outside of Rio in July.
A: I don't care about the weather! Tell me more about that good-looking Brazilian colleague of yours.
B: Well, he **can¹** be very charming. And guess what! He **could** be here in the next couple of weeks on business.
A: Really? If he's as cute as you've said he is, I'd love to meet him.
B: Well, that **can²** be arranged.
A: Who knows. This **could** turn out to be a very interesting experience!

	CAN	COULD
1.	_____	_____
2.	_____	

Here we have completely different uses of "can" and we come upon "could" for the first time in a dialog. **Can**[1] represents the idea of **capability**. First we have the idea that the temperature is capable of getting quite chilly in that area outside of Rio proper, and then we have the idea that this man is capable of being charming. Note that there's a big difference between saying:

It can get quite chilly in the hills.

and

It gets quite chilly in the hills.

or between:

He is very charming.

and

He can be very charming.

The question is, how can you explain that important difference to your students if the subject comes up? Write your thoughts on the following lines:

_____

_____

The important difference is that when we use "can" in this way, we're communicating that **there's a potential, but we're not claiming that it's always the case**. In our first example, Speaker B is saying that there's a potential for the temperature to get quite chilly in that area in July, but it doesn't necessarily mean that this is always true. In our second example, Speaker B is saying that her former colleague is the kind of person who has the potential to be quite charming, but that he isn't always like that. Actually, she might be implying that he can turn the charm on and off at will, and some listeners might even pick up a negative subtext in this case! You can see how important using or not using "can" may be to the communication.

Can[2] and **could** represent the idea of possibility, but there's a difference: **Can** once again expresses **hypothetical possibility** and often implies a conditional idea. Person B says it's possible that a meeting between her friend and the Brazilian will be arranged with the implication if things work out. **Could**, on the other hand, expresses what we call **real possibility**, that is, something that we aren't sure of or is still to come in the future. Person B uses "could" when talking about the future trip her Brazilian colleague is planning to take because it falls within the categories we've just mentioned: "It's possible that he'll be here in a couple of weeks." Likewise, Person A ends the dialog by saying that there's a good chance the experience of meeting the Brazilian will be interesting, and to communicate this idea of real future possibility as opposed to some idea in theory only, she uses "could."

Here are two sentences that demonstrate why "can" and "could" aren't always interchangeable because the focus they have on the kind of possibility being expressed is different:

1.   **With all the rain we've been having, the dam <u>can</u> burst.**
2.   **With all the rain we've been having, the dam <u>could</u> burst.**

Think about the difference in meaning between these two sentences and write down your ideas on the following lines:

_____

_____

In **Sentence 1**, "can" represents a **hypothetical possibility**. The focus isn't so much on a possible disaster which we think is about to happen as it is on the idea that we know the dam is able to hold just so much water before it bursts. In **Sentence 2**, "could" represents a **real possibility**; we're saying in this case that there's a real chance the dam is going to burst. It's more appropriate for our speaker to use "could" in this context since weather conditions have created that real possibility.

Another reason that "can" isn't used too commonly to mean possibility is that we deal with real possibilities most of the time, not hypothetical ones. This also explains why "can" isn't usually interchangeable with "could" for this meaning.

 # Troubleshooter

    Be prepared for another inevitable occurrence: many of your students will end up using "can" to mean *possibility* in every English sentence they create containing this idea. They'll produce all sorts of sentences like:

> "The weatherman says it can snow tonight."

This is most likely because the equivalent of the English modal "can" is used in many languages to mean possibility even in its present tense form unlike English, which usually uses "could" for this idea.

Just keep reminding them that "could" is more common for possibility than "can."

But we're not done with "can" and "could" yet. What uses do you find for them in our next dialog?

A: Here the weekend's coming and I've got absolutely no plans. I have no idea what to do.

B: Well, you **can** get together with your friend, Nancy. You haven't seen her in a while.

A: That's true.

B: Or you **could** clean out your closet or finish that term paper that's due soon for your social studies class.

A: Thanks, Mom. You're just full of neat ideas. Mmmm. Maybe I'll give Nancy a call.

The first question we need to ask is, how are "can" and "could" being used in this dialog? What's your idea?

"Can" and "could" are being used _____

_____

It seems that "can" and "could" are being used in this instance as a way of giving **advice** or **suggestions** but it's important to mention that these two modals leave room for other options. You'll see why this is important later on when we explore "should" and "ought to." The next question we need to ask is, why did Speaker B choose to use "can" in her first utterance, but switch to "could" in her next one? Any ideas on the subject?

_____

_____

An interesting difference can be seen in the way Speaker B is thinking. When she gives her first suggestion, she's fairly confident that her daughter will react favorably to the idea of seeing her friend, Nancy. However, when she gives her next two suggestions, she knows perfectly well that there's a very slim chance her daughter will take these ideas seriously. It turns out, then, that **we tend to** use "can" when we give advice that we believe has a good chance of being accepted, but we use "could" when we're not so sure our suggestions will be heeded. And, by the way, we'll be returning to these uses of "can" and "could" again when we discuss "should" and "ought to."

Now let's examine these two uses for "could":

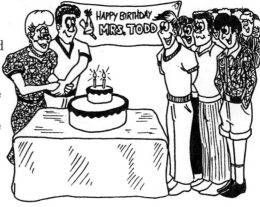

A: Hello, Mrs. Todd. Happy birthday!

B: Why, thank you, Jim. And thank you, everybody, for this lovely cake! **Could¹** you help me blow out the candles, Jim?

A: I'm sure you can manage the two of them just fine!

B: Well, I don't know . . . a woman my age. It's a good thing they didn't put one candle on the cake for each year!

A: **Could²** I ask how old you are today?

B: I don't mind telling you. I'm 72 today.

A: No way! You can't be 72!

B: Well, bless your heart. However, I'm afraid I am.

1. _____

2. _____

This use of **could¹** is what most people refer to as **a polite form for making a request**. There are other ways to make requests with modals, most notably by using "can" or "would." Most native speakers, however, perceive "could" as being more polite and formal than "can." In the sentence with our first example, Mrs. Todd is making a little joke by politely requesting that Jim give her some help blowing out the candles on her cake.

The use of **could²** is a different matter; it represents **asking for permission**. In this case, Jim is politely asking Mrs. Todd for permission to inquire about her age. Since asking a woman's age isn't something you normally do in many cultures, Jim feels the need to ask for permission to pose this question, and he soft-ens it by using the polite use of "could."

Instead of waiting for the end of the chapter to challenge you to some "Mind Bogglers," we're going to offer you one right now. Read the following two mini-dialogs and decide if the lines in bold are acceptable or unacceptable:

Dialog 1

> **A:** Could I become a doctor?
> **B: Sure you could.**
> ☐ acceptable   ☐ unacceptable

Dialog 2

> **A:** Could I borrow your pen?
> **B: Sure you could.**
> ☐ acceptable   ☐ unacceptable

Native English speakers would say that Person B's reply in **Dialog 1** is **ac-ceptable**, but Person B's reply in **Dialog 2** is **unacceptable**, yet they're exactly the same sentence. The questions that need answering are, what's the difference, and why is it that the exact same sentence doesn't work in both cases? Here's some space for you to write down any solutions you have to solve this puzzle:

_____

_____

_____

The explanations for this strange occurrence are as follows. The word "could" in Dialog 1 expresses the idea of **possibility** and is being used by Person A as he wonders about the possibility of becoming a doctor. If we continue to develop the idea in that question, we can come up with phrases like "Could I become a doctor . . . if I wanted to / . . . if medical school weren't so hard to get into / . . . if tuition weren't so high and I weren't so poor?" In any case, **"could"** **represents possibility both in the question and in Person B's reply:** "Of course you could [become a doctor if . . .]" which equals "Of course you'd have the possibility [of becoming a doctor if . . .]."

The word "could" in Dialog 2 is completely different. Here Person A is using it as a polite way to ask for **permission** to use Person B's pen. Remember that "could" represents this polite form of <u>asking for</u> permission, but it doesn't represent the way we <u>give</u> permission; for that, we use "can" (among other modals). So "could" is unacceptable in the reply to Person A's question in Dialog 2 because "could" never means "I give you permission." We say "Sure you can [borrow my pen]."

CAN in a Nutshell

 ability:
My friend Roger **can** speak three languages.

hypothetical possibility (limited in use):
If surgery is successful, it **can** mean the start of a new life for her.

advice or suggestions (which are likely to be heeded and leave room for other options):
If she's passed over for another promotion, she **can** always look for another job.

informally making a request:
Can you help me out for a moment?

informally asking for permission:
Can I take the car tonight, Dad?

capability:
He **can** be really cranky when he hasn't had enough sleep.

can't = disbelief/impossibility:
The ozone layer **can't** be disintegrating! Do you realize what that means? (disbelief)
He **can't** be there already. He only left ten minutes ago, and it's a good twenty-minute ride to get there. (impossibility)

COULD in a Nutshell

real possibility:
Yes, I see your point. You **could** be right.

advice or suggestions (which aren't likely to be heeded and leave room for other options):
Well, if you have nothing much to do tonight, you **could** take me out to dinner.

politely making a request:
Could you help me with these suitcases, please?

> ❧   **politely asking for permission:**
>   **Could** I take your picture?

> ❧   **couldn't = "softened" form of disbelief; not very probable:**
>   He **couldn't** be your brother. He looks nothing like you.

WILL / WOULD

The next two modals that we'll investigate are probably just as troublesome as "can" and "could" tend to be, but before we look at the next dialog, we want to make mention of the fact that this is a continuation of the material covered in Chapter 6. There's so much to say about "will" that it would be overwhelming to do so in one chapter.

Now let's look at the following dialog to see "will" in some uses not covered in Chapter 6 and some uses for its counterpart "would":

A: Isn't Ahmed here yet?
B: No, not yet.
A: **Would**[1] you call his house to make sure he's on his way?
B: You **would**[2] ask me to do that. He'll be here soon. Just take it easy!
A: I *will* take it easy, but I still think you should call him.
B: **Will**[1] you kindly stop nagging me?
A: You know me. I ***will***[2] go on and on when I worry. I can't help it. Please find out if he's on his way.
B: All right! All right!

Let's examine the uses of "will" and "would" the same way we covered "can" and "could." On the following lines that are numbered to correspond to the modal uses in the dialog, write down your interpretation of what these modals mean in their contexts:

WOULD   **WILL**

1. _____   1. _____

2. _____   2. _____

Would[1] and **will**[1] express **polite requests.** Many native speakers, however, perceive a slight difference between the two words. They see "will" as being somewhat more direct or forceful than "would."

Would[2] and **will**[2] are quite unusual. They represent **actions or behaviors characteristic of the person or thing you're talking about.** First, Person B says it's typical for Person A to insist on asking him to make such a phone call; similarly, Person A says she knows she has the habit of going on and on about something to the point of obsessing on it (offering this thought almost as an apology). The difference between the two modals when used in this way is that **"will" expresses this idea about a general observation** just as the simple present can do (refer to Chapter 2). **"Would" expresses the same idea as "will" and is an immediate response to something that has just occurred.**

One more unusual point about this use of the two modals is that stress can play an important role in determining meaning. When the modals are unstressed, the usual intent is simply that this is/was typical behavior. When the modals are stressed, however, there's a negative implication that can be interpreted as criticism. Compare these two sentences as more examples of this usage:

> **Whenever anyone's in trouble, she'll be the first one to help.**
> (unstressed 'll which carries no negative implication)

> **A: Why is Fred always so tired in the morning?**
> **B: Well, he _will_ stay up to watch the late night movie on TV every night. What can you expect?**
> (stressed **will** which carries a criticizing tone)

Go back to the dialog for a moment and re-read the third sentence that Person A says. The italics, in case you haven't realized it, indicate stress on those words as it would be used in the spoken language by the two people. Even though "will" appears stressed in two instances, it only changes meaning (resulting in that reproachful tone) in one instance: I _will_ go on and on when I worry." In the other sentence where this stressed "will" occurs, its meaning isn't altered at all ("I _will_ take it easy . . . ") The word is stressed in this case simply to give it an emphatic quality as a retort to what Person B has just said. Words or phrases that have their meaning changed depending on whether or not they're stressed are part of a group called "suprasegmentals," and you'll find a chapter on this phenomenon in Volume 2.

Here's something else to note about modals and stress: **you never contract modals when you want to stress them.** That's easy to understand when you consider how impossible it would be to try to stress the **'ll** when added to a pronoun (they**'ll**, for example).

Before we leave the subject of the stressed "will" that can indicate a pejorative or critical view of someone's behavior—depending on the context it's used in—we need to mention an alternative for "will" which is very typically heard in English. **Most speakers tend to use the word "do" the same way we've demonstrated "will" in this section to indicate that reproachful tone.** In other words, instead of saying "I *will* go on and on when I worry," Person A could just as easily say "I *do* go on and on when I worry."

There are four final uses for "will" that we're going to investigate now, so take a look at the following dialog and see what you can make of the modal in these cases:

A: Let me go answer the door. Someone's knocking.
B: Oh, that**'ll**[1] be Ms. Borgia. I invited her over for dinner.
A: Borgia? Oh, no! You know I can't stand her.
B: Look, she's my supervisor, and I think she's considering me for a promotion.
A: Oh, that's nice—buttering up the boss!
B: Call it what you **will**[2], I think it's just good politics and I ***won't***[3] discuss it anymore. You**'ll**[4] be nice to her and you **won't**[4] do anything to sabotage my chances of getting a promotion, right? Right!

1. _____

2. _____

3. _____

4. _____

The interpretation for **will¹** is that it represents **a deduction** or **conclusion** based on some sort of information previously known. Actually, it's just about the strongest way you can express **probability** without really knowing the facts. Person B says in this case that she's 95% sure the person knocking at the door is her supervisor.

Teaching Tips

Ask the students what they know about fortune telling, crystal balls, and palmistry. Copy the hand you see here on the board, explaining that the lines on the palms of your hands are thought to predict your future. Also explain what the different lines are and what they're supposed to pre- dict. Then ask the students to read three or four other students' palms being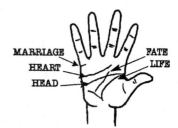
sure they use the various modals. Some typical answers are: "You'll live a long life." "You might work for the government when you graduate." "You should be more careful of what you eat." Let your students read your palm, too. Students can also write up their predictions in a short composition.

Will² is a bit tricky—and it's also a linguistic throwback to many centuries ago when the modal "will" was the Old English verb "willan," meaning "to want." That historical information gives the answer away: in this instance, **"will" means "want,"** so Person A is saying "Call it whatever you want . . . " You can often hear this use of the modal in the currently popular parenthetical expression "if you will," which is thrown into practically any kind of sentence and seems to mean "if you want to interpret XYZ as I'm explaining it." Here's an example of how the expression is used:

A: The steady destruction of the natural world, or the end of life as we know it, **if you will,** isn't just some bad dream anymore. It's real, and we've got to stop it.

B: I just hope people all over the world wake up and realize how big the disaster will be if they don't take a stand.

Won't³ represents **refusal** and, coincidentally, it can get stressed equally with its verb for emphasis in the spoken language.

Will[4] (both in the affirmative and negative) expresses **a command, an order.** Person B is saying in no uncertain terms that she expects Person A to be on his best behavior and expresses this idea with a strong, firm imperative form. Some native speakers take this use of "will" as the strongest imperative form we can muster up in English as it has the hidden meaning that the person saying it will accept nothing less than what's being demanded. We mentioned earlier that "will" can be used as a more forceful, polite request than "would" when used in a question ("Will you kindly stop nagging me?"). When we use "will" this way in a statement ("You will be nice to her . . . "), it's even more forceful.

WILL in a Nutshell

- **used for polite requests (more forceful than "would"):**
  Will you buckle your seat belt so I can start driving?
- **used for an action characteristic of the person or thing being discussed (general time observation):**
  - Jim knows how to relax. He**'ll** nap for hours under that tree.
    (unstressed **'ll** = no negative connotation)
  - Anton is such a stubborn man. He **will** have to have his way. (stressed "will" = criticism)
  - Anton is such a stubborn man. He **does** have to have his way. (stressed "do" as alternative for "will" = criticism)
- **used for deductions or conclusions (probability):**
  Can you get the phone? That**'ll** be Jim. Tell him I'm leaving now.
- **"will" = "want" in some formulaic expressions:**
  Do what you **will** with this old, ugly chair; just get it out of the living room.
- **"won't" = refusal:**
  You can nag me all you want. I **won't** look for a different job!
- **used for a command/order:**
  You **will** eat everything on your plate, and you **will** like it!

WOULD in a Nutshell

- **used for polite requests (softer than "will"):**
  Would you answer the phone, please? My hands are wet.
- **used for an action characteristic of the person or thing being discussed (immediate reaction to something that has just occurred):**
  - I should know you by now. You **would** embarrass me like that! (stressed "would" = criticism)

MAY / MIGHT

We'll continue our investigation into modals the same way we've discovered so many facts about those already covered. Let's look at this next dialog to see how "may" and "might" can function:

A: Good morning, Mr. Snodgrass.

B: Good morning, Ms. Ketchum. **Might**[1] I have a word?

A: Certainly. What is it?

B: You **may**[2] not realize it, but your dog has been going through my garbage can again and tossing the garbage all over my front lawn.

A: My Muffie? I don't believe it. I'm sure it's the work of another dog.

B: Well, it **might**[2] be, but I very much doubt it.

A: Well, Mr. Snodgrass, if **I may**[1] say so, you **might**[3] consider using a garbage can with a tighter lid!

B: And if I may say so, Ms. Ketchum, **may**[4] you never find garbage strewn all over your front lawn as I have!

Now that you've looked over the uses of these two modals in the dialog, write down your interpretation of what they mean in the different contexts on the following lines that are numbered to correspond:

MIGHT	**MAY**
1. _____	1. _____
2. _____	2. _____
3. _____	3. _____X_____
4. _____X_____	4. _____

Even though not the most common use of the word, **might**[1] is **the most polite and formal way to ask for permission—it's also the least forceful.** Some native speakers even consider this use of "might" almost too much in this somewhat overly polite way of asking for permission. **May**[1] is the more common way we politely ask for permission to do something.

May[2] expresses the idea of **possibility.** "It's possible that you don't realize it . . . " is what Mr. Snodgrass is saying to Ms. Ketchum. When we see **might**[2], it expresses **possibility** just as "may" does. The question is, do you discern any difference between "may" and "might" when they both express possibility?

Many prescriptive grammar books define "might" as being a weaker version of "may" when the meaning is possibility. The way these two modals have been used for possibility in this dialog tends to uphold that perception of "may" and "might." Mr. Snodgrass is less certain that a dog other than Muffie is the culprit than he is about Ms. Ketchum not realizing what her dog's been up to. In other words, he's using "may" for stronger possibility and "might" for weaker possibility. We want to make it clear, though, that not all native speakers discern this difference; that's probably why so many ESOL grammar books teach these two modals together to mean possibility and don't bother to dwell on any subtle differences between the two.

One further point we should make about "may" and "might" when they express possibility is that they both signify **real possibility** just as "could" does (as opposed to "can"). In fact, all three modals are usually interchangeable:

He may be late. / He might be late. / He could be late.

There's one occasion, at least, when the three modals aren't interchangeable, and that's when a rhetorical phrase is used to preface some sort of critical remark. Notice that "may" and "might" are the traditional choices for this use but that "could" isn't:

A: My English teacher says it's okay to say "I might could do it."
B: Well, she **may** (**might**) be an English teacher, but she certainly doesn't know the difference between standard and nonstandard English!

As for **might**[3] in our dialog, the modal expresses **an indirect way of making a suggestion.** Ms. Ketchum is gingerly suggesting to Mr. Snodgrass that he get himself a "dog-proof" garbage can. There are other ways to make suggestions with modals, but we'll cover those a little further on.

Finally, we come to **may**[4] which signifies a very formal way of hoping that something will happen. Mr. Snodgrass is saying in his very formal tone that he hopes Ms. Ketchum will never experience the mess he's found on his front lawn. Another thing to notice is that **this use of "may" requires a word order inversion so that "may" appears before the subject.** In fact, **"may" always appears as the first word in this kind of sentence.**

Now that we've discussed "may" and "might," look at the following mini-dialogs. Check which of **Person B's** responses is acceptable and which is not, and then explain the reasons for your decisions:

Dialog 1

> **A:** Might I ask you a favor?
> **B: Of course you might.**
> ☐ acceptable   ☐ unacceptable

Dialog 2

> **A:** Might I ask you a favor?
> **B: Of course you may.**
> ☐ acceptable   ☐ unacceptable

_____

_____

_____

Person B's response in **Dialog 1** is **unacceptable.** The reason is that we can use "might" in a super-polite request when we <u>ask for</u> permission, but we don't use it when we <u>give</u> permission since it wouldn't be appropriate to be so overly polite in this case. Person B's response in **Dialog 2** is **acceptable** because "may" is the correct way of giving permission in the formal style.

MAY in a Nutshell

- **permission (in polite or formal context):**
  Ladies and gentlemen, you **may** now take your seats.
- **real possibility:**
  You **may not** believe what I'm about to tell you, but it's true.
- **hope that something will happen (in very formal style):**
  May you be blessed all the days of your life.

MIGHT in a Nutshell

 possibility:
You **might not** believe what I'm about to tell you, but it's true.

 an overly formal way of requesting permission:
Might I sit here, please?

 an indirect way of making a suggestion:
If the regular doctors can't help, he **might** try a chiropractor.

SHOULD / OUGHT TO

It's time for another dialog! Let's see how "should" and "ought to" function in the following context. We'll work with these two modals the same way we've worked with the others, so think of explanations for how they're being used and write them down on the lines whose numbers correspond to the numbered modals:

A: I hate commuting to work every day.
B: Yeah, so do I.
A: Where's the 7:20 train? It's 7:20 now, and there's no train in sight.
B: Yeah, I know. It **should**[1] be here already.
A: Maybe I **ought to**[2] take my car to work.
B: Well, I know how you feel, but the hassles of taking your car, fighting rush hour traffic, and parking in the city **ought to**[1] stop you! Just calm down and don't let it bother you so much.
A: You're right. I **shouldn't**[2] let train delays and all this nonsense get to me so much.

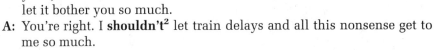

SHOULD	OUGHT TO
1. _____	1. _____
2. _____	2. _____

Should[1] and **ought to**[1] express **expectation.** Person B is saying that he expects the 7:20 train to be there already since the time is indeed 7:20. He then says that he expects all of those hassles to stop Person A from driving to work every day instead of taking the train.

Should[2] and **ought to**[2] have to do with **advisability, opinions,** or what's considered **a good idea.** Person A says that it might be a good idea for her to take her car to work. Then she says that she realizes it's not advisable for her to get so upset about such things as train delays. Both of these modals are what we call **benign advice** or **benign suggestions,** that is, when people use them to offer opinions or suggestions, they don't force their thoughts upon the listener or the person under discussion; we'll talk about a modal that can force itself upon you when we get to "must."

While we're on the subject of negatives like the one we've just discussed in the preceding paragraph ("I shouldn't let train delays . . . get to me."), there's a feature unique to "ought to" which doesn't happen to any other modal. Most native speakers, especially Americans, tend to use "should" in the negative (shouldn't) rather than "ought to" (ought not to); that's probably because "ought not to" and "oughtn't to" seem unwieldy to many people. The unique feature we're talking about is that when people do use "ought to" in the negative, they often drop the "to" probably to make the phrase less unwieldy ("He oughtn't say such things!").

Going back to whether we prefer to use "should" or "ought to," do you perceive any difference between these two modals when they both express expectation or advisability? According to prescriptive grammar books, "ought to" is perceived as being less forceful than "should" when expressing advisability, but not when expressing expectation:

You ought to get a job. (not forceful)
You should get a job. (somewhat more forceful)

The bus ought to be here already.
The bus should be here already. (no big difference)

The difference, however, is really quite slight, and that's why most ESOL grammar books teach both of these modals at the same time when they deal with either advisability or expectation.

There are even some native speakers who claim that "should" deals with straightforward advice while "ought to" carries a moral obligation with it. Look at these two sentences and see what you think:

You should call your poor mother more often.

You ought to call your poor mother more often.

It's safe to say that the choice of whether to use "should" or "ought to" in the previous two examples is really up to the individual. Always remember that each native speaker of a language has his/her own style for using the language (what linguists refer to as an *ideolect*), and that there aren't always hard-and-fast rules that we can give.

If you recall, when we were exploring "can" and "could" we said that we were going to get back to these two modals when we got to "should" and "ought to"—and here we are. Let's bring back the suggestions that the mother gave her daughter in that dialog which showed "can" and "could" as ways of giving advice:

> **You <u>can</u> get together with your friend, Nancy.**
>
> **You <u>could</u> clean out your closet or finish that term paper.**

What if we were to substitute "can" and "could" with "should" or "ought to" in these sentences? After all, they're all ways to give advice or suggestions, right? Well, let's see what happens:

> **You <u>should</u> get together with your friend, Nancy.**
>
> **You <u>ought to</u> clean out your closet or finish that term paper.**

Uh-oh! Even though all four modals can be used to give advice or make suggestions, there's definitely a difference between the first two and the second two. What do you perceive the difference to be?

_____

_____

What it comes down to is that **when we use "can" and "could" for suggestions, there's an implied idea that there are other options; when we use "should" and "ought to," however, we're clearly focusing in on just the one suggestion at hand with no implication that other options exist.** Quite an important difference indeed!

There's one last observation we'd like to make about "should," and this is one time when "ought to" can't be interchanged with it. As we demonstrated way back in Chapter 1 (see page 18), "should" can substitute for "if" in a more formal style conditional sentence:

> **If he arrives before 3 o'clock, tell him to join us.**
>
> **Should he arrive before 3 o'clock, tell him to join us.**

Troubleshooter

Even though we haven't come to the modal "must" yet, this is a good time to mention a problem that you may very well encounter with some students.

Some of your students will end up inappropriately using the modal "must" instead of using "should" or "ought to." This is probably because in many languages the same word is used to express these quite different ideas in English.

"Should" and "ought to" are modals which express soft advice as opposed to "must," which expresses a command, order, or regulation of some sort. People who have some kind of authority over others can use "must" when talking to them, e.g., parents to children, bosses to employees, teachers to students. It's not appropriate, though, for the employee to use "must" when talking to the boss or the student when talking to the teacher.

This can be interpreted as a linguistic problem, but it can also be a cultural problem—and we know that language should never be taught out of cultural context. Make sure you're prepared to explain why "must" is or is not appropriate to use in certain situations, and why "should" and "ought to" often work better.

SHOULD / OUGHT TO in a Nutshell

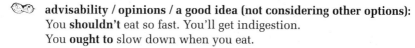 **advisability / opinions / a good idea (not considering other options):**
You **shouldn't** eat so fast. You'll get indigestion.
You **ought to** slow down when you eat.

expectation:
If her work continues to be this good, she **should** get a raise soon.
He **ought to** feel much better once the medicine starts working.

should = if (in a conditional sentence):
If the two companies merge, our stock will go up.
Should the two companies merge, our stock will go up.

MUST

We've now come to the only modal which we haven't dealt with yet. Let's do it just as we have the others, so get ready to write down your interpretations of "must" as you find it in this dialog:

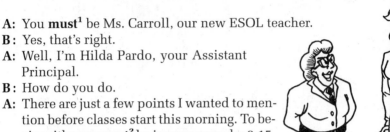

A: You **must**[1] be Ms. Carroll, our new ESOL teacher.

B: Yes, that's right.

A: Well, I'm Hilda Pardo, your Assistant Principal.

B: How do you do.

A: There are just a few points I wanted to mention before classes start this morning. To begin with, you **must**[2] be in your room by 8:15. And while I think of it, you **mustn't**[2] allow students to eat or drink in the classrooms.

B: Understood.

1. _____

2. _____

Must[1] expresses **a conclusion or deduction made from information already known.** (Recall how unstressed "will" can be used in the same way.) Ms. Pardo spots someone new at her school, knows that a new teacher is to begin working that day, and concludes that she's that new teacher, Ms. Carroll. We can paraphrase this sentence by saying *"I'm sure* you're Ms. Carroll, our new ESOL teacher." Of course, when we use "must" in this way, we wait for confirmation from the other person to be certain our conclusion is right.

Must[2] expresses **a requirement or necessity**, meaning that Ms. Carroll has no choice in the matter; she's obligated to comply or face the consequences. Even the negative of "must" in this use represents a requirement although it can also be interpreted as a prohibition.

In the last "Troubleshooter" that you came upon, the discussion dealt with the cultural difference between using the modal "must" when "should" or "ought to" might be more appropriate. When you teach "should" and "ought to," explain to your students that these are used when you give someone your advice or opinion about what to do, but that it doesn't mean the listener is obliged to take that advice. That's why we consider "should" and "ought to" as <u>benign</u> advice.

On the other hand, "must" leaves no options; when you use "must," meaning that someone is to do something, it's a <u>forceful</u> idea—sometimes too forceful if said to a person who's in a higher social or authoritative position than the speaker is. Remember, when hearing "should" or "ought to," the listener or person being discussed can take the advice or not; when hearing "must," the listener or person of the idea supposedly has no choice in the matter. True, you will hear native speakers at times say something like "Oh, you simply must see that movie! It was wonderful!" Of course, in this context, "must" isn't taken authoritatively; it simply expresses a strong suggestion that the speaker is making to a friend, for example.

Let's see how "must" can be used in other ways by looking at this next dialog. Write your interpretations of the words in bold on the lines provided.

A: Hello, Ravi? This is Selim.

B: Hi, Selim. What's up?

A: You know, I hear the surf's really great today and we can find some big waves for our surfboards. You interested?

B: But we've got school today.

A: So what? We **don't have to** be at school every day!

B: I **mustn't** be absent today, or my teacher will kill me. I've got a big test today, and she hates when someone's out and she has to give a make-up.

A: That's dumb!

B: It's not dumb. What **must** the teachers think of you, Selim, with your being absent so often?

A: I never really give it any thought—nor should you!

don't have to = _____

mustn't =   _____

must =   _____

Don't have to is a phrase which means **it isn't necessary.** This is totally different from the idea of **must not (mustn't)** which is **a requirement in the negative meaning something prohibited or not to be done.**

Remember to stress to your students that when we say something isn't required, we use "don't/doesn't have to," but when we say something is not to be done or prohibited, we say "must not" (mustn't).

Here are some more examples to demonstrate these points:

<u>deductions:</u>
He must be very happy over that news.
(We're sure he's very happy over that news.)

She mustn't be very happy over that news.
(We're sure she isn't very happy over that news.)

<u>requirements / necessities:</u>
You must be here by 9 o'clock.
(You're required to be here by 9 o'clock.)

You mustn't take this medicine without food.
(Do not take this medicine without food.)

You don't have to take this medicine with food.
(You aren't required to take this medicine with food.)

She doesn't have to see the doctor.
(It isn't necessary for her to see the doctor.)

As for **must**, the word is being used in our dialog in quite an unusual way. In this context, the question "What must the teachers think of you . . . ?" really means **"I wonder what the teachers think of you."**

MUST in a Nutshell

- **used for a conclusion or deduction:**
  Marry Arnold? You **must** be out of your mind!
- **used for requirements/necessities:**
  You **must** submit a note from your doctor if you're not at work for more than three consecutive days. (requirement)
  You **must** eat and drink in order to stay alive. (necessity)
- **used for prohibition / that something <u>not</u> be done:**
  An orthodox Jew or Muslim **mustn't** eat pork.
- **used in a question to mean *I wonder . . .*:**
  What **must** it be like on Mars?

Here are the rest of the *Teaching Tips* for the modals:

Teaching Tips

#1 Before class, create various situations about your students, other people, places, or things (a student's absence, glass on the street, a dent in your car, a bad grade, etc.). Let the students brainstorm responses to the situations using modals: "Paco might be sick." "Someone will get a flat tire if they run over the glass." "Grace should drive more carefully." "Marjorie must study very hard; she always gets good grades."

#2 Before class, create problems that contain a real-life conflict (e.g., You've just received a four-year scholarship to a very prestigious university, but you can't bring your spouse; the person you're engaged to is pressuring you to get married soon, but you want to wait; your father is seriously ill and can no longer work; you want to study sociology, but your family wants you to be a doctor, etc.). Put the problems on the board or on a handout. Divide the class into small groups and tell them to discuss the problems. Have them come up with solutions to the situations. Tell your students to use at least three different modals and have all the members of each group write down their group's suggestions. While the groups are discussing their responses, walk around the room and "visit" each group. When the problems have been thoroughly discussed, have each person in the group give at least one of their responses to the whole class. If you hear contradictory statements made between two groups while they're sharing their ideas with the entire class, note them down and go back to them after this activity is over. You can get lots of meaty material in this way for lively conversation practice.

#3 Divide the class into pairs or small groups. Give them copies of a television guide and tell them that they're going to recommend programs appropriate for various groups (children, teens, adults). After they've looked through the listings carefully, have them come up with their program schedule using modals whenever possible: "Kids shouldn't watch X, but they might enjoy Y." "An adult may enjoy Z, but I might not."

#4 Prepare a list of people that might need advice. Divide the class into pairs or small groups and have them decide what advice they'd give a newlywed, a teenager on his/her first date, a person entering college for the first time, the new owner of a large company, your English teacher, a student learning English for the first time, etc. Encourage your students to use modals.

#5 Divide the class into pairs or small groups and tell them they're going to invent a new game or sport. Have the groups write up the rules of their game/sport using modals whenever possible: "You must face each other." "You shouldn't move until the referee blows his/her whistle." "You must stay out of the game for two minutes after a foul." Have the different groups share their games/sports with the entire class.

#6 Create a questionnaire (teacher- or student-generated) about a relevant or timely topic (upcoming elections, environmental issues, exams, etc.). Have the students interview two or three of their classmates, students in other classes, their teachers, or people outside school, etc. and prepare a report on their findings. Questions should have modals in them (Should students _____? Would you rather _____? Could the President _____? What might the government _____? Should we _____ exams?).

#7 Prepare an undetailed map of a city (only the streets and any relevant natural landmarks like rivers, lakes, valleys, etc. should be shown). Provide a list of buildings that the city will have.

houses	airport	post office	municipal offices
library	night club	swimming pool	elementary school
hospital	theater	supermarket	secondary school
hotel	gas station	hardware store	jail/police station
bakery	museum	fish market	high rise apartments
zoo	train station	electricity plant	water treatment plant

Students will plan out the town suggesting where the various buildings should/would/mustn't/can't go. Let the students draw the buildings on their outline and then put them up on the board. Have various spokespersons from each group discuss their choices.

#8 Advice columns appear in many newspapers and magazines. The typical advice column has two elements: a reader with a problem writes a letter asking for advice, and a columnist responds to the letter and suggests solutions. Clip out several examples or write up several of your own. Divide the class into pairs or small groups and distribute the columns to your students. Have them write responses to the person who wrote the letter suggesting solutions to the problem. If students have trouble coming up with acceptable solutions, for homework let them ask teachers, native English speakers, students in other classes, or friends about what they might do. Encourage them to use modals in their responses.

SEMI-MODALS

The first thing we should do is list some of the semi-modals. Although there's disagreement among some linguists as to whether certain of these are semi-modals or not, we're going to include the following: *be able to, be unable to, have to, have got to, had better, need, dare, used to, would rather,* and *would sooner.*

The next thing to do is explain the difference between modals and semi-modals. Semi-modals work the same way as modals do as far as altering the meanings of verbs. Unlike true modals, however, semi-modals don't always function grammatically in the same way:

- Some semi-modals don't use the same form for the present and future as true modals do (I have to. / I'm going to have to. / I'll have to.).
- For questions, semi-modals use "do/does/did" as the typical introductory question marker (Do I have to? / Did they use to?). Others use the inverted construction typical of modals and the verb "be" (Is he able to? / Have I got to? / Need we? / Dare she?/ Would they rather? / Would you sooner?). One little note: we don't normally use "had better" in questions, preferring to use "should/must/have to/have got to" instead.
- For negatives, some semi-modals use "don't/doesn't/didn't" before them (don't have to / didn't use to), while others use "not" (haven't got to / had better not / need not / would rather not / would sooner not). One semi-modal, "dare," uses "not" in the present/future form (dare not), but "didn't" in the past (didn't dare).

We're not going to deal with each and every semi-modal in this chapter because most of them aren't particularly troublesome; what we will do, though, is make some passing observations about those that aren't troublesome.

Be Able to (Be Unable to)

Why is it that English has this expression which is synonymous with "can/ could" as long as the meaning is ability? Here are a couple of <u>ungrammatical</u> sentences for you to correct. Let's see how you correct the underlined parts:

1. **For that job at the United Nations, he needs to <u>can</u> speak at least three languages fluently.**

_____

2. **<u>Can</u>-ing speak four languages, he had no trouble getting that job at the U.N.**

_____

Yes, we know that these are two really bizarre sentences! And that's just the point. The corrections should be "he needs to **be able to** speak . . . " for Sentence 1, and "**Being able to** speak . . . " for Sentence 2. What observations can you make about why "be (un)able to" is so convenient at times?

_____

_____

In order for us to avoid such bizarre problems, **we use "be able to" instead of "can" after prepositions and when an -ing form is required**.

Along similar lines, there's a clever way we get around the problem of not being able to use two modal auxiliaries together, as you'll remember we discussed at the start of this chapter. The way we do this in certain cases is to combine a modal with a semi-modal. Look at the following examples of how this works:

We <u>must be able to</u> produce more food.

Nobody <u>should have to</u> go hungry.

Need

The meaning of "need," when it's used as a semi-modal, is the same as "must," "have to," and "have got to"; that is, something is required or necessary. Typically, in the affirmative and most questions, we use "need" as a regular verb with "to" after it ("I needed <u>to</u> see you." / "Does she need <u>to</u> apply right away?" Compare this question with the much more formal or even antiquated "Need she apply right away?"). It's in the example just cited and in the negative that "need" can sometimes be seen as a semi-modal. Look at these examples:

1. **She needn't let us know before Friday.**
2. **He need never know the awful truth.**

In both of the previous examples, "needn't" means "doesn't have to" or "hasn't got to"; in other words, something is not required. We should mention, though, that many native speakers, particularly Americans, will probably find the sentences somewhat atypical because "need" isn't commonly used in many dialects of English as a semi-modal, especially in everyday speech.

Would Rather / Would Sooner

These two expressions are used to indicate **a preference**. Some native speakers consider "would rather" more formal than "would sooner," but we think that's once again a matter of personal choice.

The grammar used with these semi-modals is a bit unusual. If only the subject is discussed, any verb that follows will be in its basic form (**I**'d rather <u>have</u> a beach house than a house in town. / **They**'d sooner <u>eat</u> chicken or fish than beef.).

However, if the subject is discussing a preference for somebody, (even him-/herself) or something else, the grammar changes radically (I'd sooner **he** <u>were</u> here than at home. / We'd rather **you** <u>didn't say</u> that word again.) The words we've underlined represent a grammatical form called the present subjunctive, but we'll deal with that in detail in Volume 2.

Mind Bogglers!

Now that you've survived the chapter on modal auxiliaries, let's see what you can make of the word "dare." "Dare" can be a verb, but it can also be a semi-modal. Study the following sentences and decide which ones have the verb "dare" and which ones have the semi-modal. Then explain how you decided one way or the other.

1. Dare I mention to the professor that his toupee is on backwards?
2. I dare you to tell the professor that his toupee is on backwards.
3. Amelia Earhart dared to be the first woman to fly round the world nonstop.
4. How dare you!
5. Don't you dare let that wet dog into this house!

Chapter 12

Troublesome Vocabulary

LAY? LIE? DO? MAKE? rob? steal?

LARGE? big? WORK? JOB? waste? lose?

a store? a shop? deliver? bring?

INJURY? DAMAGE? would like? like?

SHORELINE? COASTLINE? flesh? meat?

persons? peoples? HEAR? LISTEN TO?

people? come back? go back?

raise? rise?

GET MARRIED? BE MARRIED?

home? house? little? a little?

THIS IS TRUE? THAT IS TRUE?

borrow? lend?

garden? backyard? phenomena? phenomenas?

dirt? earth? soil? small? little?

blossom? bloom?

Out of the Frying Pan into the Fire.

You've now made it through eleven chapters of this book and have accumulated a lot of information on basic English grammar, so for this final chapter, we thought it would be nice to give you a change of pace.

Even though we've written this book to help out current ESOL teachers, ESOL teachers-in-training, or teachers from other disciplines who regularly come into contact with limited English proficient students (LEP's), nothing we've offered you will mean anything at all if it can't be easily transferred into your daily classroom teaching. The traditional "method" for training ESOL teachers back in the early '70s was to hand an unsuspecting teacher a book, fling open a classroom door, shove the teacher inside, and tell the poor soul, "Go teach!" It was no method at all but rather a real-life trial by fire, a sink-or-swim situation which was very unfair and very nerve-racking. If, however, the novice ESOL teacher had enough survival skills, creativity, and curiosity about the language he/she was now told to teach, the experience, though grueling and sometimes embarrassing, often proved to be an effective training ground in the long run. Take it from us—we were among those sink-or-swimmers! Even today this kind of trial by fire is how many teachers are introduced to and "trained" for the teaching of ESOL.

Throughout the previous eleven chapters, you were exposed from time to time to situations in which you had to assume the role of a teacher beleaguered by difficult, challenging vocabulary questions posed by bright students—the "Mind Bogglers" will remain fresh in your memory as having done this. The most challenging vocabulary questions deal with the differences between two words, differences that aren't always so easy to pinpoint and explain and ones which remain vague in the minds of even advanced ESOL students. We've ended each chapter with a "Mind Boggler" because it's such an important part of a teacher's job to give clear, simple, easy-to-handle explanations to students whose English language skills are still limited but who deserve straightforward, knowledgeable answers to their questions given in the target language.

We're going to save you from some of those trials by fire experienced in the classroom by your professional predecessors and give you the chance to sharpen your skills in responding to students' queries about vocabulary while you're still safely reading this book instead of beginning to perspire uncomfortably in front of perhaps sixty staring eyes as you attempt to create a plausible explanation on the spot. That's what Chapter 12 is all about—in fact, that's what this whole book is all about.

We've divided this chapter into two parts: The first part will list typical vocabulary questions that students have challenged us with over the past twenty-or-more years; the second part will offer our answers to these questions. Take each question and respond to it in the clearest, most concise way possible on a pad of paper or in your notebook. Then check your replies with ours and see how closely they match. Our replies are ones that we've found get through to the students with the smallest amount of head scratching, the smallest amount of aggravation, and the greatest amount of effectiveness. They may not cover every fine point, as well they shouldn't; they should simply be enough for the students to take in without giving them an overload.

We've set up the questions in realistic mini-dialogs between student and teacher (S = student; T = teacher). So put your thinking cap on, and have fun!

THE QUESTIONS

1. **S:** Can I leave early today, Dr. Killian? I have to go to my house.
    T: You mean you have to go <u>home</u>?
    S: Yes, home. **What's the difference between *house* and *home*?**

2. **S:** I need to find a second job.
    T: Oh? Why is that?
    S: My family is having terrible economic trouble now.
    T: I'm sorry to hear you're having <u>financial</u> trouble, Ali.
    S: **"Financial," not "economic"? What's the difference between the two?**

3. **T:** Well, I hope you won't need that second job for long, Ali.
    S: So do I. This is a big trouble for us.
    T: You mean a big <u>problem</u>, not *trouble*. **The difference between "problem" and "trouble" is that . . .**

4. **S:** Is the library closed now, Mr. Firsten?
    T: I'm afraid it is, Juan.
    S: Too bad. I wanted to buy my grammar workbook today.
    T: Oh! You want to go to the <u>bookstore</u>, not the *library*. You see, **the difference between the two is that . . .**

5. **S:** Mr. Firsten, did you read the newspaper report about all those old World War II mines that are floating all along the shore of my country?
    T: I think you mean your country's <u>coast</u>, not *shore*.
    S: **Aren't they the same thing?**

6. **T:** Does anyone in the class have an interesting hobby? Mehran?
    S: Yes, Dr. Killian. I build things out of toothpicks. It rests me.

T: Really? That's very interesting. By the way, you mean it <u>relaxes</u> you.
S: **Not "rests"? Why not?**

7. T: I know that most of you share household chores with your spouses or brothers and sisters. In your family, who does the dishes after dinner?
S: I do the dishes, and my husband takes out the trash.
T: If you're talking about from the kitchen, I think you mean to say the <u>garbage</u>, Jeanne. You see, **the difference is that . . .**

8. S: Mr. Firsten, I am very confused about "get." Everything in English is get, get, get!
T: I know, it's a very hard verb because it has so many meanings.
S: Yes! For example, **what's the difference between "get sick" and "get a letter"?**

9. S: Thank you, Mr. Firsten. Now that I understand "get" a little better, I have another question about it.
T: Fine, what is it, Yuki?
S: Sometimes I hear people say "get" sick and sometimes "be" sick, or "get" married and "be" married. **What's the difference?**

10. T: Did you know that my worry beads are missing, Yves? And they were a present that I really liked.
S: That's terrible. Who did you tell about it?
T: The security guards and the school's Lost and Found.
S: Who did give them to you?
T: That's "Who <u>gave</u> them to you?" I got them from Nagib, my Egyptian student last semester.
S: What did you tell the security guards?
T: That I think the beads were right here on my desk when I left the classroom for a few minutes. Maybe someone took them.
S: What does make you think that?
T: You mean what <u>makes</u> you think, not what *does make* you think. I don't know. I hope I'm wrong.
S: Why do I need to use "do" sometimes in questions but not other times? I don't understand it.
T: **Okay, I'll explain . . .**

11. S: Dr. Killian, yesterday you asked me to remember you to review pages 45 to 48 in the book.
T: Thank you, Kee-Sook. That's right, I asked you to <u>remind</u> me about those pages.
S: **Not "remember"?**

12. S: What's the matter, Mr. Firsten?
T: I thought I had some change for this vending machine, but I'm all out.
S: That's okay. I can borrow you some change.
T: Why, thank you, Reina. Oh, you mean you can <u>lend</u> me some change.
S: I'm confused. **Can't I say "borrow" for this idea?**

13.   **T:** Are you still very upset over what happened to your cousin, Kim?
      S: Yes, I am. He has a very bad wound from the car accident.
      T: No, Kim, that's an <u>injury</u>, not a *wound*. **The difference is that ...**

14.   **S:** Okay, thank you, Dr. Killian. Yes, my poor cousin. He'll be in the hospital a long time because of his damage, and his car has a lot of injury, too.
      T: Uh-oh. Kim, let me explain to you the difference between "damage" and "injury." **You see ...**

15.   **S:** Did the police find your car yet, Mr. Firsten?
      T: Not yet, Rashida.
      S: It's terrible that your car was robbed.
      T: That's <u>stolen</u>, Rashida. **The difference between "rob" and "steal" is that ...**

16.   **S:** You know, Dr. Killian, my neighbors are stranger.
      T: Well, that's true for many of us in this country, Wei-Lin.
      S: It is? That's terrible. How can that be for so many people?
      T: Well, did you know all your neighbors back in your hometown?
      S: What? I'm not talking about knowing my neighbors. I said my neighbors are stranger. They act a little crazy.
      T: Oh, now I get it! You don't mean *stranger*, Wei-Lin, you mean <u>strange</u>. **The difference between "strange" and "stranger" is that ...**

17.   **S:** Mr. Firsten, I won't be in class tomorrow.
      T: Why? What's wrong, Cleide?
      S: I have a large problem with my small girl, and I have to take her to the clinic.
      T: I'm sorry to hear that, Cleide. I hope it's nothing serious.
      S: Well, the doctors don't think so, but it's difficult for me to take her there because of large transportation problems.
      T: I see. By the way, Cleide, it's not a *large* problem; it's a <u>big</u> problem. And she's your <u>little</u> girl, not your *small* girl.
      S: Big! Small! Large! Little! These words confuse me. Can you explain?
      T: Of course. **The difference between "large" and "big," and "small" and "little" is that ...**

18.   **S:** Good morning, Mr. Firsten. I want to display you some pictures of my family.
      T: Wonderful, Astrid! I'd love to see them. By the way, you want to <u>show</u> me some photos, not *display* them.
      S: But somebody told me that "display" means "show."
      T: Sometimes that's true, but ...

19.   **T:** Any special plans for this weekend, Luigi?
      S: Yes, Dr. Killian. On Saturday night, I have an appointment with a girl in the Level 3 class. I'm very happy!

T: You mean you have a <u>date</u>, Luigi.
S: Date? **What's the difference between "appointment" and "date"?**

20. **T:** I hope that answered your question, Luigi.
    S: Yes, thank you.
    T: Are you taking the girl out to dinner?
    S: Yes, and then we will dance.
    T: You mean, you'll <u>go dancing</u>.
    S: That's what I said.
    T: No, Luigi, **there's a difference between "to dance" and "to go dancing."
    The difference is that . . .**

21. **S:** I read a very interesting article in the newspaper this morning.
    T: Oh? What was it about?
    S: About how dentists can be safer so patients don't get AIDS.
    T: And what did the article say?
    S: That dentists must sterilize all their tools with heat before using them
    again.
    T: That makes sense. Oh, and Anna, it's <u>instruments</u>, not *tools* that a den-
    tist works with. **The difference is that . . .**

22. **T:** Mr. van Straten, how's your business doing now that you've expanded?
    S: Very well, Mr. Firsten. I now have a full-time accountant and a general
    office manager, and their wages are very competitive.
    T: I'm so glad to hear it. By the way, Mr. van Straten, **we normally say
    "<u>salaries</u>," not *wages* in this case because . . .**

23. **T:** What's the matter, Birna? You look confused.
    S: I am, Dr. Killian. I don't understand the difference between "clothes"
    and "clothing." Sometimes I hear people use the two words in the same
    way, but sometimes not. Is there a difference?
    T: Well, yes, Birna. **The difference is that . . .**

24. **T:** That's a beautiful pocket watch you have, Ito.
    S: Thank you. And it's an ancient watch.
    T: No, Ito, you mean it's an <u>antique</u>.
    S: Oh. Thank you.
    T: How long have you had it?
    S: For a few years. When my grandfather got very antique, he gave it
    to me.
    T: That's <u>old</u>, Ito, not *antique*.
    S: Ancient! Old! Antique! I'm very confused now! **How are "old," "an-
    tique," and "ancient" different?**

25. **T:** Have you seen any good movies lately, Ailton?
    S: Yes, that's why I'm so tired every morning. I love movies, and I always
    watch the TV movies that start at 11:30 at night. I know I watch them
    too lately, but I can't resist them.

    T: You mean you watch those movies <u>late</u> at night, not *lately*. I think you misunderstood my question, Ailton. **You see, "late" and "lately"** . . .

26. **T:** I'd like to know what your tastes are in music, class. Pierre, what kind of music do you like?

    S₁: I know that not many young people like this, but my favorite is classic music.

    T: Oh, you like <u>classical</u> music? What about you, Sophie?

    S₂: Not me. I prefer rock and roll, especially the classical songs of the 1950s and 1960s.

    T: Uh, that's <u>classic</u>, Sophie, not *classical*.

    S₁: Mr. Firsten, why did you change my word from "classical" to "classic," and Pierre's word from "classic" to "classical"?

    T: That's a good question, Sophie. **The difference between "classical" and "classic" is that** . . .

27. **T:** Let's have a class outing one evening soon and go to a restaurant together so that all of you can practice ordering in English. Does anybody have any suggestions where we should go?

    S: How about going to that Thai restaurant near school, Dr. Killian? They have some very interesting plates.

    T: You mean <u>dishes</u>, Carlos, not *plates*. Have you eaten there before?

    S: I used to work there. I had a part-time job. I was the platewasher.

    T: No, you were the <u>dish</u>washer, Carlos, not the *plate*washer.

    S: **What's the difference between "dishes" and "plates"?**

28. **S:** Thank you for the explanation, Dr. Killian.

    T: You're welcome, Carlos. By the way, if we decide to have dinner at the Thai restaurant, should we make reservations?

    S: Yes, we should. They are busy every night. Many times the clients have to wait a long time before they can get a table if they don't have reservations.

    T: You should say <u>customers</u>, Carlos, not *clients*. **The difference between a "customer" and a "client" is that** . . .

29. **T:** Is anybody doing anything special over the holidays? Elizabeth?

    S₁: Yes, Mr. Firsten. I'm going to go camping with my girlfriend in one of the national parks.

    T: That sounds great! What about you, Hans?

    S₂: I'm just going to be at the beach with my boyfriend.

    T: No, no, Hans. You mean just <u>friend</u>, not *boyfriend*.

    S₂: But Elizabeth said "girlfriend" and that was okay. **Why can't I say "boyfriend"?**

30. **S:** You look very tired today, Dr. Killian. Didn't you sleep well last night?

    T: No, actually, I didn't. Sometimes I have a little insomnia.

    S: Oh, I never have that problem. As soon as I lay down and I lie my head on the pillow, I'm asleep!

T: Well, I wish I could fall asleep so easily. By the way, you should say that you <u>lie</u> down and <u>lay</u> your head on the pillow.

S: Could you explain the difference?

T: Well, **the difference between "lie" and "lay" is that . . .**

31. **S:** Did you watch TV last night, Mr. Firsten?

    T: No, I didn't, Diego. Why? What was on?

    S: I saw a wonderful movie about spies. It was a very good history.

    T: It was a <u>story</u>, not a *history*.

    S: Oh? Okay, *story*. It took place during the time of Napoleon.

    T: Really? I wish I'd seen it. I like the history of that era very much.

    S: Excuse me, Mr. Firsten. **Why could you say "history," but I couldn't?**

32. **T:** Tell me, Yoko, why do you look so tired every morning?

    S: I have a new work and it's at night.

    T: You mean you have a new <u>job</u>. Well, what are your hours at work?

    S: From 4:00 to 11:00 five days a week. But **why did you say "work" and I have to say "job"? What's the difference?**

33. **T:** Now do you see the difference, Yoko?

    S: I think so. Thank you.

    T: So where do you work?

    S: At a grocery shop.

    T: That's a grocery <u>store</u>, not *shop*, Yoko.

    S: Oh, yes, a grocery store. I used to work at a butcher store, so they put me in charge of the meat department.

    T: Oops! It's a butcher <u>shop</u>, not *store*. You see, **the difference between a "shop" and a "store" is that . . .**

34. **T:** Is anything wrong, Stanislav?

    S: Yes. I'm angry because I got two tickets driving to school!

    T: What happened?

    S: The policeman said I didn't stop completely at a stop signal, and he said that I went through a traffic sign that was red.

    T: Gee, that's too bad, Stanislav. But you've confused the words *signal* and *sign*. Let me get your mind off of your driving problems by explaining to you how you've confused the two words. **The difference between a "signal" and a "sign" is that . . .**

35. **T:** Let's talk about romance today, class. Have any of you done anything romantic lately?

    S: Leila has, Dr. Killian!

    T: Oh? What was that?

    S: She stayed up all night with her boyfriend and watched the sun raise.

    T: You mean <u>rise</u>, not *raise*.

    S: Doesn't "raise" mean "go up"?

    T: Yes, and so does "rise," but in a different way. **The difference is that . . .**

36. **S:** Mr. Firsten, do you ever watch that TV program "Wanted!" where they show criminals who the police are looking for?

    T: Sometimes. I understand that many criminals have been caught because their pictures were shown on it.

    S: Yes, and a person who calls in with information can get an award of $1,000.00 for his help. I really like "Wanted!" And you know, they've won many rewards for their service to the public.

    T: I'm afraid you've confused two words. You should say that the person who calls in will get a <u>reward</u> for helping the police, and that the show has been given many <u>awards</u>.

    S: I'm really confused. **What's the difference between "award" and "reward"?**

37. **T:** Is this your new baby, Sonia?

    S: Yes.

    T: What is it?

    S: What do you mean, "What is it?" My baby's not an "it"!

    T: No, no, Sonia. Don't get insulted. I don't know if it's a boy or a girl, that's all.

    S: You see? You said "it" again! My baby's not an "it"; he's a boy!

    T: Okay, okay, now I can say "he."

    S: I don't understand. **Why did you say "it"?**

38. **T:** Why didn't your brother come to class today, Min?

    S: Because he did bad on Monday's test.

    T: That's <u>badly</u>, Min; he did <u>badly</u>.

    S: Oh, yes. He did badly on that test.

    T: And that's why he didn't come to class today?

    S: Yes. He feels very badly about it.

    T: Guess what, Min. This time you need to say <u>bad</u>, not *badly*.

    S: Now <u>I'm</u> beginning to feel "bad." **When should I use "bad" and when should I use "badly"?**

39. **T:** Aren't you going home now, Seshu?

    S: In a few minutes. My friend Hiro is driving me home.

    T: But you've got your own car, don't you?

    S: Yes, but it broke on the way to class.

    T: That's too bad. I hope it isn't going to cost you a lot to fix. And it's <u>broke down</u>, Seshu, not *broke*. **The difference is that . . .**

40. **T:** Why are you so sad today, Dalia?

    S: My parents prohibit me from going out with Jorge anymore.

    T: Oh, I see. Why do they <u>forbid</u> you to see him again?

    S: They think he's lazy, but I keep telling them he isn't. Oh, Dr. Killian, why did you say "forbid" and not "prohibit"?

    T: Well, they're different. **The difference between "prohibit" and "forbid" is that . . .**

41.   **S:** These cookies are just great. Do you like some, Mr. Firsten?

　　T: Thank you, Masha. I'd like just one, please. And, Masha, the question should be <u>Would</u> you like, not *Do* you like. There's a big difference between saying "I like" and "I'd like."

　　S: Oh? **What's the difference?**

42.   **T:** You know, Paolo, I don't get too many students that have read as many books as you have.

　　S: Really? Oh, I love to read. I read whenever I have the chance. I even read while I'm expecting the bus before and after class.

　　T: You mean, while you're <u>waiting for</u> the bus, Paolo, not *expecting* the bus. **The difference between "wait for" something and "expect" something is that . . .**

43.   **S:** You know, Dr. Killian, I really enjoy taking English classes here.

　　T: Why, thank you, Nils.

　　S: It's wonderful because I have a chance to meet people from all over the earth.

　　T: That's from all over the <u>world</u>, Nils, not the *earth*.

　　S: Why not the "earth"?

　　T: You see, **the difference between the "world" and the "earth" is that . . .**

44.   **S:** You saw the movie "*E.T.*" last night, didn't you, Mr. Firsten?

　　T: Yes, Hiroko, that's right.

　　S: How was it?

　　T: Actually, quite good.

　　S: I thought it was very good, too.

　　T: No, I said it was <u>quite</u> good, not *very* good.

　　S: What's the difference?

45.   **S:** I'm sorry to annoy you, Dr. Killian, but I have just one more question about tomorrow's test.

　　T: No, Ursula, the expression is "I'm sorry to <u>bother</u> you," not *annoy* you.

　　S: Is there a difference between "annoy" and "bother"?

46.   **T:** Have all the plans been made for the class picnic?

　　S: Yes, Mr. Firsten. Everybody knows what they should deliver to the park.

　　T: Not *deliver*, Miguel, <u>bring</u>. You can't use "deliver" in that way.

　　S: Why not? **Doesn't "deliver" mean the same thing as "bring"?**

47.   **T:** Oh, no! Look at that big crack in the chalkboard!

　　S: This is too bad, Dr. Killian, but the school can get us another.

　　T: You mean, <u>that's</u> too bad, Rawia. The problem is that we're having a budget crisis right now, and a good board can cost something like two hundred dollars.

　　S: Do they really cost this much?

　　T: You mean, <u>that</u> much, Rawia, not *this* much.

S: <u>That</u> much. Do they?

T: I'm afraid they do.

S: That's a real problem then.

T: No, Rawia, you should say "<u>this</u> is a real problem," not *that*.

S: Excuse me, Dr. Killian. I should say "that" much, not "this" much, but I should say "this" is a problem, not "that" is a problem. Why?

T: When you use "this" and "that" as you did, the difference is that . . .

48. **T:** I'm sorry that no students can stay inside the classroom during a break, but that's one of the school board's regulations.

    S: I sometimes think there are too many regulations in the world. My parents have many regulations for me and my brother, too.

    T: You mean, your parents have many <u>rules</u> for you and your brother to follow, not *regulations*.

    S: I don't see a difference between "rules" and "regulations." Is there one?

49. **S:** I'm sorry that I was late again for class, Mr. Firsten, but I lost my bus.

    T: You mean you <u>missed</u> your bus, Juan.

    S: Yes, I missed my bus, and I had to wait almost thirty minutes for the next bus. I hate to lose my time like that!

    T: You mean you hate to <u>waste</u> your time, Juan.

    S: Why does English have so many words? **How are "miss," "waste," and "lose" different?**

50. **T:** Do you mind if I sit here at your table for lunch, Aïda?

    S: Yes, I do.

    T: Oh. You mean I can't sit here?

    S: No. Please sit here.

    T: Wait a minute! Aïda, I think you're confused about the expression "Do you mind." You should answer "no" when you mean "yes."

    S: Huh?

    T: Let me explain . . .

THE ANSWERS

1. **What's the difference between *house* and *home*?**

    House usually refers simply to a structure, a building; *home* has an emotional attachment that *house* doesn't have. *Home* is where you feel protected and safe. In addition, a *home* doesn't have to be in a house; it could refer to a region of a country, a city or town, or anywhere a person or even an animal decides to live.

    Examples: — Most birds make their homes in trees.
    — There's no place like home.
    — I think my house needs a new roof.

2. **What's the difference between *financial* and *economic*?**

    We normally use *financial* when we talk about money or budgets in a personal way or about where we work; we use *economic* when we talk about the country or something on an international level.

    Examples: — Now that Karim is rich, he has a financial advisor.
    — The President has just appointed a new economic advisor.

3. **The difference between *problem* and *trouble* is that . . .**

    we can count *problems*. In other words, we can use *problem* in the singular or the plural. *Trouble*, however, is a non-count noun, and non-count nouns are generally not found in the plural.

    Examples: — Our company has two problems that we need to solve soon.
    — If we don't solve those two problems, we're going to have trouble with our creditors.

4. **The difference between *library* and *bookstore* is that . . .**

    a *library* is a place which <u>lends</u> books to readers who can take them home for a while; a *bookstore* is a place that <u>sells</u> books.

    Examples: — I have to return these books I borrowed from the library or I'm going to have to pay a fine for every day they're overdue.
    — Bookstores always do a lot of business during the Christmas season.

5. **Don't *shore* and *coast* mean the same thing?**

    Not really. The *shore* is the land that meets a body of water which can be an ocean, a bay, or a lake. Moreover, when we think of the *shore*, we usually picture that one spot where the land and water meet. On the other hand, the *coast* usually refers to the whole line of land that meets the ocean or other very large body of water such as a gulf.

    Examples: — We just bought a little house on the shore of Lake Lucerne.
    — Government marine patrols search for drug smugglers all along the coast.

6. **What's the difference between *rest* and *relax*?**

    You *rest* when you're physically tired. You might want to lie down and take a nap, or sit down and just do nothing for a while. You *relax* when you do some activity such as a hobby or sport that frees you from tension or takes your mind off of problems.

> Examples: — I was so tired after planting all those rose bushes that I went back into the house and lay down to rest.
> — Some people relax on the weekends by playing tennis.

7. **The difference between *garbage* and *trash* is that . . .**

we usually use the word *garbage* to mean any food or empty food cans, boxes, or wrappers that we've decided to throw out, while *trash* means anything else that we decide to throw out. Another word for *trash* is *rubbish*.

> Examples: — We have to keep a tight lid on the garbage can in our kitchen because our dog loves to go through it after dinner to find scraps.
> — I had so much trash after cleaning out the closets that I didn't know where to put it all until I could get rid of it.

8. **What's the difference between *get sick* and *get a letter*?**

Even though we use *get* in both of these phrases, the word means completely different things. In the phrase get *sick*, the verb means "become"; in the phrase *get a letter*, the verb means "receive" or "obtain."

There's a simple rule that can help you remember when *get* means "become" and when it means "receive":

get + an adjective = become / get + a noun = receive

get thirsty	get a message
get angry	get a present
get busy	get a prize

9. **What's the difference between *get* married and *be* married?**

As we said in No. 8, *get* means "become" when it's followed by an adjective. The word *become* means that there's a change in a condition or state of being; in other words, something that existed previously is now being changed. The verb *be,* on the other hand, deals only with the state of being at a certain time and has no reference to what conditions were like before.

> Examples: — Antonio got angry with Sara when she embarrassed him.
> (= the moment when his mood changed)
> — Antonio was angry with Sara for a couple of days.
> (= the period of time that his anger lasted)

10. **When do we use *do* and when don't we use *do* in wh-questions?**

These four wh-words, *where, when, why,* and *how* (excluding "how much" and "how many"), always require the question auxiliary words *do, does,* or *did* when the question is in the simple present or simple past.

> Examples: — **Where did** you go last night?
> — **When do** tulips bloom?
> — **Why does** he get here so late every day?
> — **How do** you say "hello" in Amharic?

These other wh-words, *who, whose, what, which, how much,* and *how many* don't always require the auxiliary.

The rules that govern when we use *do, does,* and *did* and when we don't are as follows:

a) If one of these wh-words is the <u>subject</u> in the question, we don't use the auxiliary *do, does,* or *did.*

> Examples: — Who **gave** you the worry beads?
> — Whose (mother) **gave** you the worry beads?
> — What **makes** you think a student took them?
> — Which (person) **took** them?
> — How many (students) **saw** the beads on your desk?
> — How much (stealing) **takes** place here every day?

b) If one of these wh-words is the <u>object</u> in the question, we must use the auxiliary *do, does,* or *did.*

> Examples: — Who **did** you tell about the theft? ("you" = subject)
> — Whose (worry beads) **did** you say they were?
> — What **did** you tell them?
> — Which (department) **did** you report the theft to?
> — How many (people) **do** you suspect?
> — How much (money) **does** a strand of worry beads cost?

Teaching Tips

#1 This is a good activity for the early days of a new course, especially if the students don't know each other. Before class, prepare a questionnaire that contains items that you'd expect them to see on an application form. Hand out one or more of the questionnaires to the students and tell them to find out the information from two or three classmates. Stress the fact that they can't just hand the questionnaire to a classmate for him/her to fill out. The students need to ask appropriate yes/no and wh- questions to get the information. When all the questionnaires are filled out, have the students introduce one another using the information collected.

#2 Have the students come up with names/occupations of people they would like to interview. Stress the fact that they'll actually interview one or more of these people, so they have to suggest feasible names and occupations. Some possibilities from your school are the lunchroom personnel, school secretaries, the principal, or another teacher; in your community these could be a parent of another student, a banker, a fireman, a farmer, or a businessperson. Contact some of the people your students have indicated an interest in and see if they'd be willing to be interviewed. Have the students prepare questions for their interview, interview the person(s), and finally prepare an oral report based on the interview. **Note:** If you're working on a specific vocabulary topic, say banking, a banker, a teller, and a customer would be the perfect people to interview. Students will then practice two things, question formation and the vocabulary that they're learning.

Variation

This activity is also one that's good in the early days of a new class. Before class, prepare a blank chart like the following one. If you don't want to prepare the charts, have the students make their own. To do the activity, ask the students what they'd like to know about their classmates. Select several of the best questions and write the information on the board. Have the students fill in the requested information about themselves and then have them circulate around the room and ask their classmates about themselves. Make sure that the students actually ask questions to get the information. It's not unheard of for a student to have classmates just fill in the blanks themselves without a word being exchanged! Let the students give oral reports on their findings after the interviews have been conducted.

NAME	AGE	HOBBY	FAVORITE FOOD	MARITAL STATUS	NATIVE OF	FAVORITE SUBJECT	FAVORITE BOOK	ETC.	ETC.
me									

#3 A crime has just been committed (your grade book has disappeared, the museum's most prized painting has been stolen, one of the students' cars was hit and no one has confessed to the accident, etc.). Get two volunteers to be the "accused" and have them leave the room to prepare their alibis. (Tell the volunteers that [1] one of them will be found guilty, so they need to prepare airtight alibis, and that [2] they need to decide which one of them will be the real criminal.) The rest of the class will be the "investigators"; their job is to prepare questions that will help to break the alibis of the accused. Because it's impossible for all the appropriate questions to be thought of before the investigation begins, tell students that they'll have to improvise questions as they go along. When you're ready to begin the investigation, divide the class into two groups and get the groups to sit as far away from each other as possible. (This will help prevent eavesdropping.) One suspect is interrogated by one half of the class while the second suspect is interrogated by the other half. Encourage note-taking; this will help the students decide who is really guilty. After an appropriate amount of time has been spent quizzing the suspects, switch suspects and questioners and repeat the process. **Note:** Because the two suspects are being interrogated separately, questions might come up that they didn't plan for while they were creating their alibis. They should be encouraged to answer them, but be aware that they may incriminate themselves. When the two suspects have been fully interrogated, have each group decide who the guilty person is. Compare results and then have the guilty party reveal him-/herself.

#4 Before class, record a news report on audiotape. At appropriate spots, go back and either erase bits of the recording or record static or other people speaking over those bits. The "appropriate spots" are those places in the recording which would take a variety of wh- or yes/no questions to reconstruct. (The following is an example of how you can alter a text: "Good evening, ladies and gentlemen. Tonight's news is brought to you from ***##@@&&%%** downtown. We'll have an interview with the mayor **##@@&&%%**. Now, . . ." The original script is: "Good evening, ladies and gentlemen. Tonight's news is brought to you from the new city administration building downtown. We'll have an interview with the mayor later in the program. Now, . . .") The students' task is to fill in the lost information by asking you questions.

#5 Record or create your own announcements typical of those given at airports or train or bus stations. The best announcements are those that are actually recorded at the location because they're often garbled and sound like they're in an echo chamber. In other words, they're "real." Prepare questions about the announcements and have your students answer these questions after they listen to them.

#6 Before class, write up a list of answers to imaginary questions. Your answers should be varied; in other words, they should be answers to as many different wh- question words as possible (e.g., [1] because of hunger; [2] 3.1416; [3] a device for opening cans; [4] 2,000 mi. off the coast of Chile; [5] 60 seconds, etc.) Have the students work in pairs to create the questions to your answers.

#7 Have the students bring in an item they want to show their classmates. The item can be anything that's important or interesting to them (a travel souvenir, a picture, or a part of an item that is unrecognizable

on its own, but when put back in its place is obvious as to what it is—e.g., a picnic basket handle). The student shows the class the item. Each student then thinks up two questions he/she would like to ask the owner. The purpose of having the students think up two questions is so that every student has the opportunity to ask a question if someone else has thought up the same question. The owner of the item then answers the questions. **Note:** This activity can get boring quickly if you plan to do it all on the same day. To avoid this, have volunteers bring in their items on different days throughout the term.

Variation

The previous activity can be done as "20 Questions." 20 Questions is a game where the object is to discover the identity of an object that one person has in mind by asking a maximum of twenty yes/no questions. To begin the game, students should first discover if the object is "animal," "vegetable," or "mineral." (An "animal" is an actual animal or a product made from an animal, e.g., a kangaroo or alligator shoes. A "vegetable" is any plant or plant product, e.g., broccoli or a flower arrangement. A "mineral" is a mineral or a product made from a metal, e.g., a piece of quartz or a wedding ring.) Once that broad distinction has been established, students can then ask more and more specific questions to zero in on the object. To help the students remember what they have learned about the object, write the questions and answers on the board. A variation is to let various students write the questions and answers on the board.

#8 Before class, find a picture that's vague enough so that a good variety of questions can be asked and answered about it. Divide the class into small groups and have them write up a list of questions they want answered about the picture. Exchange the questions and have the groups answer their classmates' questions. Return the answers to the original questioners so they can see what their classmates have come up with.

11. **What's the difference between *remember* and *remind*?**

Remember is something that a person does him-/herself; *remind* is when you make another person remember, or when something makes a person remember.

    Examples: — I remember that he left the restaurant before me.
                 — You remembered my birthday. Thank you!

                 — He reminded his wife to pick up her dry cleaning.
                 — Your sneezing just reminded me: I have to get a flu shot.

12.   **What's the difference between *borrow* and *lend*?**

Borrow means to <u>take</u> something from someone temporarily. *Lend* is the opposite; it means to <u>give</u> something to someone temporarily.

   Examples: A: Can I borrow five dollars from you until pay day?
                    B: Okay, but I'll lend the money to you only if you promise to pay me
                    back on Monday.

13.   **What's the difference between *injury* and *wound*?**

An *injury* is usually something that happens to you in an accident and it can be external or internal. We think of things like a broken arm or leg or a brain concussion. A *wound* is usually something you get when a sharp object penetrates your body like a knife or a bullet.

   Examples: — She received several serious injuries in the car crash.
               — The soldier received some terrible wounds during the battle.

14.   **What's the difference between *injury* and *damage*?**

We use the word *injury* when talking about a body, human or animal. We use the word *damage* when talking about things.

   Examples: — During the tornado, the Carters received some minor injuries.
               — During the tornado, the Carters' house received a lot of damage.

15.   **What's the difference between *rob* and *steal*?**

You *rob* the victim or place (a person, a bank, a gas station, etc.), but you *steal* something valuable (money, jewelry, documents, etc.).

   Example: Somebody robbed my house last night. They stole my TV, VCR, and
             some jewelry.

16.   **The difference between *strange* and *stranger* is that . . .**

strange is an adjective which means unusual, different, or not normal. *Stranger,* which is a noun, means a person you don't know. The person can be perfectly normal, but you just don't know him or her.

   Examples: — Did you ever notice that Clyde talks to himself when he thinks
               nobody's around? I think he's a little strange.
             — In the Hollywood westerns, nobody liked it when a stranger came
               to town; they were always suspicious of him.

17.   **The difference between *large* and *big,* and *small* and *little* is that . . .**

all four words refer to physical, concrete things with real dimensions, but only *big* and *little* can refer to abstract or figurative things.

   Examples: — You have a very large/big house. How do you keep it clean?
               — Can you fit that piano in such a small/little space?

               — Don't listen to a word he says. He's a big liar.
               — Just have a little patience; the doctor will see you soon.

There's one more thing to say about these adjectives: when you speak about a child, *big* and *little* refers to the child's age or maturity, not just physical size.

Examples: — I'm proud of you for not crying when the doctor gave you that shot. You're a big boy now.
— Her little girl is the teacher's pet.

18.   What's the difference between *show* and *display*?

Show simply means to bring something to another person's attention and let him/her see it, but there's no special meaning in the word. *Display,* however, means to put something special in a place that's made to look nice so that it will attract people to come and look.

Examples: — Dr. Killian, let me show you my report.
— When you go to a department store, you find lots of the merchandise displayed in glass cases or under special lighting.

19.   What's the difference between *appointment* and *date*?

We normally use *appointment* for business or formal reasons, although you can use the word at times for meeting friends. We normally use the word *date* when we're speaking about meeting or going out with someone we're romantically involved with.

Examples: — I have an appointment with my lawyer at 1 o'clock.
— I have a date with my girlfriend, Midge, at 7 P.M.

20.   There's a difference between *to dance* and *to go dancing*. The difference is that . . .

to *dance* simply means to move your body to some music, but *to go dancing* is the name we give to a whole social activity which involves going to a night club, disco, or some other place where you'll join other people who are dancing.

Examples: — Ah! They're playing my favorite song. Let's dance!
— I relieve the stress and tension I get at work when I go dancing with my husband on Saturday nights.

21.   What's the difference between *tools* and *instruments*?

Tools are normally those items which are used by tradesmen such as carpenters, plumbers, and auto mechanics. *Instruments* are finer in design and usually more delicate than *tools* and are used by people such as surgeons and dentists.

Examples: — Because some of his tools were old and rusty, the mechanic went to a hardware store and bought some new wrenches, screwdrivers, and hammers.
— A set of brand new surgical instruments costs a great deal of money.

22.   The difference between *salaries* and *wages* is that . . .

salaries are usually figured on a regular basis, normally a yearly basis. *Wages,* on the other hand, are usually figured by the hour. If you're out sick and you earn a salary, you'll still receive the same amount in your paycheck on pay day (that is, assuming you have sick days coming to you), but if you receive wages, you normally get paid only for the hours you actually work.

> Examples: — He works on construction projects whenever they need some extra hands. His wages aren't very good, though.
> — As an administrative assistant, she gets a decent salary.

23.   **What's the difference between *clothes* and *clothing*?**

When we talk about *clothes,* we usually discuss individual items we're thinking of or the particular articles that we're looking at or wearing. When we talk about *clothing,* we're usually thinking of the collective idea, not individual garments. Sometimes, however, the words are used the same way, so there's a bit of a gray area.

> Examples: — You don't need to pack those heavy clothes in your suitcase; the weather's warm where you're going.
> — Eskimos used to make all of their clothing out of the skins and other parts of the animals they hunted.

24.   **How are *old, antique,* and *ancient* different?**

Old refers to something that we've had for a long time or that's in bad condition now because of its age. It's a word that's very relative—what one person thinks is old, another person may not. When we talk about things that are *old,* we can use the word with a negative implication.

Antique (or *an antique*) refers to something that's old (one hundred to a few hundred years or so) and usually in good condition. The difference is that most of us agree that it's very valuable because it <u>is</u> old and somewhat rare. An *antique* can also have nostalgic meaning to its owner.

Ancient, on the other hand, is more than *old* or *antique.* It's something that's thousands of years old and, because of that, has a value that can't be estimated. Archaeologists deal with places and things that are *ancient.*

> Examples: — That jacket's really old. Why don't you throw it out and buy yourself a new, fashionable one?
> — You'll never guess what I bought at the auction! An *antique* vase from England that must be at least a hundred and fifty years old.
> — The *ancient* tombs of Egypt have revealed many fascinating details about Egyptian civilization 3,000 years ago.

25.   **You see, *late* and *lately* . . .**

have no connection in meaning, even though many students think that *lately* is the adverb form of *late.* You know what *late* means, so I don't have to go into that. *Lately* really means "recently," and I was asking you if you had seen any good movies <u>recently</u>, not if you had seen any good movies late at night.

> Examples: — He got to the office late because the traffic was so heavy.
> — I've been thinking lately about changing jobs.

There's an interesting secondary use of *late* as an adjective. We put it with the article *the* before the full name or title of someone to show that the person is dead: the late Greta Garbo; the late Mr. Kepler; the late queen.

Note that *lately* is normally used with the present perfect or present perfect progressive.

26.   The difference between *classical* and *classic* is . . .
that *classical* refers to some aspect or period of a civilization or culture which is recognized as being of superior quality and style and has been esteemed by every generation since then. *Classic,* on the other hand, refers to a perfect example of something. In this case, Pierre meant that he liked the European music which has been continuously recognized by Westerners as being of superior quality and style (e.g., Mozart and Beethoven), but Sophie was talking about those rock and roll songs of the 1950s and 1960s which have been recognized as being perfect examples of that sort of music.

Examples: — Every civilization has what it considers to be its classical period, an era that people look back upon with nostalgia as a time of great learning, art, and architecture which epitomizes the very best of that civilization.
— The music sung by Elvis Presley and Little Richard is classic rock and roll.

27.   What's the difference between *dishes* and *plates*?
We can use the word *dish* for more things than we can use *plate*. A *dish* can be: (1) the same thing as a plate if it's the rather flat object made of china, ceramic, or glass that we put food on and serve to each person who's about to eat; (2) some prepared food, usually a combination of things that have been made with a recipe; (3) in the plural, *dishes* are all of the plates, bowls, cups, and saucers that are used for serving food; (4) *to wash* or *to do the dishes* means to wash all of those items mentioned in (3) after eating.

Plates, on the other hand, only means those rather flat objects made of china, ceramic, or glass that we put food on and serve to each person who's about to eat.

Examples: — I just bought a new set of dishes made in Japan. Aren't these dinner plates just beautiful?
— Did you hear that loud crash coming from the kitchen? Well, I just broke a dish. Now the pieces are everywhere!
— We had the most wonderful dish last night at that new Mexican restaurant that opened up near our house.

28.   The difference between a *customer* and a *client* is that . . .
a *customer* normally is someone who buys a product (in a store it would be merchandise; in a restaurant it would be the food), whereas a *client* is normally someone who pays for a service (from a lawyer, a private detective, or agencies of one kind or another). There are notable exceptions, though. Banks refer to these people as *customers.*

Remember that we have special words for the clients of doctors and dentists—we call them *patients.*

29. **Why can't a man call another man his *boyfriend*?**

Remember how we've said on various occasions that language is a reflection of culture and can never be taught in a vacuum? Here's a perfect example of that. In English-speaking communities, it may not be considered unusual for two women to hold hands as they walk down a street or dance together. Women can also kiss one another when greeting or saying good-bye.

Men, however, have different rules of social behavior in these instances. In English-speaking communities, it would be considered unusual for two men to hold hands as they walk down a street, and they would never be seen dancing together or kissing. That's just the way it is in English-speaking societies.

The language reflects these rules of social behavior. The term *girlfriend* can be used by one woman talking about another and is simply another way to say *friend.* Note that there's no romantic implication when a woman uses the term.

For men, though, it's a very different matter. For some reason, because of the way English-speaking communities have developed their mores, there <u>would</u> be an apparent romantic implication if a man should say "my *boyfriend*" just as there would be if a woman should say "my *boyfriend.*" So, oddly enough, women have a choice (*my friend, my girlfriend*), but men don't (*my friend*).

30. **The difference between *lie* and *lay* is that . . .**
lie only refers to what the subject is doing, which means being in a horizontal position. *Lay,* however, focuses on the direct object, something you put down.

> Examples: — After work, <u>she</u> lies on her couch and takes a little nap.
> ("She" is the subject, and we're focusing on what she herself is doing.)
> — Please lay <u>the phone book</u> on that table.
> ("The phone book" is the direct object, and we're focusing on what is to happen to the phone book.)

31. **Is there a difference between *history* and *story*?**

There certainly is! We use the word *history* when we speak about events that took place in the past, usually events that refer to cities, countries, or civilizations, but the word can refer to a person's past, too. The word *story,* however, can refer to something from literature, the theater, or movies, and it's also used when recounting something that happened to a person.

> Examples: — The history of China goes back thousands of years.
> — She has a fascinating family history.
> — Let me tell you a story about what wonderful things happened to me on my last trip to Peru.

32. **What's the difference between *work* and *job*?**

Work is a non-count noun and a general term that really refers to anything other than *play.* We use the word for everything from household chores and garden chores to tasks we have on farms, in factories or offices, or other places where we earn a living. The word can even refer to the place where we earn a living.

In these meanings of the word, *work* doesn't have a plural form since it's a non-count noun.

The term *job* is a countable noun that refers to the specific tasks, assignments, or duties that we have, and since it's countable, we can use the word *job* in the plural.

> Examples: — He gets to work about 8:30 in the morning.
> — This work should be completed by next Friday.
> — I don't like my job, so I'm going to look for another one.
> — Because he needs extra money, he has two jobs.

33.   The difference between a *shop* and a *store* is that . . .
a *shop* tends to be relatively small and usually specializes in one type of merchandise or has some kind of theme; a *store* tends to be larger than a *shop* and carries all sorts of merchandise. Unfortunately, there are a great many exceptions to these neat-and-tidy definitions, probably because the way we identify almost all places where products are sold has become formulaic in English.

> Examples: a butcher shop, a hat shop, a flower shop, a barber shop
> a drugstore, a pet store, a shoe store, a candy store

34.   The difference between a *signal* and a *sign* is that . . .
a *signal* usually depends on electricity to function because it normally has a light in or on it. Moreover, it almost always has to do with traffic and doesn't necessarily depend on the written word. A *sign,* however, is composed of words or pictures painted or drawn on some flat surface. One notable exception is a *neon sign,* which has lights.

> Examples: — Stop the car! Don't you see the railroad signal flashing?
> — In the U.S., a stop sign is always octagonal in shape.

35.   The difference between *rise* and *raise* is that . . .
just like with "lie" and "lay," *rise* focuses on the action of the subject, but *raise* deals with what the subject does to the direct object.

> Examples: — The sun rises in the east.
> ("The sun" is the subject.)
> — He raised his hand to ask a question.
> ("His hand" is the direct object.)

36.   What's the difference between *award* and *reward*?
You get an *award* to honor you. It's a way for people to give you special recognition for something you've done very well, perhaps better than anybody else. Some examples are the Nobel Prizes, the French Légion d'Honneur, and the Congressional Medal of Honor. Awards are usually things like certificates, plaques, trophies, and letters of commendation. (The Nobel Prizes are exceptions because they include money, too.)

You get a *reward* as a way to say thank you or to encourage repetition of a certain behavior. A reward can be given to a person or an animal, and it always has a real, practical value for the recipient.

Examples: — Elmer won an award for coming in first place in his school's science fair. His exhibit was terrific.
— The Carlsens gave little Henrik a reward for finding their lost dog.
— When the Carlsens' dog does a trick well, he gets a dog biscuit as a reward.

37.   **Why did you call my baby an "it"? My baby's not an "it"!**

English is one of those languages that must have some sort of subject—even if only a pronoun—with every verb, unlike languages such as Portuguese or Italian which don't always require subjects or pronouns with verbs. When I saw the baby for the first time and didn't know what sex the infant was, I had to use some pronoun to ask the question about gender, and in English I had no choice but to use *it.* That's why I asked what *it* was, to find out if *it* was a boy or girl. Now that I know the baby's a boy, I'll refer to the little bundle of joy from now on as *he,* not *it.*

By the way, we have to do the same thing in English (showing that we don't know the gender of a person or animal) when making other questions or talking about something because English requires us to have that pronoun as a subject.

Examples: — Someone's knocking at the door. I'll go . . . Who is it?
— That's a beautiful dog you have. What is it?

38.   **When should I use *bad* and when should I use *badly*?**

As you know, *bad* is an adjective (a word which describes a person, animal, place, or thing), and *badly* is an adverb (a word which describes an action). Knowing when to use these two words isn't always so simple, but the key lies in the definitions we've just reviewed. A verb like "feel," when used the way it appears in our dialog, falls into the category we discussed in Chapter 2 called stative verbs. Because stative verbs aren't actions, they don't use adverbs to describe them. That's why we have to say "He feels *bad.*" The verb "do," on the other hand, represents activity of some sort, so it will take an adverb; that's why we say "He did *badly* on the test."

39.   **What's the difference between *break* and *break down*?**

When something *breaks,* we usually find it in two or more pieces, or at least cracked. *Break down* is a verb we use to mean that a machine or motorized vehicle has ceased functioning.

Examples: — The rudder of our boat broke when we crashed into those rocks.
— If that copy machine breaks down one more time, we'll replace it with a different model.

40.   **The difference between *prohibit* and *forbid* is that . . .**

prohibit is a verb we usually apply to what a government or other regulatory body says we aren't allowed to do. We use the verb *forbid,* however, when this command meaning not to do something comes on a more personal level. Sometimes, as with religious teachings, there's a gray area which we could consider a more personal level or a regulatory body.

> Examples: — The government's new policies on smoking prohibit passengers from smoking on all domestic airplane flights.
> — Our teacher forbids us to chew gum in class.

41.   What's the difference between saying *Do you like* . . . ? and *Would you like* . . . ?

The difference is that when you say *you like* (*do you like?*), you mean that you find something to be good or you prefer something; when you say *you would like* (*would you like?*), you're really saying that *you want.*

> Examples: A: Do you like vanilla ice cream?
> B: Yes, I do. It's my favorite dessert.
>
> A: Would you like some vanilla ice cream now?
> B: Yes, I'd like a big bowl of it, if you have enough!

42.   The difference between *wait (for)* and *expect* is that . . .

wait (for) means you're somewhere and you plan to stay there until something arrives or happens in the near future. *Expect,* on the other hand, means that you think something is going to arrive or happen in the near future, but it doesn't mean that you have to stay in one place until then.

> Example: A: Why are you standing at your front door, Fritz?
> B: I'm waiting for the mailman. I want to tell him that I'm expecting a package from home and that he can just leave it here at the door if I'm not here when he delivers it.

43.   What's the difference between *the earth* and *the world*?

When we say *the earth,* we're referring to the actual physical, natural astronomical object we call a planet. When we say *the world,* we're referring more to the inhabitants of the planet than to the physical planet itself. Saying "from all over *the world*" is really another way to say "from every country."

> Examples: — Those astronauts traveled around the earth hundreds of times.
> — Our rich neighbors are planning to take a cruise around the world.

44.   What's the difference between *quite* and *very*?

In order to answer this question, we really should look at a whole group of words or phrases that we call **intensifiers** and **adverbs of degree**. These are additions to adjectives and adverbs of manner which do exactly what the name "intensifier" suggests: They intensify the strength of the adjective or adverb of manner. Let's look at how they work by making a scale which goes from the most powerful way of describing an adjective to the most negative way of describing that word. As an example, let's use the adjective *funny*:

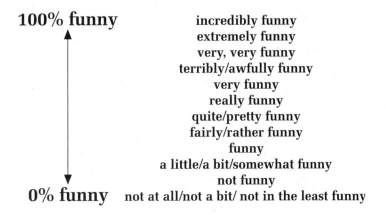

100% funny

incredibly funny
extremely funny
very, very funny
terribly/awfully funny
very funny
really funny
quite/pretty funny
fairly/rather funny
funny
a little/a bit/somewhat funny
not funny

0% funny   not at all/not a bit/ not in the least funny

So now you can see the difference between *quite* and *very*, especially when you compare them with the rest of the words and phrases in our list.

We have some other intensifiers, too, such as *greatly, absolutely, completely,* and *particularly.* We even have an idiomatic use of the word *dead* which is as high on our scale as you can go when it's used with a select group of adjectives: *dead serious, dead drunk, dead right,* and *dead tired,* to name a few!

45.   **Is there a difference between *annoy* and *bother*?**

There isn't a big difference, but there is a difference. When you *annoy* people, they usually become irritated or even angry because you're doing something they just don't like. When you *bother* people, it normally means that you're interrupting them from something they're doing or breaking their concentration, but it doesn't necessarily mean that you're irritating them or making them angry. You can also think of it this way: *annoy* can carry a stronger idea with it than *bother* can.

Examples: — If I'm bothering you with all these questions, just let me know, and I'll get back to you when you're not so busy.
— You have the terrible habit of humming while you work. I can't tell you how much that annoys me!

46.   **Doesn't *deliver* mean the same thing as *bring*?**

Yes and no. Even though their basic meaning is the same, we use *deliver* in a specialized way when we're talking about taking something from one place to another, generally for business or official matters.

Examples: — I can't leave the house this afternoon because I'm waiting for the new couch and love seat I bought to arrive. The store's delivering them today.
— When you come back from the kitchen, could you bring me a glass of water?

47.   **When you use *this* and *that*, the difference is . . .**
we're dealing with a very unusual phenomenon of language called **deixis**. To explain it simply, deixis has to do with our perception of what is "near" or "far" from us. At times, it can be literal, as when I say "this book" for a book that I have in my hand or "that book" for a book farther away from me. At other times, we can apply this concept of "near" and "far" to abstract things.

We normally say "<u>That's</u> too bad" because we're talking about a situation which we can separate ourselves from and "that" refers to the situation. (In the case of the cracked chalkboard, "that" refers to the terrible crack.) Moreover, "That's too bad" has become a formulaic or pat sentence which we don't have other ways to express except to substitute "That's" with "It's."

The way Rawia used "this much" when referring to the amount of money needed to replace the board was incorrect; she should say "that much" because she doesn't have the money in front of her—she's not looking at the actual money as she speaks. If, on the other hand, Rawia has two hundred dollars spread out in front of her or is holding a receipt in her hand, she can say "this much."

When Rawia says "That's a real problem," she's distancing herself and the teacher from the problem, but the teacher feels that the problem is *their* problem and is going to affect them immediately and personally; that's why the teacher says "<u>This</u> is a real problem" to bring it closer to them.

Another interesting way deixis can be noticed is in the response "That's true." When someone has made a statement that you agree with, you say "<u>That's</u> true" because the other person said it, not you. In recent years, however, many people have started saying "This is true," and even though it isn't the standard response, people are probably using "this" instead of "that" to show even greater agreement with what the other person has said by bringing it *closer.*

48.   **I don't see a difference between *rules* and *regulations.* Is there one?**
There certainly is! *Rules* are guidelines we use for behavior or how to do something. They're also less formalized and can be more personal as with a parent and child or teacher and students. *Regulations* are formalized and are like orders coming from some institutionalized authority such as a school, a branch of the military, or a section of the government.

Examples: — Our teacher has a rule that we can't use the classroom pencil sharpener while someone is talking in class.
        — It's a school regulation that students aren't allowed to leave school until 3 P.M.

49.   **How are *miss, waste,* and *lose* different?**
These verbs can be quite confusing to many students whose languages may only have one verb or two for our three in English.

Miss, as it's being used in our dialog, means not reaching something or somebody or not making contact with something or somebody. *Waste* means to use something in an unproductive way or to use it badly or unwisely. *Lose* means be unable to/can't find; it also means the opposite of *win.*

Examples: — Because I walked just a bit too slowly to the bus stop, I missed the bus by maybe a minute.
— Even though he's a college graduate, he's decided to work in a fast-food restaurant. All that education, wasted!
— Has anybody seen my keys? I think I've lost them.
— I'm sorry to say that they lost a lot of money at the casino.

50.   **With the expression *Do you mind . . . ?*, you should say "no" when you mean "yes."**
This tends to be a hard expression for students to figure out and respond to appropriately. What they need to understand is that the verb *mind* means *to object to* or *to object if . . .* So, "Do you mind?" really means "Do you object?" Once the students understand this, they shouldn't have so much trouble responding appropriately to the question.

Examples: A: Would you mind waiting outside?
(Do you object to waiting outside?)
B: Yes, I mind! I'd rather stay right here!
(Yes, I object!)

A: Do you mind if I sit here?
(Do you object if I sit here?)
B: No. / Not at all.
(No, I don't object. = It's all right.)

Mind Bogglers!

1.   As far as the kinds of words that follow them, what's the difference between **prefer** and **would rather?**

2.   We can say: *We use a saw to cut down trees.*

We can also say: *We use a saw for cutting down trees.*

We can say: *I've come to this school to learn English.*

But we can't say: *I've come to this school for learning English.*

Why not?

APPENDIX 1

Picture Files

The single most useful teaching aid you can have is a picture file, which doesn't cost much to make. All you need is magazines, some glue, sturdy paper or other backing material, and a pair of scissors.

PUTTING YOUR FILE TOGETHER

Choose magazines that have lots of pictures and cut out anything you find of interest. Don't overlook simple ones because even the simplest may have various teaching points to focus on. Use large pictures in front of the entire class; use large or small ones for individual or small group work. Trim the edges and glue the pictures onto sturdy backing sheets. (Construction paper or tag board is excellent for this.) On the back of each mounted picture, list the teaching points that the picture can be used for.

Let's take a look at one picture that we took out of a magazine and we'll show you what teaching points we can use it for.

Courtesy of Quaker Oats Company.

Vocabulary Items

School:
—teacher, student, desk, notebook, book, textbook, pencil
Colors:
—red, blue, green, orange, purple, brown

Grammar Points

Present Progressive:
— He's pointing, writing, sitting, standing, lecturing, listening, smacking his lips, wearing a cap/glasses
Count and Non-count Nouns:
—paper, a piece of paper, papers, hair, glasses
Active and Passive Voice:
—The teacher is lecturing about "Kibbles and Bits."
—An eager student is taking notes.
—Are the different flavors being mentioned?
—Medley, Inc. published the biology book.
—The biology book was published by Medley, Inc.
Past Tense:
—The lesson started 30 minutes ago.
—He wrote "bits" 8 times.
Simple Present:
—Dogs love "Kibbles and Bits."
—Good students take complete notes.
Present Perfect:
—The professor has taught this lesson many times.
Present Perfect Progressive:
—The professor's been lecturing for 30 minutes.
Wish vs. Hope:
—The student wishes that he were at lunch right now.
—The student hopes the lesson ends soon.
Modals:
—The professor says that dogs should be fed "Kibbles and Bits."
Prepositions:
—on the chair, at his desk, on the wall, under the pictures, at the podium, to the chart, on the chart, in front of the class

Pronunciation

/ɪ/ **vs.** /i/:
   —/ɪ/: bit, sit, listen, lip
   —/i/: seat, see, read

/s /, /z/, vs. /ɪz/:
  —/ s /: books, caps, talks, points
  —/z/: arms, eyes, listens, studies
  —/ɪz/: glasses, pages, teaches, watches

See how much you can do with one picture? But don't overlook simple pictures on plain backgrounds. They can be productive, too.

Once you have a stack of pictures ready to go, number them. Then make a master list of the teaching points you've found in the pictures. Next to each point, list the numbers of all the pictures which fit that teaching point. In other words, your master list will tell you what topics (grammar, vocabulary, pronunciation, etc.) your files contain and what pictures can be used to demonstrate these points. This way, when you teach a particular lesson, you can go through your file quickly and pull out the pictures you need. Any time you add to your file, you can easily update your master list.

Here's an additional comment about writing the teaching points your pictures represent on the back of the pictures. When you hold up a picture and the teaching point appears on the back for you to see, you don't have to strain your neck to look at what it is you're holding up. The students see the picture; you see the teaching point!

Why do all of this work to create a picture file? A teacher-made picture file suits you, your needs, your students, and the subjects you're teaching. Commercial sets of pictures could never give you this personalized touch at a price that most teachers can afford. Moreover, if a picture goes out of date, is lost, or is destroyed, replacing it doesn't require that you buy a new set; just find another magazine, and there you have your replacement.

RUBE GOLDBERG

In his heyday Rube Goldberg was called the "Charley Chaplin" of twentieth century cartoonists. So successful was he as a cartoonist in the early part of this century that he earned in one year what another equally famous cartoonist, Thomas Nast, earned in ten. What made his humor work was an obvious fondness for slapstick and the ridiculous. His most famous character, Professor Butts, defines his style of humor. His inventions always over-complicated the simple, and it's for this over-complication that we've included two of his inventions in the discussion about picture files. There's a lot to choose from when looking at a Rube Goldberg cartoon. Be creative and imaginative and enjoy using them with your classes.

How to Keep Shop Windows Clean

A passing man **(A)** slips on a banana peel **(B)** causing him to fall on a rake **(C)**. As the handle of the rake rises, it throws a horseshoe **(D)** onto the rope **(E)**, which sags, thereby tilting the sprinkling can **(F)**. Water **(G)** saturates the mop **(H)**. The dog **(I)** thinks it is raining, gets up to run into the house and upsets the sign **(J)**, throwing it against a non-tipping ashtray **(K)**, which causes it to swing back and forth and swish the mop against the window pane, wiping it clean. Reprinted with special permission of King Features Syndicate.

Back Scratcher

The flame from the lamp **(A)** catches on the curtain **(B)**. The fire department sends a stream of water **(C)** through the window. Dwarf **(D)** thinks it's raining and reaches for an umbrella **(E)**, pulling the string **(F)**, which lifts the end of the platform **(G)**. The iron ball **(H)** falls and pulls another string **(I)**, causing the hammer **(J)** to hit the plate of glass **(K)**. The crash of the breaking glass wakes up the puppy **(L)** and the mother dog **(M)** rocks him back to sleep in the cradle **(N)**, causing the attached wooden hand **(O)** to move up and down along your back. Reprinted with special permission of King Features Syndicate.

Appendix 2

More Strategies and Activities That Work

This book has dealt with some of the most troublesome features of the basics of English grammar, and Volume 2 will carry on with some of the most troublesome areas of more advanced grammar. A point we'd like to stress from the outset is that this book, even though a grammar book, was not written with the intention of telling you that you should teach grammar as a separate entity in your ESOL classes. On the contrary, we feel that grammar should be an integrated part of your lessons. A teacher can plan that he/she will teach the present progressive or articles or whatever this week and break the topic down into individual lesson plans. In doing so, however, the teacher shouldn't overlook an essential point, namely that **language should be taught in meaningful context.** You can handle the present progressive or modal auxiliaries or whatever is being taught very effectively within the context of meaningful situations that your students can relate to—and that's the key element: **situations or topics that your students can relate to.** We've usually been able to get to know the kinds of students we've had in any given class after only a short time, and if you can do this too, you should be able to determine where their interests lie as a group and what subjects "turn them on."

Even if you teach the grammar component in an intensive English program which separates the four basic language skills into different classes (grammar, reading, writing, conversation), you can still teach each grammar point in the context of something cultural, scientific, or topical. Use introductory dialogs like the ones you've found abundantly in this book. Create exercises that deal with the grammar points in sentences related to the topic. Plan activities such as the ones featured in the *Teaching Tips* that relate to the topic. By planning your teaching in this way, you'll be doing your students a tremendous service because they'll experience the grammar realistically and meaningfully, they won't feel burdened by grammar drill after grammar drill, and they'll learn something important for their growth and development besides language.

On the following pages you'll find samples of various types of exercises that have proven very effective in reinforcing specific points of grammar or in developing more holistic practice for the students. As you know, there's really nothing very new under the sun. The exercises selected for this appendix aren't revolutionary, but they're solid, reliable, adaptable exercises that you can create with very little effort once you've mastered their styles.

You may notice that the exercises that follow progress in a certain direction, and the reason for this bears explanation. Over the years, we've found that the best language teaching methodology and most practical approach to teaching and reinforcing specific grammar points are accomplished through the use of **mechanical, meaningful,** and **communicative** exercises as championed by Christina Bratt Paulston and Mary Newton Bruder, two eminent leaders in the field of TESOL to whom all of us owe a debt of gratitude. These concepts deal with a "weaning process" in which the teacher gradually turns over control of the language to his/her students. This is how they work:

Mechanical.   The teacher has complete control of the responses and knows exactly what the correct ones should be. There's only one possible correct response to each item. The students have no choices to make. They plug in some words or carry out a transformation, but they don't even have to understand all the vocabulary in order to do the exercises correctly.

Example: *Make this sentence negative:*

> He **likes** to study the environment.

> He **doesn't like** to study the environment.

Meaningful.   The teacher relinquishes some control of the responses but knows that there's a limited number of correct ones and can anticipate what they'll be. The students now have a few choices to make, which may change the meaning of their responses to some degree, thereby allowing them to show some individuality. The students assume partial responsibility for the utterances they produce.

Example: *Fill in the blank:*

> The ozone layer _____ disappear.
> 's going to / isn't going to / will (won't) / might (not) / may (not)

Communicative.   The teacher relinquishes all control of the responses and can't always anticipate what they'll be. The students are now in complete control of their responses and can be as individual as they wish. They now assume full responsibility for the utterances they produce.

Example 1: (T=teacher; S=student)

>   T: *Isn't it awful that the rain forests are being destroyed?*
>   S₁: I know it.
>   S₂: Why don't we do something about it?
>   S₃: I'm going to write to my government.
>   S₄: That's a good idea.

Example 2:   T: *I had a great weekend. How about you?*
                S$_1$:   It wasn't so good. I had to work.
                S$_2$:   It was fine. I went to a great party.

SLOT SUBSTITUTIONS

This type of exercise is to be used for <u>oral</u> practice. In these exercises, the teacher does the following:

1.   models the basic structure
2.   has the class repeat the model
3.   calls out the first substitution(s)
4.   calls on a student to insert the substitution(s)
5.   calls out the second substitution(s), etc.

Why use slot substitutions? Actually, there are lots of good reasons. To begin with, they help sensitize the students to English word order. (You have to know where words can be inserted in order to give correct responses.) Second, they're wonderful for listening comprehension. (If you don't hear it right, you can't repeat it right.) Third, they sensitize the students to changes that many kinds of words must make to conform to the new versions of the sentences. Here's what we mean:

T: He**'s** going to the dentist tomorrow.   THEY

S: **They're** going to the dentist tomorrow.   YESTERDAY

S: They **went** to the dentist **yesterday.**

Single Slot Substitution

(**T** = teacher;   **Ss** = whole class;   **S** = student)

T: I'll probably stay home this evening.

Ss: I'll probably stay home this evening.

T: go to a movie

S$_1$: I'll probably go to a movie this evening.

T: write some letters

S$_2$: I'll probably write some letters this evening.

T: watch TV

S$_3$: I'll probably watch TV this evening.

Double Slot Substitution

T: She bought a hat last week.

Ss: She bought a hat last week.

T: you / dress

S₁: You bought a dress last week.

T: I / jacket

S₂: I bought a jacket last week.

T: the neighbors / car

S₃: The neighbors bought a car last week.

Multiple Slot Substitution*

T: Her blouse has flowers on the front.

Ss: Her blouse has flowers on the front.

T: his shirt / buttons / cuffs

S₁: His shirt has buttons on the cuffs.

T: my jacket / a dragon / back

S₂: My jacket has a dragon on the back.

T: their shoes / taps / heels

S₃: Their shoes have taps on the heels.

Moving Slot Substitution

T: He's going to a movie tonight.

Ss: He's going to a movie tonight.

T: show

S₁: He's going to a show tonight.

T: last night

S₂: He went to a show last night.

T: they

S₃: They went to a show last night.

*Go cautiously with the multiple slot substitutions. After all, there are three pieces of information for the students to remember in each item, and lower level students will probably find these too tough.

CLOZE PROCEDURES

Another type of exercise that should become a "staple" to language teachers is called the *cloze procedure*, and it can play a very important role in mechanical and meaningful exercises. Actually, there are two types of cloze, the pure cloze and the modified cloze. This is how you create them:

Pure Cloze.   Take any passage (or create your own) that's as close to 350 words in length as you can get. Leave the first and last sentences intact. Beginning with the second sentence, take out every 5th, 6th, or 7th word and replace it with a blank. All your blanks should be of equal length. It's a more difficult exercise if every 5th word is omitted than if every 7th word is omitted. You'll probably prefer to eliminate every 7th word.

As far as correcting the cloze exercises that the students have completed, there are two lines of thought on the subject. Some people insist that only the exact word that was eliminated should be accepted as the correct answer. Others, however, argue that any word which completes the idea appropriately should be accepted.

Just in case you'd like to know, here's the current thinking on the two methods of correction just mentioned. Accepting any appropriate word while correcting a cloze seems, at least on the surface, the only fair way to go. Why shouldn't teachers accept any answer that works? Why should students be penalized for not being able to read the mind of the person who wrote the text? Here's why:

1. Accepting any appropriate word is much harder to correct because the teacher needs to keep in mind the entire context while trying to focus on each answer;
2. Correcting in this way takes a lot more time; and,
3. Using this method is only slightly more statistically reliable. So you be the judge.

The most important use of pure cloze procedures is to test your students' overall mastery of the language (whole language). Since a blank may be in the place of any kind of word, only the overall competence and comprehension that your students have will allow them to figure out what possible item can go in each blank.

Modified Cloze.   Write your own sentences or passages in which you plan to focus on any given point of grammar. The length of the sentences or the whole passage depends on your knowledge of what your students can handle. If you're dealing with prepositions or articles or the like, eliminate whatever words are being targeted and keep the blanks equal in length throughout. If you're dealing with verbs, draw in each blank and write the verb to be used in parentheses before or after the blank. The students will quickly learn that they're to use the verbs in parentheses to fill in the blanks.

As for correcting, a rule of thumb is that any appropriate words or forms of verbs that work to complete the sentences are acceptable.

Some Tips About Cloze Procedures

1. Don't "spoonfeed" your students. For example, don't tell them in the parentheses to use a negative form of a verb; let them figure that out through the context. (Of course, make sure that the context is clear.)

2. Don't focus on more than one discrete point in a <u>modified</u> cloze procedure. In other words, don't eliminate prepositions in the same exercise in which you eliminate verbs. Don't blur your focus.

3. Always treat two-word- or three-word verbs (phrasal verbs) as single entities so that your students will view them in this way. For example, don't put the verb "look" in parentheses and its allied preposition outside:

_____ (look) at

_____ (look) for

It's always better for the students to view phrasal verbs as whole items and learn them in that way:

_____ (look at)

_____ (watch out for)

4. Tell your students to read <u>everything</u> at least twice before filling in any of the blanks. This is important for them to get an idea of the context. If they don't do this first, they'll probably make avoidable mistakes.

That's all we have to say about these exercises. Following are some examples of cloze procedures. We hope that you find them to be useful, clear examples of the kinds of exercises you can easily create for your classes. By the way, if you'd like to, feel free to copy them out of this book and use them in class to get you started.

PURE CLOZE PROCEDURE

Fill in the blanks with appropriate words to complete the sentences.

Yuri had been in the United States for just three months. Now he was having mixed emotions _____ whether it had been a good _____ to leave Russia after _____ . He was sitting in the school _____ , having his lunch, and looking at _____ faces of all the other students. _____ were laughing, clowning around, and having _____ great time, but Yuri wasn't. He _____ understand English well enough to get _____ jokes, and he always had the _____ —even though he knew it was _____ —that the students were talking about _____ . It wasn't supposed to be like _____ . What had happened to all the _____ and enthusiasm he had felt about _____ to America? Why was he beginning to feel _____ towards all the other students? He _____ know the answers to those questions; _____ that things didn't look very good.

Yuri glanced up at the clock _____ the wall and knew that the _____ was going to ring any minute, _____ he didn't feel like going to _____ next class. It was social studies, _____ Yuri's inadequate knowledge of English made _____ difficult for him to follow the _____ or keep up with the rest _____ the class. He was seriously thinking _____ cutting class and just hanging out _____ the park near his home.

No, _____ had always been a good student _____ in Kiev, and he didn't want _____ get in trouble for cutting classes. _____ a deep, sad sigh, Yuri got _____ off his chair, collected the pieces _____ aluminum foil that his mom had

_____ to wrap his sandwich and apple_____,
closed his lunch box slowly, _____ started heading toward the
trash barrel _____ always sat near the cafeteria exit.
_____ stopping to throw away his garbage, Yuri _____
the wrappers up in the air _____ some legendary American bas-
ketball star about_____ make an incredible trick shot, and
_____ up hitting his classmate, Anna, right _____
the head with the messy wrappers. _____ expected a scene: she
was going _____ yell at him and call him _____,
but she didn't. She just started laughing, and for the first time since his arrival
in this country, Yuri felt a part of something.

MODIFIED CLOZE PROCEDURES

The first of these exercises is for discrimination practice between the simple past and present perfect. It's in the form of a letter.

Example 1

Fill in the blanks with the verbs in parentheses. If no verb appears in parentheses, think of one that will fit.

Dear Pam,

It _____ (be) a long time since I _____ (write) you. I _____ (have) any time to write you last month because I_____ (be) extremely busy. The school year _____ _____(just / end), and during the last three weeks of the semester, I _____ (have) a chance to do anything except correct papers, hand in final grades, and sleep. Besides all that, over the past week and a half, I _____ (write) twenty-two letters of recommendation for various students and _____ (interview) three candidates for the position as my new secretary. In my last letter I _____ (tell) you that I _____ (need) a new secretary, _____ ?

So, Pam, how _____ (your life / be) since we last _____ (correspond)? _____ (you / make) any plans for your vacation yet? The last time you _____ (write) me, you _____ (say) that you _____ (want) to get away for a month or so during the summer. _____ (you / decide) where to go? I _____ (decide) to stay home this summer and grow flowers in my back yard!

Write me soon, and let me know all about your summer plans.

Love,

Artie

Example 2

This second example is for practice with prepositions. The sentences have been numbered for ease of identification during review.

Cooking with Carmen

Fill in the blanks with appropriate prepositions. Some of the prepositions are parts of two-word verbs.

1. Carmen decided to make a chef's salad _____ dinner.

2. She took all the vegetables she had _____ her refrigerator and put them _____ the kitchen counter.

3. She got _____ a large salad bowl, a cutting board, and a sharp knife.

4. First, she washed her lettuce _____ the kitchen faucet and drained it thoroughly to get all the excess water _____ .

5. Then, she got a clove of garlic _____ the basket she had hanging _____ one corner of the kitchen, took _____ the skin that covered it, and rubbed the garlic clove all _____ the inside of the salad bowl.

6. Next, she tore the lettuce leaves _____ little pieces and put them all _____ the bottom of the salad bowl because she wanted the lettuce _____ all the other vegetables.

7. She cut tomatoes _____ wedges, cucumbers and scallions _____ slices, and some zucchini and American cheese _____ long, thin pieces, and placed all these items _____ the lettuce _____ the bottom of the bowl.

8. After that, she threw _____ lots of pieces of cooked turkey and ham and slices of hard boiled eggs and added some sliced radishes and mushrooms _____ the bowl as well.

9. Finally, she shook her salad dressing and poured it all _____ everything. Carmen knew she had created a work of art!

Example 3

This is a dialog for overall verb practice. It's a useful instrument for the recycling technique that we have already discussed.

Fill in the blanks with the words in parentheses. If there are some blanks without words after them, think of what you can write in those blanks.

Bob: Hello.

Ann: Hello, Bob? This _____ Ann.

Bob: Oh, hi, Ann! Long time no see. What _____ (happen)?

Ann: What _____ (you / do) next Saturday night?

Bob: Nothing special. Why?

Ann: I _____ (think about) _____ (have) a party at my

place, and I _____ (wonder) if you _____ (like)

_____ (come).

Bob: I _____ (love) to. Who else _____ (come)?

Ann: Well, I _____ (call) anybody else yet. You _____

_____ the first one.

Bob: The first one? I _____ (flatter)! _____ there any-

thing I _____ (bring)? Some drinks or food or something?

Ann: No, thanks. I _____ (already / take care of) all that. By the way,

_____ (you / like) _____ (bring) a date?

Bob: Sure.

Ann: _____ (you/still/see) that girl I _____ (meet) at

your house a couple of months ago?

Bob: No, we _____ (stop) _____ (see) each other three

weeks ago.

Ann: Oh, I _____ sorry _____ (hear) that. She

_____ (seem) very nice.

Bob: Yeah, well, that _____ the way it _____ (go).

Ann: Okay then. I _____ (see) you Saturday night around 8:30.

Bob: Great! See you then! Bye.

INCOMPLETE DIALOGS

Exercises like the ones that follow work best when students pair up and put into practice that old proverb which says "two heads are better than one." These exercises really get the students thinking. The students should first read the <u>entire</u> dialog at least twice before attempting to fill in the missing parts. Stress this helpful hint: **The line that follows the blank area they're about to work on probably contains information that will help them figure out what may work logically in the blank.**

Why incomplete dialogs? There are some very compelling reasons which make them such effective exercises. They serve as marvelous activities for reading comprehension, for sensitivity to language components, for reasoning, and for critical thinking. They also allow the students that special freedom found in meaningful and communicative activities. Here's how each of the skills just noted come into play through the use of incomplete dialogs:

Reading Comprehension: The students are forced to read thoroughly and find clues within the dialog which place the situation and enhance understanding of what's going on. Attention to punctuation is also very important as meaning can change depending on what punctuation has been used and where it's been placed. Here's an example:

A: Acme Plumbing. Jim _____ . _____?

B: Yes, please._____.

A: I'm afraid that job's been taken.

Let's see just how much there is for the students to deal with in the previous excerpt which was taken from a longer exercise. To begin with, the readers have to determine what the situation is (Are the speakers face to face? Are they on the phone?) Because of the way Person A starts the conversation, the readers should deduce that the speakers are on the phone.

Now, from what is referred to in reading pedagogy as "knowledge of the world," the readers must decide what Jim could possibly say in the short blank following his name. Thinking back to similar situations they've experienced on the phone when calling a company, the readers should understand that Jim is saying something to identify himself ("Jim speaking." or "Jim here." or "Jim talking.").

Next we have a long blank ending in a question mark. The readers must see the question mark (and it's surprising how many students fail to do this at first glance), realize there must be a question in that blank, and determine what would be appropriate for Jim to ask at that moment. Harkening back once again to their "knowledge of the world," the readers should figure out that Jim is probably saying something like "May I help you?" or "What can I do for you?" But wait a minute! The following line begins with Person B saying "Yes, please." That means we have to eliminate "What can I do for you?" as a possible question for Jim to ask because "Yes, please" wouldn't be an appropriate response to "What can I do for you?" We must conclude that Jim has said "May I help you?" and then Person B's response works just fine.

Finally, how can we figure out what Person B says next? To do this, we need to look at Person A's (Jim's) reply; that's where we'll get the hint we need to fill in the next blank. Person A says "I'm afraid that job's been taken," and this gives us quite a bit of information to work with. If he mentions "that job," Person B must have asked about a specific job, so we know that we've got to think of a specific job to mention in the blank. In addition, Person A says he's afraid that job's been taken, and this information leads us to the conclusion that Person B was attempting to apply for that job—otherwise, Person A would have no reason to make that statement. So we have these two pieces of information: Person B wants to apply for a job, and it's for a specific job he/she knows about, not just any job. (Everything we've been discussing, especially in this paragraph, demonstrates clearly how important critical thinking can be to reading and language learning in general.)

So what can we put in that final blank? Possibilities are: "I'm calling about the ad I saw in the paper for a plumber's assistant." or "I'd like to know if you're still looking for a plumber." or "A friend of mine told me he saw your ad for a secretary."

Notice how the situation we've been working with is deliberately left quite open; that's to allow the students to come up with different ideas.

While the students are paired up and working on one of these dialogs, walk around the room and offer assistance when the students seem stuck. When they're finished and you've checked over their work, have the best of the lot presented to the class in the final versions. The students will find it interesting to compare what they've come up with to what their classmates have created.

Sensitivity to Language Components: The readers must search out clues within the dialog which set the tense or aspect of verbs, and those words which students typically rush over, like prepositions, take on an importance which the students don't often realize they have. Just look at the following examples:

> A: Who are you sending that fax _____ ?
> B: Our main office.
>
> A: Who are you sending that fax _____ ?
> B: My boss. She said to get it out right away.

The students are forced to become more sensitive to language by having to figure out which prepositions will work in these blanks in order to elicit the responses provided. This is another use of critical thinking.

The following examples of incomplete dialogs get progressively more difficult. You decide which difficulty level is most appropriate for your students.

Work with a classmate and complete the following conversations.

Example 1

A: I just dropped my glove. Would you mind _____ ?

B: Why don't you _____ ?

A: Can't you see that _____ ?

B: Oh, I didn't notice. All right. Here you are.

Example 2

A: That's not your jacket; it's my jacket. _____ !

B: Aw, can't I _____ for this evening?

A: No, you can't. You should have _____ first.

Example 3

Tom: Hi, Pat! _____ ?

Pat: Oh, everything's fine, thanks. _____ ?

Tom: She's fine, too.

Pat: _____ ?

Tom: To that little restaurant across the street for lunch.

Pat: _____ ?

Tom: Sure! I'd love to have some company.

Example 4

Ken: _____ ?

Hal: Really? When?

Ken: _____ .

Hal: Well, that's wonderful! Let me be the first to congratulate you!

Ken: _____ .

Example 5

Sam: _____ ?

Ben: To the grocery. I need to get some dog food and paper towels.

Sam: You don't look so good. _____ ?

Ben: Not really.

Sam: What's the matter?

Ben: _____ .

Sam: That's awful! _____ ?

Ben: Just two days ago.

Sam: _____ ?

Ben: Actually, there is something you could do. _____

_____ ?

Sam: Sure, no problem. I can't guarantee anything, but I'll see what I can do.

Ben: _____ .

Sam: Don't mention it. And cheer up. Everything'll be all right.

Ben: _____ .

Sam: Well, see you later.

Ben: _____ .

Sam: You don't need to say that again. What are friends for?

Appendix 3

Games

Appendix 2 offers you straightforward, serious, time-honored activities that you can use to teach or reinforce any grammar point you choose to focus on; Appendix 3 offers you fun ways to deal with grammar as a change of pace. We hope you find these activities as much fun and as effective as we have over the years. The time and effort it might require to create the materials for each game will be well worth the while, and from then on, you'll always have the materials available to you whenever you feel it time to "lighten up" your classes. Enjoy these changes of pace!

TIC TAC TOE (BRITISH "NAUGHTS & CROSSES")

Tic Tac Toe is a good game for a practice or wrap-up session and can be played by students at any proficiency level. The object of the game is for one team to be the first to get three X's or three O's in a row horizontally, vertically, or diagonally. Here's how you play it.

Before class, select nine pictures from your picture file on one teaching point and prepare them for play. For example, if you're practicing the simple past, you may want the class to practice two points, the simple past and wh-question formation. But how can you get the students to use what you may have in mind for them (both regular and irregular verbs, a variety of wh- question words)? Look at a picture you have chosen from your file. Think of wh- words and verbs that can be used to make questions about that picture. Cut a sheet of paper into small slips. On each slip, write down one wh- word and one verb that the group can use to make an appropriate question. Now, using paper clips, attach these slips onto the front of the picture anywhere that won't obscure the scene.

To begin the game, lay the nine pictures face down on the floor in three rows of three. Cut a piece of paper into eight smaller pieces, writing an "X" on four of them and an "O" on the other four. Divide the class into two teams (the X's and the O's) and have the team members stand on opposite sides of the pictures. Flip a coin to see who goes first. Let's say the X's start. The X's choose one of the pictures, turning it over and leaving it on the floor for the whole class to study. The team then has to perform what is asked of them on the pictures. The team looks at their chosen picture and as a group prepares their response. Give them enough time to work out a response that is acceptable to the entire group. A single spokesperson gives his/her team's question and answer in order to win the square.

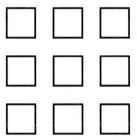

You should rotate spokespersons so that as many students as possible have a chance to speak and be accountable for their grammar and pronunciation. If you have a large class, you can double the number of spokespersons by having one student give the question and a second, the answer. You should let the spokesperson have two chances to give the group's responses; this way he/she can correct the responses if necessary and you're sure to hear what's said.

If the question and answer are correct, the team puts an "X" on the picture, which is now out of play. If the responses are wrong, the picture is turned back over and it's the "O" team's turn to play. They can choose the picture that's just been turned back over or they can choose another one. Remember—both teams have the opportunity to study and discuss the picture that was chosen earlier. This gives both teams the opportunity to discuss the teaching point even if only one team is actually playing that picture. This may seem like an unfair advantage, the second team having all that additional time to formulate correct responses, not to mention the chance of hearing an incorrect response, but this doesn't always prove to be the case. Frequently, the second team makes mistakes on the same picture, even with that extra time to study it. Part of the object of any ESOL activity is to give as many students as much opportunity to practice the language as possible.

The game continues until one team wins three pictures in a row or a tie occurs.

CONCENTRATION

Concentration is a matching game that does take a good amount of time to prepare initially, but once you make the playing cards, you can use them again and again. The object is for students to match as many pairs of cards as possible.

To prepare the playing cards, find thick paper (index cards, old computer punch cards, tag board, etc.) that can't be seen through when placed face down on a table. Cut the cards into a size that can be seen by all the students playing the game. We recommend that you use cards that are approximately 2$^{1/2}$" or 8 cm. square. You'll want between twenty to twenty-five pairs of cards per teaching point. If you have fewer, the game's not very challenging; if you have more, it's too hard (see **NOTE** that follows).

The Concentration game we describe here is a review of irregular verbs in the simple past and past participle forms. Choose twenty irregular verbs you want your students to review; put one past tense form on each card. Put the corresponding past participles on the other twenty cards. Now you have forty verb cards:

If you have a large class, you'll want to make additional sets of cards. We recommend that you have no more than six or seven students per set of cards, otherwise, one round takes too long and the students get restless waiting for their turn to come up again. Now you're ready to play.

Shuffle the cards well and lay them face down in neat rows on the students' desks or on the floor. It's important that the cards be in some sort of order because the students need to remember where they've seen each verb once it's been turned over. One student starts by turning over two cards and leaving them face up for everyone to see. If the cards match, the student gets to keep the pair, earning 1 point. The same student can keep on selecting pairs of cards until he/she makes a mistake. If the two cards don't match, the student must return them to the exact position they were in to begin with. This will help the other students remember where the cards are when it's their turn to play. Students keep on playing until all cards have been matched; the one with the most points/pairs wins the game. **Note:** Sometimes students aren't quite sure whether the two cards they've chosen make a match, so it's important for you to walk around the room and monitor the game and give advice when needed. This also helps if you have more than one game going on—we've done it with five games going on at once! Don't be afraid to circulate to keep everything going smoothly.

THE CLOTHESLINE

The "Clothesline" can be used to introduce, practice, or review grammar. Regardless of how you use it, what you need to begin with is a clothesline, a way to hang it, and some scrap paper.

For our example, we'll show how you can introduce yes/no questions.

Before class you'll need to prepare the vocabulary words you'll be working with. Each word will be written on a separate piece of paper, so don't choose words that are too long or paper that is too small. The back of scrap paper or used paper is perfect for this activity.

Your vocabulary for this lesson will include subject pronouns, the verb "be," and adjectives. You'll also want to have the appropriate punctuation marks on hand. Write each word on the bottom half of a piece of paper and fold it in half.

| he | they | is | are | cold | tall | ? | etc. |

Stack all the pronouns together, all the verbs together and all the adjectives together. Attach the clothesline, hang up the vocabulary in separate stacks, and you're ready to teach yes/no questions.

Stand behind the clothesline and ask the students to repeat the sentence they see after you've said it. Some teachers attach the clothesline to the board, but the disadvantage is that you might block the view for some students, even if you're off to the side of the clothesline. And, if you're in front of the line, your arms can get in the way when you're changing the words. If at all possible, we recommend hanging the clothesline so you can stand behind it.

Ask the students to repeat the sentence they see after you.

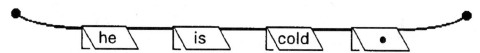

Begin showing students how English makes yes/no questions by rearranging the subject and verb papers. Don't forget to adjust your punctuation!

Continue these rearrangements and substitutions until the students are comfortable with the changes.

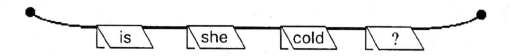

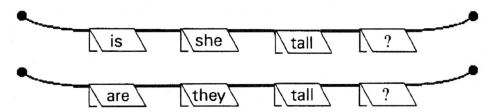

Note: You can make this a "substitution drill" by pulling off the vocabulary words that you previously stacked up on top of each other one by one.

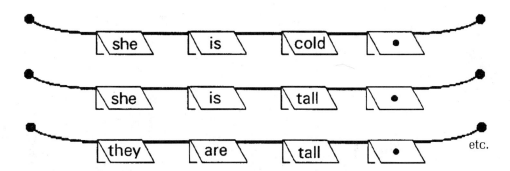

etc.

Later, you can test their comprehension of the new grammar by taking all the vocabulary and punctuation marks off the clothesline and distributing them to the students. Ask one student to go up to the clothesline and hang up his/her word. Then ask the other students to add their words one by one, making sure that each addition makes sense. Be sure to have plenty of cards with punctuation marks on them so the students will be forced to make both statements and questions.

ORAL MATCHING

Use this activity as a review or practice activity. Before class begins, you'll need to prepare questions and statements and their logical responses. They can be complete sentences or partial sentences. Put the sentences or parts of sentences on individual slips of paper and mark each one with an "A" or a "B" (A = beginning phrase; B = finishing phrase). Make enough pairs for each student to have at least two slips. This example will focus on two-word verbs.

> A: Where do I catch the #25 bus?

> B: You can pick it up at the corner.

> A: You look like you need a ride, Ben.

> B: I sure do. Can you drop me off downtown?

> A: Mister, this is where you get off the bus!

> B: At this stop? Thanks!

Make sure to remember that "A" slips and "B" slips can be either questions or statements. A closer look at the examples will show you what we mean. And keep a master list of your dialogs so you can monitor the students' responses more easily or prompt them when they get confused or make mistakes.

Hand out the slips and have a student with an "A" slip read it aloud. The other students need to listen carefully, but only the one who has the matching "B" slip responds. (A challenging variation is to have the students memorize the information on their slips so they can recite their parts of the dialogs by heart.) Continue until all the matches have been made.

SCRAMBLERS

A "Scrambler" is a take-off of a **Jumble**©, a scrambling activity that's fairly easy to prepare. Here's how you do it. Let's say that you've been working with your students on question forms. Choose a target word related to question forms that will be the final answer to the puzzle; since we're working on question forms, let's use the word QUESTION as our target. Come up with a sentence, phrase, or clue that uses your target word. You might want to use an illustration to help your students solve the following puzzle. Next, think of four or five words which together contain the letters needed to spell out QUESTION. These words can be, but don't have to be, related to the topic.

Scramble the letters of each of the four or five words. Next to each scrambled word, write a blank space corresponding to each letter. In your mind's eye, picture where each letter falls on the blanks when the word has been unscrambled. Then underline only those blanks which have the letters needed to spell out the target word. Now put the activity on the board or on a handout. What the students need to do follows the two sample Scramblers. The first Scrambler is on the topic of "questions" and the second, "holidays."

Do You Have Any Questions?

E A L T I O S   __ __ __ __ __ __

E R R E U I Q   __ __ __ __ __ __ __

C I R O N A G   __ __ __ __ __ __ __

E H A B E T N   __ __ __ __ __ __

WHAT THE 5 W'S PRODUCE...

Who? What? Where? When? Why?

" __ __ __ __ __ __ __ __ __ __ __ __ **responses**"

Scrambler

A C H I M R S S T

— = — — — — — = —

A A D E E I L N N S T V Y   ,

— — — = — — — — = — — — —

A E E N R S W Y __ __ =   __ __ = __ __ ' __

A A B D L O R Y __ __ __ __ __ __ __

Why we are doing this . . .

It's __ __ __ __ __ __ __ __ __ __ __ !

Now it's the students' turn to work. First, tell them what the topic of the Scrambler is. Next, have them unscramble each word and put one letter in each corresponding blank. When they have unscrambled all the words and filled in all the blanks, tell them to write the underlined letters out in a line and unscramble them to find out what the target word is.

Appendix 4

Mind Boggler Answer Key

CHAPTER 1, page 21.

STOMACH vs. BELLY vs. TUMMY

All three nouns mean the same thing: in scientific and conversational terms, the large, saclike organ of digestion located between the esophagus and small intestine; also in conversational terms, the area on the front of the body between the chest and the top of the loins.

Stomach is considered the standard word. *Belly* is considered an informal word when speaking of that part of the human body and can also refer to a fat stomach; it can be considered a standard word when referring to the underside of an animal. *Tummy* is a word normally used by children or by adults when speaking to children.

NECK vs. THROAT

Neck is the term we use for the outside, or visible, part of the body between the head and shoulders. *Throat* is the word used for the inside of the same part of the body.

CHAPTER 2, page 59.

SEE vs. LOOK AT

See is the involuntary action of using the eyes; when you open your eyes, you see. *Look at* means to pay visual attention to a stationary object or an object that isn't involved in any special activity. *Look at* is also the more commonly used verb in the imperative when we want someone to pay attention to someone or something.

LOOK AT vs. WATCH

Look at and *watch* mean basically the same thing: paying visual attention to some object. The difference is that *look at* focuses on the object per se, but *watch* focuses on what the object is doing. Some people also discern that *look at* has a shorter duration than *watch*.

CHAPTER 3, page 79.

1a. "Mr. van Straten is on the phone, sir."

The speaker knows Mr. van Straten personally or at least knows who he is.

1b. "A Mr. van Straten is on the phone, sir."

The speaker doesn't know this person named van Straten. We can communicate this fact to a listener by using the indefinite article before someone's name or someone's title and name.

2a. She's going to have a baby.

She's pregnant.

2b. She's going to have the baby.

She's in labor. / She's decided not to have an abortion.

CHAPTER 4, page 105.

1. **FEW FRIENDS / A FEW FRIENDS**

   Few = not many, and in the phrase *few friends,* there's a negative or unhappy connotation.

   A few = not many, but in this case there isn't that negative or unhappy connotation. In fact, there are those who say that *a few* + countable noun is practically synonymous with "some" (I have a few dollars on me. / I have some money on me.).

2. **LITTLE MONEY / A LITTLE MONEY**

   Little = not much, and it can have no special connotation (It costs little money to start a stamp collection.) or the same negative or unhappy connotation as *few* does (He makes little money at that job).

   A little = not much, and this phrase also lacks that negative or unhappy connotation. In fact, just as with *a few*, there are those who say that *a little* + non-count noun is practically synonymous with "some" (I have a little money on me. / I have some money on me.).

3. **REMEMBER TO DO / REMEMBER DOING**

   Remember + an infinitive verb (to do) = recall the need for something to be done in the future.

   Remember + -ing form of the verb = recall that something was done or happened before.

CHAPTER 5, page 130.

1. **Jim's <u>enough old</u> to vote.**
   Change to: **old enough.** The syntactic rules for using *enough* are:
   — adjective / adverb + *enough* (old enough / fast enough)
   — *enough* + noun (enough money), and less commonly: noun + *enough* (money enough)

2. **It's *such* hot that I can't sleep.**
   Change to: **so.** The rules for *so* and *such* are:
   — *so* + adjective / adverb (so hot / so quickly)
   — *such* + (indefinite article) + (adjective) + noun (such a liar / such a big liar / such liars)

3. **He makes <u>much</u> money.**
   Change to: **a lot of / lots of / a great deal of.** Most ESOL grammar books fail to mention the fact that we rarely use *much* in an affirmative sentence, preferring instead to use one of the three phrases listed above. In the negative, however, *much* is commonly used: **He doesn't make much money.**

4. **I ate <u>too many</u> chicken<u>s</u>.**
   Change to: **too much chicken.** Certain animals which are normally countable nouns, become non-count nouns when they're turned into fare for our tables. There may be *too many chickens* on the farm, but we need to use the non-count form and say *too much chicken* when talking about the food item.

5. **That's the <u>expensivest</u> car I've ever bought.**
   Change to: **most expensive.** The rules for making the comparative and superlative forms of adjectives are:
   — one-syllable adjectives: add -er / -est (small, smaller, smallest)
   — one-syllable adjectives ending in "e": add -r / -st (ripe, riper, ripest)
   — two-syllable adjectives ending in a consonant +"y": drop the "y" and add -ier / -iest (happy, happier, happiest)
   — other two-syllable adjectives or adjectives with more syllables: use "more / less" or "most / least" before the adjective (more expensive, most expensive / less thoughtful, least thoughtful)

   What most ESOL grammar books fail to mention is that there are some adjectives which have optional forms even though they go against the traditional rule about two-syllable adjectives. The following examples can use "more / less" and "most / least" in front of them, or they can have the -er / -est endings added onto them: *clever, common, gentle, handsome, narrow, quiet, simple, stupid.*

6. **The woman is sleeping. / the sleeping woman**
   Both of these are perfectly grammatical. In the sentence, the verb is in the present progressive (real present) to communicate that the activity is taking place right now. In the phrase, the -ing verbal adjective is being used to describe the "doer." (Refer to Chapter 3 for more information on verbal adjectives.)
   The woman is asleep. / the asleep woman
   The sentence is grammatical, but the phrase isn't. The adjective used in both cases (asleep) belongs to a special group of adjectives which all begin with the letter "a" and can only be used <u>after</u> stative verbs like "be," "become," "seem," "turn," and

"feel." In other words, these special adjectives can never be used before the nouns they describe: *afraid, afloat, aghast, alike, alive, alone, ashamed, asleep, awake,* etc.

CHAPTER 6, page 156.

1. **"I'm <u>coming</u> back to my country."**
   Change to: **going.**
2. **"Who's <u>here</u>?"**
   Change to: **there.**

These two changes deal with the concept of deixis (mentioned in Chapter 12), which deals with the perception of whether something is near to or far from the speaker or whether something is coming towards or going away from the speaker. This might include concrete things or abstract things. In the first sentence, the idea is that the speaker is talking about his country which is "there," not "here." Because of this, the verb "go back," which means "return," must be used (go <u>there</u>). "Come" can also be used to mean "return," but in a different context. Its meaning is "here" (come <u>here</u>) and would be inappropriate in this case.

In the second sentence, the speaker has to consider whether someone is on his side of the door or on the other side. His side of the door signifies "here," while the other side of the door signifies "there." Since the person knocking is on the other side of the door, it's more appropriate for our speaker to ask "Who's <u>there</u>?"

CHAPTER 7, page 173.

SAY vs. TELL

Although both verbs basically have the same meaning, the construction of the phrases they're in is quite different. Students look for simplification, not complication, and keeping that in mind, here's the easiest way to explain the difference in how these two verbs are used in indirect or reported speech:
— *say* + (that) + clause: He said (that) we should wait for him.
— Although it's possible to have this construction, say + to + listener + (that) + clause [He said to me (that) we should wait for him.], most people consider it awkward and too wordy, and therefore opt for the verb *tell* with its phrase construction.
— *tell* + listener / reader + (that) + clause: He told me (that) we should wait for him.
— *tell* + listener / reader + infinitive verb: He told us to wait for him.

The point to stress to the students (even though some may feel it's too simple) is that, in normal usage, we always mention the listener after the verb *tell* (he told <u>me</u>), but we don't mention the listener after the verb *say* (he said).

TALK vs. SPEAK

Talk and *speak* really have the same basic meaning, to "converse," and in this sense, they can be used interchangeably (I talked to him about the problem. / I spoke to him about the problem.) However, even though there's no hard-and-fast rule about it, we tend to use *speak* with the names of languages (I speak Japanese) rather than *talk.*

HEAR vs. LISTEN (TO)

The same distinction that we made between *see* and *look at / watch* applies to these two verbs. *Hear* is the involuntary activity that the ears do; if there's sound anywhere within your range, you hear it. *Listen (to),* on the other hand, means to pay attention to certain sounds or concentrate on those sounds.

CHAPTER 8, page 201.

a bee's sting	:	a wound which can be inflicted by a bee
a bee sting	:	an actual wound already inflicted by a bee
a dog's kennel	:	a specific place for a specific dog to live in, e.g., in someone's backyard
a dog kennel	:	a place created to board or house dogs, often as a business
a sheep's skin	:	the skin of a living sheep
a sheep skin	:	the skin which came from a slaughtered sheep; a diploma
a cow's hide	:	the hide (thick skin) of a living cow
a cow hide	:	the hide which came from a slaughtered cow

There's an interesting phenomenon going on with all of these pairs—a distinct change in stress. When we say the phrases with the -s genitives, there's more or less equal stress on both the noun with the -'s and the head noun (a BEE'S STING / a SHEEP'S SKIN). However, when we say the compound noun phrases, the stress is placed only on the first element (a BEE sting / a SHEEP skin).

CHAPTER 9, page 244.

Isn't Mr. Spock a character <u>on</u> *Star Trek*?

In this sentence, *Star Trek* refers to the television series. Use *on* for television or radio shows.

Isn't Mr. Spock a character <u>in</u> *Star Trek*?

In this sentence, *Star Trek* refers to the movie. Use *in* for movies or books.

Almost all paper is made <u>from</u> wood pulp.

We use the expression *be made <u>from</u>* when we can no longer identify the material that was used just by looking at the object. When you look at a piece of paper, there's no way to tell that it started out as wood pulp.

That old dresser is made <u>out of</u> knotty pine.

We use the expression *be made <u>out of</u>* when we can identify the material that was used just by looking at the object. When you look at that dresser, you can tell immediately (by the look, grain, and color) what kind of wood was used—if you're familiar with different kinds of wood, that is. (Note that *made of* is an alternate form.)

This paint is made <u>with</u> latex.

We use the expression *be made <u>with</u>* when we mention one or more ingredients.

CHAPTER 10, page 261.

DIRT

A word synonymous with "earth" and "soil," it's the actual substance you can hold in your hand. It also carries a negative connotation and can be considered a marked word because of that (Look at that dirt on the floor!).

EARTH

A word synonymous with "dirt" and "soil," it doesn't carry any negative connotation (There are many creatures that live in the earth, such as certain worms and insects.). It also means the name of the planet we live on (The earth's ozone layer is in big trouble.).

GROUND

This word stands for the solid surface of the earth, with emphasis on the word "surface" (Man is the only creature that always stands with just two feet planted firmly on the ground.). Students sometimes confuse *ground* and *floor*. The ground is natural and always found outside; a floor is man-made and found inside or as part of some sort of man-made construction outdoors.

LAND

Land has quite a few uses that distinguish it from the other words under discussion:

— the opposite of the sea (Some people travel by land; others travel by sea.)
— a piece of the ground that you can buy or own (He just bought some land outside of town.)

— a country or nation (This is the land of opportunity.)

— an area or region (Florida is a state containing a good deal of swamp land.)

SOIL

This word is synonymous with "dirt" and "earth" in the sense that it's the substance you can hold in your hand, and, like "earth," it doesn't carry any negative connotation as a noun (I just got some potting soil so we can transfer those mums to larger pots.).

CHAPTER 11, page 295.

1. **Dare I mention to the professor . . . ?**
   the semi-modal: inverted question form; no infinitive marker on following verb
2. **I dare you to tell the professor that . . .**
   the verb: followed by direct object and infinitive marker
3. **Amelia Earhart dared to be the first woman . . .**
   the verb: regular past tense ending added; followed by an infinitive marker
4. **How dare you!**
   the semi-modal: inverted question form (used here as an exclamation)
5. **Don't you dare let that wet dog . . . !**
   the semi-modal: not followed by the infinitive marker

CHAPTER 12, page 325.

1. PREFER

can be followed by an infinitive verb (prefer to swim) or an -ing verb (prefer swimming); can also be followed by a noun (prefer roses)

WOULD RATHER

can be followed only by a base-form verb (would rather swim)

2.   We use a saw <u>to</u> cut down trees.

We use a saw <u>for</u> cutting down trees.

In both of the above sentences, we are focusing on the **purpose** or **use** of a saw. When we speak about the purpose or use that something has, we can use either *to* or *for* followed by the appropriate verb form.

I've come to this school <u>to</u> learn English.

I've come to this school <u>for</u> learning English.

In both of these sentences, our focus is different. Although many ESOL grammar books state that we use *to* + verb and *for* + noun when we speak of purpose

(I went to the store *to buy bread.* / I went to the store *for bread.*), this can be a bit simplistic and dangerous. Why dangerous? Because the second sentence in our first pair clearly has *for* + verb, not noun, and the sentence deals with purpose.

The reason *for* doesn't work in the last sentence is because our focus is not on a purpose or a use; it's on an **intention.** Granted, there's certainly some overlapping between purpose and intention, but there is a difference. We seem to use only *to* when we're more concerned with intention than with purpose or use.

Index